Advance Praise for

OUT *of the* SHADOWS

"Timea Nagy's harrowing story deeply reports the ugliness of human trafficking. But it's ultimately a remarkable tale of survival and resilience, with lessons for a country that considers itself to be a safe place for immigrants."

—Pauline Dakin, bestselling author of
Run, Hide, Repeat

"*Out of the Shadows* is a story of survival in the face of unimaginable circumstances. In a voice that is heartbreakingly innocent and honest, Timea Nagy inspires us to recognize the strength of purpose and resilience, and redemption."

—Jackie Kai Ellis, bestselling author of
The Measure of My Powers

OUT *of the*
SHADOWS

OUT *of the* SHADOWS

a memoir

Timea E. Nagy
and Shannon Moroney

Doubleday Canada

Doubleday Canada and colophon are registered trademarks of Penguin Random House Canada Limited.

Library and Archives Canada Cataloguing in Publication

Nagy, Timea, author
   Out of the shadows / Timea Nagy and Shannon Moroney.

Issued in print and electronic formats.
ISBN 978-0-385-69258-8 (softcover).—ISBN 978-0-385-69259-5 (EPUB)

   1. Nagy, Timea. 2. Human trafficking victims—Canada—Biography.
3. Hungarian Canadians±Biography. 4. Human trafficking—Canada.
5. Prostitution—Canada. 6. Autobiographies. I. Moroney, Shannon, author II. Title.

HQ281.N34 2019   306.3'62092   C2018-906355-6
                                             C2018-906356-4

Cover design: Leah Springate
Cover images: (flowers) Gregory Adams; (background) Pinghung Chen / EyeEm, both Getty Images

Printed and bound in the USA

Published in Canada by Doubleday Canada,
a division of Penguin Random House Canada Limited

www.penguinrandomhouse.ca

10 9 8 7 6 5 4 3 2

Penguin
Random House
DOUBLEDAY CANADA

To all the victims and survivors of human trafficking,
and to my mother, who gave me life and the strength to survive
and live to tell my story.

—T.E.N.

CONTENTS

A NOTE FROM THE AUTHORS

THIS IS A WORK OF NON-FICTION, recounting traumatic events that took place between ten and twenty years ago. There is no such thing as a perfect memory, particularly through times of trauma—some images and conversations are imprinted on the mind and heart with great clarity, while others are blurred. As such, we made every effort to check dates and other facts in police reports, court documents, and media articles when they existed, as well as with friends and professionals who were there at the time. Yet, there are periods of time about which there are no records of anything and we had to rely on memory. We worked closely together, recording hours of interviews in person, plus countless phone calls, email messages, and time together at Timea's presentations, sorting and examining memory and emotion, and reconstructing dialogue to the very best of our abilities. We have changed the names and identifying characteristics of certain people to protect their privacy. Because of the high level of trust between us, and the benefit of time and continued trauma healing, the story we have written in these pages is the most fulsome account of Timea's experience on record, and may at times vary in detail from past accounts or interviews. Some memories are shared here for the first time.

This is one woman's story of being trafficked and it bears both similarity and difference to the stories of other victims and survivors the world over. With reverence and respect to all people affected by human trafficking, we thank you for reading. Please visit www.timeascause.com for references and recommended reading, should you need them.

Timea Eva Nagy and Shannon Moroney
March 2019

PROLOGUE

IN THE MIDDLE OF A FREEZING January night in 2010, my phone rang, startling me out of sleep. I pulled back my warm duvet, sat up straight and cleared my throat. Despite the time, I wanted to sound alert and ready. My heart was already beginning to pump adrenaline through my system as I answered.

"Is this Timea Nagy?" a deep male voice asked. I knew immediately that the caller wasn't a victim, since I always gave my alias—Christina—to the people I was helping. It was to help prevent traffickers from finding me if victims were caught by them and forced to implicate me. The tables had turned and I was now a threat to the traffickers. I was still getting used to that idea, to the fact that I didn't have to be afraid all the time.

"Yes, this is Timea," I said confidently.

"My name is Mike Viozzi. I'm an investigator from the vice unit at Peel Regional Police. I'm sorry to call at this hour, but we're wondering if you can come and speak with a sixteen-year-old girl we have here at our station. It's a difficult situation. We could use your help."

"I'll be right there." Five minutes later, I was in my car and backing out of my driveway through the snow. I'd grown up with snow, but the snow in Hungary was nothing like Canadian snow. In Budapest, it was wet and mushy, and did nothing to soften the sound of the Russian soldiers' boots on the pavement as they patrolled the streets around my family's apartment complex. Here in Canada, where I'd lived for a dozen years now, the snow was so many things. Tonight's was old, and with the temperature well below zero, it had frozen into flakes so hard that they squeaked when pushed together under my tires, like the sound of fingernails on a chalkboard. My hands gripped the steering wheel, and I could see my breath as I headed toward the highway. I wanted to race to the rescue, but I kept an eye on the speedometer. If I hit ice and slid off the road, I'd be no good to anyone, and I was the only one the police had to help a victim of human trafficking, especially someone who'd been forced to work in the sex trade. I already knew that was the case without being told. The police called me because I was a survivor myself.

Half an hour later, I pulled into the police station in Brampton, a suburb of Toronto. I took my volunteer badge out of my purse and walked around to the trunk where I kept my box of supplies—soap, hand cream, clean clothes. I grabbed a pear-scented hand sanitizer—something a young girl might like—and tossed it into my bag with some snacks. Small items like this helped comfort someone in crisis and build trust. If I won a girl's confidence, the police and I had a chance of saving her. But if she got scared, we could lose her. She could run from us, and back to danger.

Inside, Detective Viozzi came out to greet me. "Thank goodness you're here," he said. He briefed me on the case as he led me through a maze of corridors to where the girl waited.

"We found her on the side of one of the main streets not far from here, wearing only a tank top, yoga pants and a pair of very high heels.

She was looking for help. She saw one of our cruisers, ran to it and jumped inside before the officers realized what was happening. She told them that she was running from her boyfriend and that he'd be after her soon." *Boyfriend*, we both knew, meant pimp.

"I see," I said. "Good thing that car happened to be there."

"Yes, that was pretty lucky. One of the officers had attended your trafficking training session. He knew not to ask questions, just to give her his jacket and drive away fast. Then he called me."

That was one of the things I always stressed when talking to police officers—don't scare a victim away by asking too many questions and making her feel as if everything is her fault. The first thing to do is take her somewhere safe, make her feel protected. Only then can you ask for her story.

"All we know is this girl is from outside Montreal," the officer continued. "She'd wanted to make a little extra money and a 'new friend' said his cousin was looking for extra help at his store in Toronto for the Christmas season." I knew those ploys well. There was no store; it was a nightclub.

"She told us her money was taken from her, and her life was threatened. She was sold by the first guy to another guy, who was a lot scarier than the first. He kept her in a motel, where he used her as his personal sex toy when she wasn't at the club. He put a gun on the table every night to remind her she was not to go."

Unbidden flashbacks of my own experience in the motel entered my mind. I could feel this girl's fear, exhaustion, hunger, pain and humiliation.

"Thank you so much," I said, interrupting the detective before he gave me more details. "That gives me a good sense of where she's at emotionally. Where are things at on your end?"

"She told us where the motel is. We sent officers over there and, after a chase, they arrested her pimp. He'll be arraigned tomorrow morning and will most likely have a bail hearing in two days. There's so much money in these rings that someone will probably post bail for him, though. You know how it is. He'll be out looking for her in just a few days. And if she's out on the streets . . ." He didn't need to finish that thought.

Detective Viozzi opened the door to the interview room and ushered me through. The girl was seated in a chair, slumped over a table in front of her, trying to rest. She looked so tiny under the big winter police coat she was wearing. She jumped at the sound of the door opening. I recognized the reaction—a victim can never let her guard down.

I smiled at her. "I'm Christina," I said gently, pulling out a chair across from her and carefully putting my bag on the table. "I'm here to help you. Are you hungry or thirsty?" *Always offer something to a victim before asking her for anything.* It was one of my golden rules.

She nodded yes, her brown eyes filled with terror. She was very pretty, with dimples and long, brown hair. At thirty-three, I wasn't really old enough to be her mother, but I was overcome with the mothering instinct. I wanted to take care of her and keep her safe.

I opened my bag and showed her what was inside: chocolate, chips, water, gum, hand sanitizer.

She looked at me in disbelief. "Is this all for me?"

"Of course, honey. Everything is yours."

She was still for a few moments, cautiously taking it all in. I knew exactly what she was thinking. Who is this woman? What does she want from me? What will she make me do if I eat this bag of chips?

I interrupted her thoughts. "You are very, very brave. What happened to you is not your fault—I know that because this happened to me too. I'm not a police officer. I was a girl who was forced to work the way you were. But now I work with the police to help girls like us."

Big tears began to roll down her cheeks as I pulled my chair next to hers and put my arm around her shoulders.

"You're safe now," I said, pulling her close. "I'll take you home."

———

It was almost twenty-four hours later when I pulled back into my snowy driveway, exhausted from supporting the girl through giving a statement and then driving her to Montreal to reunite her with her parents, yet also exhilarated. I climbed into my bed, pulled the duvet back over myself, and felt overwhelming gratitude. I'd been given another chance to help save a girl—a girl so much like me. Over the coming months and years, I would be given this opportunity hundreds of times. And every time, I would also shed some of those same big tears, when I thought of the girl I'd been—the good little communist, the police officer's daughter, the award-winning student, the budding TV star and, finally, the girl on the plane, coming to Canada to be a babysitter, believing in the promise and hope of a new adventure—and everything that had happened to her.

Part I | LURED

I WIPED MY SWEATY PALMS ON MY JEANS and then pulled the cuffs of my Pink Panther sweatshirt over my hands and placed them in my lap. It was April 27, 1998, and even though I was turning twenty-one in June, this was my first time on a plane. Growing up under communism, I'd only ever left Hungary on a bus to go to summer camp in other Eastern Bloc countries, and in the nine years since the Berlin Wall had fallen, I'd not yet ventured into the Western world. Buckled into my window seat, I was nervous, excited and very hopeful.

"Is London your final destination, or are you going somewhere else?" My seatmate, a cheerful middle-aged woman, spoke to me in Hungarian.

"I'm going to Toronto," I said confidently. Saying the words aloud was surreal. My travel plans had come about so quickly. Three weeks ago I barely knew the difference between the United States and Canada, and now I was going to spend three months in the country's biggest city.

"Me too," she said with a smile. "I live in Toronto. It's a great city." She looked around. "Are you travelling alone?"

"No, I'm with a friend." I gestured toward Bianka, who was sitting a few rows back and across the aisle. The woman looked at her and then back at me quizzically.

"That's your friend?" I understood her reaction. Bianka and I were very different from one another. She had teased, bleached-blonde hair, big, fake boobs and wore heavy makeup and a miniskirt; I had a tiny frame, my hair was cut into a plain dark bob, and I was wearing lip gloss and jeans. Bianka was twenty-five but looked thirty, and I was twenty but looked fifteen. It was obvious that we came from different walks of life.

"What are you going to do in Toronto?" The woman now sounded suspicious, which annoyed me. My mother, brother Zoli and boyfriend Ádám all disapproved of Bianka; I didn't need a stranger questioning our friendship and plans too. We'd even checked in separately at the airport, just to avoid my family's judgmental comments as they sent me off. It was why we didn't get seats together on the flight.

"We're with an agency. We're going to be babysitters." My statement was true for me, but only partly for Bianka. We were both with the same agency, and Natasa, the recruiter we'd met in Hungary two weeks ago, had told us they had lots of jobs for Hungarian girls: babysitting, housekeeping, and dancing in nightclubs. I'd signed up for babysitting, but Bianka had chosen dancing. She lived closer to the edge than I did.

The woman looked concerned. "You've got to be careful—do you know where you're going exactly? What part of the city are you staying in?" Her tone had sharpened and she was acting like my mother, who was a cop and usually cynical instead of seeing me as independent and adventurous. I was an adult. I was annoyed, but also felt a little silly. I didn't actually know the answer to her questions.

"Well, I don't have the exact address . . ." My voice sounded weaker than I wanted it to.

"You're going to Canada and you don't know where you're going to sleep? Which agency are you with?" She sounded incredulous, which made me feel foolish.

"Um . . ." I paused, realizing for the first time that I didn't know the name of the agency. I hadn't asked Natasa during my interview at McDonald's, nor when I saw her again yesterday to sign my contract and get my plane ticket. It was probably on my contract, which was in my bag, but since I couldn't read or speak English, Natasa had quickly translated the most important parts and pointed out the boxes I was to fill in: my personal information and emergency contacts, and where to sign my name, Timea Nagy.

"Look," I said, firmly but politely, the way my mom had taught me, "it's a Hungarian agency, so there's nothing to worry about. They're helping their own people. Thank you so much for your interest." With that, I turned away, stuffed my little airplane pillow between my head and the window, and closed my eyes. But I couldn't sleep. The woman's questions—now circling through my mind—had planted a seed of worry. I should have known the answers, but everything had been so rushed over the last couple weeks. And the last several months had been so stressful, I'd hardly slept. *Relax*, I told myself. *Everything is going to be great.*

When I opened my eyes an hour later, the woman pressed a small piece of paper into my hand.

"What's this?" I asked.

"My address and phone number. Just in case."

I thanked her, and pretended to put the paper into my pocket. Instead, I let it fall below our seats. I had my plan. I didn't need someone else trying to mother me when I already had my own mother to please. I didn't need some stranger raining on my parade.

Bianka and I got seats together on our connecting flight from London. She was able to doze for a little while, but I was too nervous and excited to sleep. I had more questions, and when Bianka woke up, we pondered them aloud. What would our apartment be like? Would we go straight there, or to the agency office? And what would Canada be like?

Growing up, I'd been taught that the Western world was a big, dark, scary place. The United States was the worst, where no one had health care and everyone had a gun. My friends and I didn't want to go there. But then the Berlin Wall came down, all the Russian soldiers left and American commercials came on TV, and suddenly it didn't look so bad. In fact, it looked wealthy, exciting, modern and delicious. The technology took our breath away— home computers, cordless phones and VCRs were all new to us. Everything Western was flashy and thrilling. We could put on a pair of Levi's and love would come to us. We could drink a Coca-Cola and be so happy we'd feel transported to a tropical beach. Under communism, wearing Levi's and drinking Coca-Cola—black market products—could get us arrested. So everyone wore the same Soviet-brand clothes and ate the same generic foods, and there was nothing to *feel* about anything.

Movies had been the most exciting Western influence for teenagers like me. A couple of families in our apartment complex got VCRs, and at least fifteen of us would huddle around the TV watching, completely captivated. Somebody would pass around the Mars bars they'd saved up for, and with our mouths full of caramel and milk chocolate, our eyes would grow wide at the images on the screen. "Look at the size of those cars!" we gasped and whispered to each other. We were in constant disbelief. "Look at those houses—everyone is so rich!" America was freedom and prosperity. We raced to catch up, watching movies and wearing clothes from the 1980s even though we were in the nineties.

My favourite movies were *Cobra* (I loved the cars), *Rocky* (I loved Stallone) and *Dirty Dancing* (I loved *everything*). We'd watch black market versions that were no longer illegal—poor quality and dubbed into Hungarian by a single, monotone narrator. Famous lines were devoid of the punch they had in English. "Nobody puts Baby in a corner" just didn't have the same effect when the voice coming out of Patrick Swayze's mouth belonged to a middle-aged Hungarian man, but we didn't care. We watched those movies so many times that the tapes wore out. When a tape broke, we would all wait nervously as the most nimble-fingered of our group would painstakingly even out the edges of the ripped tape, glue them back together and then carefully wind it back onto the reel. In the replay there would be several seconds or even a minute missing, but we knew the movies so well that we could fill in the gaps from memory. It was all we had, so we made do and were happy. Making do with less was something we were all used to—under communism there was never enough of anything, except vodka, which created its own problems among adults, my parents included.

Even though Natasa the recruiter had told Bianka and me that Canadian winter was over by April, as we flew through the clouds over the Atlantic, I imagined a beautiful, frozen landscape of evergreen trees and groups of fun-loving young people wearing sweaters and smiles waiting for me in the distance below—something like what I'd seen watching the 1988 Winter Olympics in a city called Calgary. Was it close to Toronto? I knew so little about the country I would call home for three months. Would I feel like a Canadian in that time? Would I learn English? I was most anxious about not speaking a word of the language, but I reassured myself with what Natasa had told me: there were many nice Hungarian-Canadian families that needed babysitters, so I would mostly be speaking Hungarian. Maybe the children I'd be caring for could help me learn the basics of English until I had time to take a real class.

I loved kids and had always had a good way with them. I'd been a babysitter since I was eleven, caring for my neighbour's baby and toddler after school and on weekends. For a time, I'd even wanted to be a kindergarten teacher. That was before everything had become so complicated. I folded my hands, suddenly nervous about the next three months. *It's only hard at the beginning. You can get used to anything, and soon you'll be having a great time.* That's what my mom would say when she put me on the bus to the communist summer camps, straightening my tie and badge sash as she sent me off. She'd always been right. Besides, I didn't even need to have a great time in Canada—I just needed to make as much money as I could, pay everyone back and get out of the huge mess I'd made. Then I could start living my life the way I wanted to. Then I could be free.

I'd never known true freedom. Growing up under the oppressive Soviet rule was challenging, but it was all I knew, and my childhood wasn't so different from anyone else's. Coping with scarcity and fear was normal, and neither my generation nor my parents' knew any different. Our grandparents complained the most, because they knew what democracy was like. They'd survived the Germans in the Second World War only to lose their freedom to the Russians in 1957, and they were still angry about it. But my parents' generation was too young to remember what life had been like before, and I'd been indoctrinated to fear democracy and capitalism, raised instead to be a good little communist. I followed the rules, saluted the flag and sang my heart out to the Russian anthem. I was obedient, hard-working and community-minded. I loved school and aimed to please my teachers. I earned the most badges in our communist version of Girl Guides, *Kisdobos*—the Little Drummers—and proudly wore my uniform with the blue tie. When I was older, I graduated to the Trailblazers, wore a red tie and continued to earn the most badges and was awarded a spot at the coveted leadership camp. Outgoing and positive, I made friends easily and joined every extra-curricular I could fit into my schedule; with chorus quickly becoming my favourite. Singing filled me with energy, and I loved the praise I'd get for my clear, strong voice.

I would sing at home too, trying to break the tension that always hung in the air and to distract my parents from quarrelling. They'd met when my mom was only nineteen, just a little younger than I was now. She and my dad both worked for the Hungarian public transit company; my dad drove a streetcar and my mom was a transit police officer. One rainy day, she jumped onto my dad's streetcar to escape a downpour and he let her into the driver's cabin. According to her, she fell in love with him immediately because of his good looks. According to my dad, it wasn't as much love at first sight on her part as it was an opportunity to get away from home, poverty and, quite literally, the rain.

Mom was six years old when her father was killed by a bullet to his head in the 1956 revolution. She never spoke about his death except to say that it was terrible, and that, afterwards, the family was very, very poor. When I complained about my brother teasing me or taking my toys, she would try to put things in perspective. "It could be worse, Timea. I had six older brothers to tease and torment me," she'd say, her tone compassionless. "We lived on the fifth floor and they made me go all the way down to the cellar to get the coal and potatoes, and then they wouldn't share." I quickly learned not to complain, even though our situation had many challenges too.

Other than that, neither of my parents spoke about their child-hoods, or their engagement or wedding, probably because they didn't like each other much after they were married—at least, it seemed as though my mom didn't like my dad. There was only one photo of them on their wedding day, a black-and-white shot where my mom is smiling widely—a smile that looks like mine—and is wearing a sixties mod-style white minidress and a veil. My dad, who was a handsome man with high cheekbones, olive skin and bright green eyes he got from his Roma mother, is wearing a suit and looks serious, like a man who had just taken his vows. They are standing in front of a fancy car—the most expensive one my mom could find parked on the street in front of the church. She pulled my dad in front of it and pretended it was theirs, that they had more than they really did.

The early years of our family life were spent living in the poorest part of Budapest in a tiny, mouldy flat with a shared bathroom at the end of a hallway, which we had to line up for with all the other neighbours. My mom washed me and my brother, Zoli, in the kitchen sink, and the four of us slept in one bed.

Even as a child I knew that my mother was very proud, but her moods and behaviours were opaque and unpredictable. She could be loving and affectionate—especially when I was sick—but she was also quick to get angry, often without warning. I wanted to see her smile like in her wedding photo, so I did things I thought might spark that, like singing or showing her the little red book all students had to carry. In it, our teachers wrote comments about our behaviour. Mine were always positive, and that pleased my mother. I would also run to hug her when she got home from work, but I was rebuked as often as I was embraced. When I was younger, I'd wonder if she'd had a bad day, or if I'd done something wrong, but over time, I learned to wait for her to initiate affection. Unfortunately, she'd more often instigate a fight.

"This place is a mess!" she would begin immediately after walking in the door. "No one does anything around here except me!" I would start tidying up, even when things were already as neat as a pin. I took her coat from her and hung it on the hook by the door. I put the kettle on to boil water for tea. Anything I could do to please her.

When I was six, my mom was promoted from transit officer to full-fledged police constable. She'd worked hard to follow the rules, take initiative and develop her leadership, and her efforts were rewarded by the communist regime. Her promotion meant better housing and living conditions for us. The government had undertaken extensive building projects and constructed concrete, high-rise apartment complexes in many parts of the city. The buildings were typically sparse and uninspiring, but they were generous in room size and, overall, a vast improvement over where we'd been living. They were clean, had their own bathrooms and, most importantly, were free of mould, so I wouldn't suffer from as many asthma attacks or lung infections.

We were moved to one of these new apartments in the twenty-first district on Csepel Island, in the middle of the Danube, just south of where it divides the city into two, Buda and Pest. Buda is mountainous, where the rich people live in big expensive houses; Pest is flat and more middle-class, but still beautiful. Nine bridges pull the two sides together like stitches, seaming the city into one. My parents were kind of like that—two different sides sewn together—but their stitches were loose and the move only temporarily relaxed the distance between them.

For me, the move improved not only my health but also my happiness. I became part of a community, because in these Soviet apartment complexes everyone knew everyone else and there was very little privacy. This might have bothered the adults, but we kids loved it. Each floor had three families, and there were several floors, which meant that there were always enough kids to make two teams for any game or sport. In the summertime, we knew it was bedtime because every parent called down to the community yard that it was time to come in. While I hated being called inside and ending a game with my friends that wasn't quite over, I liked getting into my pyjamas and cuddling into bed with my dad on nights my mom was working. He would play with my hair when I was falling asleep, wrapping my straight strands around his fingers to make ringlet curls that would hold for only a moment. We both relaxed without Mom there.

Our apartment block was considered cooler than all the others because our elementary school, just a two-minute walk away, was the biggest and newest on the island. It had a Hall of Fame where pictures of the best students were hung. My picture was there more than once as the top student—not just for my grades but for my school spirit. I worked hard and enthusiastically participated in activities and volunteer projects. I won many competitions in solo singing, chorus, poetry reading and gymnastics. All of this made me popular with my classmates, and I enjoyed every minute of it. I loved people, social activities, group projects—I was a true extrovert. People knew me best for my big smile, and they always smiled back, which made me feel good, especially because things were so difficult at home.

I learned quickly that getting good grades was not only essential to survival under my mother's rule, but also essential to surviving communist rule. Education was everything, and the better you did in school, the better your chances of getting a job you liked in the future. Unemployment wasn't allowed, so if you weren't able to find a job on your own, you would be given one by the government—and it wouldn't be a good job if you hadn't earned it. If you didn't work, you would be sent to jail. If you didn't go to school, your parents would be sent to jail. Sometimes I overheard adults, like our neighbour, complain about communism. He had a food stall in the market and couldn't always get the supplies he needed to make his business a success.

"Damn these Russians," he'd say under his breath. "Won't trade with anyone outside Eastern Europe! Don't they realize we can't grow fruits and vegetables all year round?" We had all the apples, potatoes and onions we wanted, but were without greens for most of the year. Bananas—I'd never tasted one. They grew in the tropics of the Evil West, I'd learned at school. Our neighbour's criticism of the government made me nervous. It wouldn't be good if soldiers on foot patrol overheard. My mother wouldn't like it either.

Despite the improvement to our living conditions that moving had brought, things continued to be tough. In her new role, my mom was on call 24/7; whenever her police detachment needed her, she went. She worked a lot, and when she was home she mothered like she was still wearing her badge, ordering us all around and seeming to care about nothing but keeping the house tidy and taking care of the building and everyone in it. My father's demeanour was softer, but his attitude was much the same, duty-wise. Communism required us to be dutiful, so when the community needed something, we all showed up, no matter where or what time. If there was an earthquake, we had to volunteer—the whole family got in a bus and you went and helped, no questions asked. This kind of community support sounds idyllic, but the reality was that you didn't have a choice. There was never a question of if you *wanted* to go help; you went because you were told. You couldn't speak freely. You couldn't make your own decisions. You couldn't leave. It was what it was.

Those rules bled into family life, since the government controlled everything: housing, employment, what we could buy and eat, our utility use and what we watched on TV. It even aimed to control parenting—every night, a uniformed teddy bear came on TV at eight o'clock to read a story, and then tell all children to brush their teeth and go to bed. We did what we were told.

From the start of their marriage my dad had tried to persuade my mom to move to the countryside, where he'd grown up, so he could farm and work with his hands, but her career was important to her, and her promotion only entrenched us deeper into urban life. They fought more and more, and finally decided to ask the government for a separation when I was nine. Dad was put on a long waiting list for a new apartment, but until one was available they were ordered to maintain separate bedrooms within our apartment and to share the kitchen, living room and bathrooms. This living arrangement lasted for two difficult years. My mom constantly picked on my dad, and she would lose her temper with him over every little thing. In response, he began to avoid being at home. Then he began drinking. He never drank at home, but he'd come home drunk, and that meant he and my mom would have huge fights. They didn't hit each other, but glasses and furniture were sometimes broken.

My mom was stressed and angry, Zoli and I were scared, and my dad was lost. Over the following year, he lost his job, then another, and then another, proving to my mom that he was the complete failure—to both our family and to the state—she thought him to be. Utterly loyal to communism, she called the government to report my father's unemployment, and he received a letter in the mail letting him know that he would be arrested in a few days and taken to jail. After that letter arrived, Dad immediately stopped drinking and mom became very quiet. They didn't speak another word to each other. He packed a bag, showered and shaved, tidied his room, finished fixing a couple of TVs and radios for the neighbours, and then filled the rest of the waiting time by reading. He let me curl up in his lap and put my head on his chest, trying to assuage my fear. He told me that he was going to "police camp" and that it was nothing to worry about—just a place for people who didn't have enough work. It wasn't for scary criminals.

When the police came to take him away, they helped him with his bag. It was very civilized, maybe because the officers were my mom's co-workers and we knew them. After Dad was gone, Mom went around the building proudly telling everyone that she'd sent him to jail because he was a lazy, stupid drunk who was a traitor to our family and to the communist party. Dad had told me he'd be home in a few months, but my mom said he'd never be back, and that ended up being the truth.

Mom should have been happier once Dad was gone, but things only seemed to get worse. In his absence, she picked on Zoli and me and always seemed to be angry about something. She worked long hours, which gave us breaks from her criticisms, but left us to take care of ourselves. Sometimes she would send officers from her unit to check on us and bring us food. I was grateful for this; Zoli liked to start fights with me, and many of them became physical, but the officers made me feel safe.

My mom's eldest brother and his wife—my godparents—helped keep an eye on us too. They often picked us up on weekends and took us to their house in a small village outside Budapest called Vecsés, where we played in the fresh air and ate sausage and cheese sandwiches on homemade bread as well as our national dish, *paprikás*. In the summers, my mother enrolled me in the camp that was run by the police association in the countrysides of Hungary, Poland, Romania and other Eastern Bloc countries. We stayed in cabins and had our own little beds with trunks at the foot for uniforms and a few personal belongings. Each day was filled with organized activities like sports and crafts, and many opportunities to salute the Russian flag, sing the anthem and songs, and march around the meal hall past posters of Lenin, Khrushchev and other communist leaders.

Unlike my home life, camp life was predictable and I thrived there. I was praised daily and recognized with badges and awards for my good behaviour and participation. At home, if I did something good, I was either praised or criticized, depending on my mom's mood. But at camp, I knew the rules: if I did something good, I was rewarded; if I made a mistake, I received a demerit point. There were three meals a day, every day, and we ate together at big tables. I learned to be organized, take risks, be adventurous and to become adaptable in unfamiliar surroundings. I was taught outdoor survival skills such as how to build a fire and how to get out of a cave. It felt really good there.

But as much as I loved camp, it wasn't my home, and I missed my family, my own bed and my mom's Sunday soups. Sunday afternoons were the good times—Mom didn't have to work and we would all be home together, curled up on the couch, watching TV. She was relaxed, and that's when I'd feel her love and affection most. During the week, she was different—I knew what kind of an evening we were going to have by the way she put the key in the lock and how she called me when she opened the door. It wasn't, "Hey kids! I'm home!" It was "Timea! Zoli! Where are you? Why are your shoes by the front door?" I never knew quite what to expect, or which mom I was going to see. And I couldn't risk complaining about anything or being in a bad mood myself, so I would lie on my bed or go out on the balcony and look up at the sky, wishing I could hop on a cloud and drift away into a dreamland where everything was bright and clean and all the people were happy, especially my family. I longed to have two parents again, even if they fought, but Dad never came back. I saw him once after he got out of jail, but he never returned to our family like he said he would. It would be a long time before I understood why.

It hurt to remember my dad's absence, so as the plane began its descent toward Toronto, I pushed the pain down and imagined reconnecting with him one day. He would be so proud of his daughter who went to Canada, learned English and made a lot of money. He would never know about the debt I'd gotten into in the last year, and I would forgive him for leaving me. We could start over. And if my plan worked, Mom would never have to know about my troubles either. I would soon be in Canada, where I would fix everything. Maybe she and I could start over too.

2 | The Border

EVERYTHING IN TORONTO WAS DIFFERENT than in Hungary, starting with the smell. It was fresh, clean and cool. It smelled *young*. Bianka and I smiled at each other as we walked up the gangway into the airport terminal, but we didn't say a word. We just took it all in, following the crowd and the signs depicting a person in a uniform, looking for that word Natasa had written down in the little journal I'd bought for my trip: *immigration*.

I really wanted to go to the bathroom first, and asked Bianka where she thought it was. She shrugged her shoulders, looking around and trying to make out the signs. She'd never been out of Europe before either. We searched for the W/C signs we were used to, but could only see a blue-and-white sign showing a person above a doorway that seemed like it could lead to a bathroom. I went inside and discovered, to my embarrassment, that it was for men only. I scurried out and Bianka pointed to a sign on the opposite wall, this one with a person wearing a skirt. Once inside the women's bathroom,

I was struck by how different it was from those in Hungary. The toilets were in stalls, but they weren't fully enclosed from ceiling to floor like they were at home. I looked for the pull-chain to flush the toilet, which should have been hanging from a tank up on the wall, but there wasn't one. In fact, there was no tank at all. I could hear other people in the bathroom. *Should I ask someone?* But I couldn't speak English. As I weighed my options, the toilet suddenly flushed completely on its own and I jumped up and shrieked; the force was so strong I thought it might pull me in. How was I going to take care of children if I didn't even know how to work a Canadian toilet? Maybe I was in over my head.

Washing my hands brought the same feelings of insecurity. The faucet had no knobs, and I had no idea how to turn it on. I watched another woman wave her hands under the tap until it came on by itself. I followed suit. The automatic hand dryer was so loud I jumped again.

Bianka was outside waiting for me. "Things are so different here!" I said. "I don't understand how anything works."

"Just stay calm," Bianka said. "Breathe."

I tried, but my stomach felt queasy as we walked toward immigration. I got my passport and agency contract ready. We were the last from our flight to get in the long line. When we finally reached the front, Bianka was directed toward one customs officer and I to another. My officer was a short black woman with glasses. She looked at me closely, then sternly said something I didn't understand and then held out her hand for my passport and papers. I gave everything to her. A minute or so passed as she rifled through the documents. I glanced nervously at Bianka, whose officer was doing the same thing. The customs official was reading my contract carefully. She said something to me again, but I couldn't make it out so I shrugged.

"Sit down," she said, louder and slower, pointing to a wide corridor off to one side of the main customs area. Grey chairs lined both sides, a few of them taken by other weary-looking travellers.

At the end of the corridor there were four doors, each with a number above it. There was a clock on the wall opposite me.

I obeyed. Bianka was ordered to sit down too, but was pointed to a chair across the hall from me. It seemed that they didn't want us to talk to each other. I started to feel sick to my stomach, as if I was in trouble for something, but I didn't know what. Ten minutes passed, then twenty, then half an hour. Was this normal for people getting work visas? Something about it didn't feel normal. I looked over at Bianka and mouthed, in Hungarian, "*Mi történik?*"—"What's happening?" She shook her head and shrugged her shoulders.

An hour passed and with each minute my heart rate rose, but despite feeling very worried, I was still fascinated by everything around me. The workers and guards in the airport were all from different cultures and had different skin colours; some were even wearing turbans. I'd never seen such diversity. We'd grown up with only one significant minority, the Roma, who were looked down upon by many and called gypsies, but not by me. My grandmother was Roma; plus, I didn't like to judge. At one point, an officer walked down the corridor carrying a cardboard tray with four cups of coffee—just like I'd seen in police movies. I glanced at Bianka. *Wow!* We were both impressed. The officer went into the interview rooms at the end of the hall, delivering a cup to each. This was a different world—I could already tell. Even though I was anxious, I was still excited. I also wanted one of those cups of coffee. It was dinnertime to me but only late morning in Toronto.

My first glimpse of the Western world had been in June 1989, nine years ago. Mom brought home our first colour TV just in time for my twelfth birthday, and we watched Eastern Europe transform from black-and-white communism to colourful democracy and the free market. First, we saw the removal of the barbed-wire fence that had separated Hungary from Austria for almost thirty years. Then, six months later, on November 9, all eyes were glued to the screen as the Berlin Wall came down, and people from East and West Germany were reunited, crying with joy and climbing over the rubble to see their loved ones. With my mom, brother and a few other families in our building gathered in our apartment, we watched in amazement as men and women tore at the cement blocks with their bare hands, breaking through to freedom before our very eyes. We all cheered for their reunion, but I could sense uncertainty and worry around me. The adults spoke in hushed tones and wore concerned expressions. No one knew what was going to happen next, how our lives were going to change, or who we would be in the new world.

For a while not much changed for the country—we had a free election, so a new government was elected, yet the Russian presence was still strong—but a lot changed for me. Gymnastics had become my second love, after chorus, and I loved to compete. I was warming up for a big competition when a boy I had a crush on came to the door of the gym. I decided to show off and impress him by running through my routine—The Big Cat—one more time. I made sure he was watching me before stretching my arms up, pointing my toe and running toward the springboard where I was to propel myself onto the pommel horse, form a handstand, open my legs into the splits and then push myself off into a double somersault and land on the mat, arms raised in victory. But I didn't make the landing. Instead, thinking more about the boy than about calculating my speed and timing, I overshot the pommel horse, tripped as I flew over it, and landed on my back. I heard the crack before I felt it, and then immediately passed out from the pain. When I woke, the teacher was kneeling over me and a crowd had gathered. I couldn't move. Everyone thought I was paralyzed. I started crying—for the pain and fear that I would never walk again; for the humiliation of having failed, disappointing my coaches, teammates, mother and myself; and for embarrassing myself in front of my crush.

I spent almost six months (including my thirteenth birthday) in the hospital, most of the time in a back brace. I was lonely, but I did have visitors. Once, I thought I saw my dad at the door, but then figured I'd been dreaming. I learned to walk again, and in the fall, I was released to convalesce at home while all my friends started grade eight. I grieved the loss of my social life, as well as my plan to become a kindergarten teacher. I would never be able to recuperate in time to pass the physical education entrance test that was required to go to high school and then university, nor the mandatory gymnastics audition. Then there were my grades in math and physics. I'd managed to keep up my marks in the arts and language by doing my schoolwork in the hospital with the help of friends and teachers who came to visit, but not in the subjects that came less easily to me. I would have to go to trade school instead of high school. My dreams were crushed.

A neighbour dropped by one day when I felt particularly down, and he gave me a cassette tape of a Hungarian musician named Pierrot, who dressed like the famous black-and-white sad clown but sang beautiful, uplifting songs. I fell in love with his voice and lyrics—ballads that comforted me and filled me with hope. I quickly learned every song by heart and would sing to myself all the time. They spoke to me and my situation, encouraging me to find a new passion and move forward with my life.

As I changed and tried to make new dreams, life on Csepel Island, in Budapest, across the country, and all through Eastern Europe began to change rapidly too. We struggled to adjust to new freedoms: freedom of speech, freedom of religion, free self-expression and a free-market economy. It was exciting but also frightening, because with all these freedoms came a loss of protection. The Russians no longer regulated anything. The cost of living began to rise drastically—Western and multinational corporations moved in with better, more expensive products and either bought the Hungarian companies or put them out of business altogether. All of Eastern Europe was behind technologically, and almost no one spoke English. We had a lot of catching up to do with the rest of the world.

I was getting caught up though, and life was starting to have meaning for me again. I started trade school, and for my fourteenth birthday, my friend Aniko and I got tickets to see my beloved Pierrot perform a concert in downtown Budapest. I had never been so excited! I screamed and squealed as only a teenage girl seeing her idol could. After the concert, I managed to get us backstage and in front of the musician himself, where I asked him if I could start his official fan club. He agreed, probably just to be nice, but I showed him that I was the real deal. With Aniko's help—and to my surprise, my mother's—I hand-drew posters and distributed photocopies of them all over the city, advertising the fan club's first meeting. It started small, but over time its membership grew to hundreds. I devoted all my free time to promoting Pierrot's music, even getting him airtime on local and national radio and TV stations by making cold calls and being irrepressible. I was only five feet tall, but I had the energy and stamina of someone twice my size. Soon, Pierrot released a single that reached the top of the charts, and he brought me along to interviews and press conferences, introducing me as his de facto agent. It was exhilarating. I loved the world of music and promoting, and I wanted more.

Aniko and I started a school newspaper and I wrote the music column, featuring not only Pierrot but many other bands as well. I called publicists and actually got interviews with some big names, taking pride in asking them questions and sharing the answers in the newspaper for my peers. Over the next year, Pierrot's fan club grew to include more than a thousand people, and we held monthly concerts on Sundays at the community centre, featuring him and other musicians. I did the bookings and the promotion, and I interviewed the bands that came through, publishing them in our newspaper.

When I was sixteen, a small cable TV station opened on Csepel Island and advertised for volunteer technicians and crew. I signed up right away, thinking it would be a good way to learn skills. Before I knew it, my bubbly personality and high energy caught the attention of the manager, and I was offered an on-screen job interviewing Budapest teenagers about problems they faced and issues that were important to them—like where to get cheap clothes, how to find a summer job, what to do about pimples and how to handle dating. The biggest issue was where to go after school and what to do with free time. Now that communism was truly over, our lives weren't nearly as structured, and there were far fewer planned activities. The school day was shorter too, without all the assemblies, flag ceremonies and the Trailblazer club. Suddenly, I wasn't only interviewing anymore—I was being interviewed. The local paper did a feature on me as an up-and-coming youth because of all the projects I was involved in and my role as host of the TV show. After it was printed, kids began stopping me on the street and asking for my autograph! It was thrilling to know that I was becoming somebody—somebody with a voice, ideas and even influence.

The program expanded and we started focusing on music and created an MTV-like video program. I was hired as the VJ, introducing videos and interviewing guests who came on the show. I couldn't believe my luck. I loved the excitement and pace of the job, and rising to each new challenge I was offered. I decided I would make my career in the music industry—publicity, production or journalism. Now that I worked for a TV station and had access to a crew, I was asked to film one of Pierrot's performances and make a video. My schoolwork was easy—courses in art, drama, cooking, first aid and child care—and I was able to juggle my classes and assignments with work. My life was going somewhere again, and it was somewhere of my choosing.

That same year, 1993, two new guys, only a little older than me, came to the station to work on my show. Endre was seventeen and a sound technician; Ádám was eighteen and a cameraman. We instantly hit it off, and soon pitched a new program to the manager called *Fresh*, which was geared toward youth and would be about both current issues and music. We were given airtime, a tiny budget and a volunteer's salary. We didn't care—it was a great opportunity. The guys showed me how to edit and do live-to-air shows, and how to put in graphics and background music; I even got a clothing sponsor. Soon the show was a success and we began to be paid for our work. I graduated from trade school at seventeen and started working at the TV station full-time.

Western music videos were making their way into Hungary—Mariah Carey, Soul Asylum, Metallica—and so were the musicians themselves. Simply Red, Bon Jovi and Queen all performed in Budapest. Michael Jackson came to shoot a video for a song on his *HIStory* album. Because of this emerging scene, Endre, Ádám and I decided to make music videos for our show. Without a well-honed strategic plan, but with passion and zeal, we started experimenting. We loved the way the Western videographers shot their sequences, but they had modern equipment and technology. All we had was a giant, heavy Soviet camera that was straight out of a 1960s newsroom, and time. We spent hours trying to figure out how to create the softness and romance of ballad videos with our limited resources. We tried techniques like stretching a fishnet stocking and plastic food wrap over the camera lens to create blurred effects. When we had what we thought were winning videos, we spliced them into a demo reel to showcase our concepts and style, gave ourselves the name Independent Movie Makers, and started driving around Buda to the record labels, hoping we could convince them that we could make good-quality videos for less money than the big names. We were rejected over and over, but we didn't let it get us down, and eventually we got the opportunity to film a music video for a Colombian band called Carpe Diem, which only made us busier and more in demand. We made ourselves fancy black business cards and started fantasizing about fame, fortune and the office space we'd rent with a view of the Danube. Soon, we were hired to accompany up-and-coming bands on their tours and to produce their videos. We managed to do this while still working at the TV station three days a week. We were making decent money and giving most of it to our families. Like typical young people, we spent the rest on eating out and on clothing, rather than saving it. That could come later, when we were *really* successful.

At some point, through the late nights, constant togetherness and genuine attraction, Ádám and I became a couple. It was a great relationship at first, but soon it was negatively affected by stress in our work life. We began arguing a lot—mainly about money, how to run our business, and the little things about each other that got on our nerves—and I found myself struggling to find happiness within tension that closely resembled the home environment I'd grown up in. I began to feel that I was never good enough for him, no matter what I did. We depended on each other, and I was worried that if we broke up, our business would break up too. That just simply could not happen, so we continued as we were—unhappy.

At home, things had also taken a downward turn. My mom seemed unable to be happy for my success, and she cried easily and often. While my schedule was so busy it left me little time to see my friends and family, her schedule had opened up. Her shifts at the police station had been cut back because of the flailing economy, and without work to keep her busy, she began feeling quite down. I didn't know how to help. We had a high-conflict relationship, but I wanted her to be happy. My brother was called up for his mandatory eighteen-month national army service, leaving me alone with Mom. In addition to her mental health problems, she also developed heart problems and was admitted to hospital for a few weeks. I had a medical crisis at the same time: my appendix burst one day while I was alone at the TV station. I called for an ambulance but none were available, so I walked the half hour to the same hospital, gripping my right side in agony, almost blinded by the pain.

When I finally got there, I was operated on almost immediately. A week or so later, my mom and I were both discharged and sent to convalesce at home, but our dynamic was anything but healing. She was always yelling, blaming me for everything from her heart problems to her unhappiness. Then I developed an infection and was on strict bed rest for two weeks.

Mom decided that my health condition was serious enough for her to call my dad and ask him to come and see me. I hadn't laid eyes on him in eight years, and I wasn't prepared for his arrival—he just showed up and sat at the end of my bed. Upon seeing his face, I started crying and couldn't stop. I didn't know what else to do with the mix of grief, loss and feelings of abandonment that suddenly rose to the surface. I had so many questions—about where he'd been, why he'd never visited and whether or not he loved me—but I was too overcome with emotion to get them out, and he didn't offer up any information, only that he'd missed me. I don't remember anything else he said. He held my hands for a few minutes, urged me to stop crying and then, as quickly as he'd come, he left. I cried on and off for days.

After my father's visit, my mom's mental health spiralled even further downward, and she was diagnosed with major depression. She began to check herself into the hospital for days at a time. I brought her crossword puzzle books, clean pyjamas and her favourite magazines to try to cheer her up. With both my brother and mother mostly gone, Ádám began to stay overnight at the apartment with me often, more so that we could come and go from work together than for romantic reasons. We argued constantly, but breaking up was never an option.

Near the end of the summer, my mother took a turn for the better. She was smiling more, was kinder, and there was a lot less crying. "I'm in love, Timi," she confessed when I gently commented on her improved mood. "I bumped into my old boyfriend a couple of months ago—the one I had before I met your father—and our spark was still there." Her whole face smiled as she spoke. I was astonished at her revelation, and couldn't help but smile back.

"That's wonderful, Mom," I said, reaching to squeeze her hand. "I'm really happy for you."

As far as I knew, she hadn't dated anyone since my father had left, so I was truly happy for her. Soon she was away every weekend at her boyfriend's place in downtown Budapest, and I was alone in the apartment until Zoli eventually returned from the army and moved back in. My mother took this opportunity to make a permanent change.

She gave us two options: either her boyfriend would move in with us, or she would move in with him and come to visit us on Sundays. Zoli and I chose the latter. We'd met her boyfriend a few times, and although he was a very nice man, we were both uncomfortable with the idea of having someone we barely knew come and live with us, especially after all the tension and fighting we'd seen between our parents growing up. Mom transferred all the bills and the rental agreement to the apartment into our names, and my brother and I, nineteen and seventeen, were officially on our own.

Zoli had trouble finding work, so I worked harder than ever. Independent Movie Makers continued to grow, and we got jobs that actually paid. Two years went by, I turned nineteen, and we decided to hire a bookkeeper to help keep track of our income and expenses—we'd never been taught how to do that. Endre, Ádám and I eagerly met with her after she'd looked at our papers, imagining a healthy bottom line. Instead, it was the opposite.

"You owe a lot of taxes, you know," she said seriously. We didn't know. We had no idea. She slid our income statement across the table and pointed to a large figure in red. It was stunning. We didn't have anywhere near that amount of money. How could we have been so naive? So stupid? I was angry at all of us and scared, too, about what this debt meant for our future. We had no idea how to make back that kind of money, let alone get ahead. Our rising star began to fall, and I knew we needed to stop it.

To alleviate some of the financial strain, I asked my brother if we could move to a smaller, less expensive apartment, and he readily agreed. He had been unable to make his half of our rent and bills. Within a few weeks, we settled into a new apartment in the same complex along with two stray cats I named Philemon and Dolores, and things felt slightly more optimistic. I set up house and was particularly proud of our kitchen, where I displayed oversized, colourful ceramic mugs I'd started collecting when I believed I had money to spend. The American sitcom *Friends* had arrived on one of our many new channels, and I adored Central Perk where the six twenty-somethings met up daily to talk through problems over giant mugs of coffee. I imagined that one day—when I'd paid off my share of the tax bill—I would move out on my own and get an apartment like Monica and Rachel's.

Hope continued to rise when I was hired by a band to do their PR and marketing, much like I'd done for Pierrot. I had to travel to their offices in Buda, which took time and money, but it was worth it because the work paid well—even if I'd have to wait three months to be paid, which is what they told me. I had to borrow money from a friend at the studio just to afford transportation, which embarrassed me, but the pride and passion I felt for my work made up for it. My optimism returned in full force, until three months came and went and I didn't receive a paycheque. Another month went by. The band assured me I would be paid by November, and then pushed it back to December. At some point it became clear that they were never going to pay me, and I quit. By then, because of all the time I'd spent working for them, my profile at the TV station had diminished, along with my paid shifts. Not only was I less available, but I was also less cool. Nothing Hungarian seemed cool anymore—everything needed to be more Western.

Christmas approached in a grey gloom, and all I could do was cry and pace. We saw my mom and her boyfriend on Christmas Day. I did my best to pretend everything was okay and to enjoy my mom's new life, but it was hard. I had almost no work to keep me busy or to keep my hopes up. By the new year, I was alone most of the time, as Zoli was out looking for work, playing soccer with his friends, or in bars. I worried he was going down my dad's road toward alcoholism. Ádám and I spent time together at the TV station and at my apartment, but there was so much tension over our business that it seemed all we did was argue. I felt lost and desperate.

It was then that I met Bianka.

3 | Befriended

BIANKA MOVED IN TWO FLOORS above us and was a character as bright and bold as my colourful mug collection. I'd never seen anyone like her in real life. She looked like Sharon Stone—tall and blonde, with perfect makeup and those big, fake boobs. Everyone else in the building gossiped about her in the elevators or the mailroom, saying she was a stuck-up snob because she never talked to anyone, but that didn't deter me; I wanted to talk to her. So, one day, when we got on the elevator at the same time, I said hello and introduced myself.

We hit it off right away. She was very chatty and friendly, and I began to look forward to running into her in the hallway or in the elevator. It was just small talk, but it was nice. I'd lost touch with many of my friends from school, and I'd distanced myself from friends at the TV station. All I could think about was the tax bill, and the overdue notices that had arrived about it and other bills, like our utilities, all of which now had interest charges on them. I felt like I was drowning.

One day, Bianka and I were talking about movies and she asked if I'd ever seen *Gone with the Wind*, which I hadn't. She'd rented it and was planning to watch it that evening, so she invited me over. Her apartment was sparse, with only basic furniture and very few personal items around. As we made snacks and poured drinks, I noticed her cupboards were almost bare—just a few boxes of biscuits and cans of beans. I was surprised; her high-maintenance, polished look had made me think she was rich. She told me about how her mother had moved to Germany years before, when Bianka was only seventeen. She was on her own, just like me. She also had a young son, who, that night, was with his father.

"Do you ever see that fancy black car pull up downstairs?" she asked. I nodded. I'd noticed it a few times, mostly because it looked so out of place in our neighbourhood. "That's my ex-husband." I was surprised—she seemed too young to have been married and divorced, to have a child.

"What does he do?" I asked casually, trying not to sound too nosy. I didn't want to seem like one of the gossips in our building.

She shrugged. "He's a mafia guy," she said, as if I was supposed to know what that meant. I thought the mafia were only in the movies or in Russia. Again, I acted nonchalant so she wouldn't know how naive I really was.

"What do you do?" I asked.

"I'm a call girl in Sweden," she responded, just as casually as she'd told me her ex-husband's line of work. It was like she'd just said that he was a doctor and she was a lawyer. I was taken aback, wondering if I'd heard her correctly. *A call girl?* I didn't really know what to say next, but I'm sure my face gave away my disbelief. Reading my expression, she filled in some of the blanks.

"It's no big deal—I go to Sweden for two or three months a year, work as a prostitute, and make enough money that I don't have to work for the rest of the year so I can take care of my son." She took a sip of her soda, calmly watching for my reaction, seeming unconcerned about what it might be.

"Wow," I said slowly, fumbling for the right response. I liked her, and I didn't want her to feel judged. "Um . . . are you okay?"

"Yeah. You have a drink, you close your eyes, you don't think about it and you're fine." She spoke breezily, and I tried to take it all in just as coolly, but I was shocked. I'd never spoken to a prostitute before, never thought about them as women with apartments and children. I'd thought it was sad when I saw women selling themselves on street corners in the red light district on the few occasions I'd driven through that area of Pest, but I'd never stopped to think about their lives beyond the horrible way they had to make money. Now, for the first time, with Bianka sitting in front of me—a mother, neighbour and friend—I did. I couldn't wipe the look of bewilderment off my face, but I didn't think I could, or should, pose any of the questions that were swirling in my mind.

"Look, I make a lot of money and I can take care of my son," she continued, sounding a little defensive. "No one cares about me, so I'm on my own."

"As long as you're okay," I said. I really did want to be friends.

We settled in to watch the movie but I could scarcely concentrate on the storyline, thinking about what Bianka had just disclosed and wondering about her life in Sweden. What she described sounded awful to me. While we'd never really received any sex education at school, and our culture didn't talk very openly about relationships, the predominant view was that sex should happen in the context of loving and committed relationships. It was something to take seriously. It was something both people had to agree to, and had to want. I knew what a prostitute was, of course, but they existed in a dark underworld that I'd never imagined I would encounter.

I'd had a few negative sexual experiences over the years, beginning one night when I was twelve. A group of kids from our building was gathered together on couches in the common room, watching a movie. Sitting next to me was the uncle of one of my friends. During the movie, he fondled me under the blanket, reaching his hands into my pants. I'd been shocked and confused, not knowing what was happening or how to stop it. When it was over, I felt ashamed. I didn't tell anyone, not even my mother, the police officer. What would I say? I must have invited the man's attention, though I didn't know how. I shut the experience out of my mind and prayed it would never happen again. I saw him a few times after that and always managed to avoid him.

Then a couple of years ago, when I was seventeen and working late at the TV station, one of the guys working there found me alone in the studio and tried to force himself on me. I'd been saved by a phone ringing, and he'd left. Again, I didn't tell anyone. I was too embarrassed, so I tried to forget, tried to imagine that it had happened to someone else—a different Timea. Yet another time, one of my mom's colleagues made some unwanted advances while I waited for her to finish her shift, and I'd had to push him off me. With Ádám, despite our other problems, intimacy was respectful and was a connection we enjoyed. I couldn't imagine having sex with someone for money, like Bianka did.

Nonetheless, I began spending more and more time with her. She was intriguing, and she made me feel older and more mature, like she needed my friendship as much as I needed hers. Ádám didn't like that I was hanging out with Bianka, nor did my brother, who would say she was trouble. All they saw was her appearance, and they thought she might be a bad influence on me. But I liked and cared for her. She opened up to me about her life, about her troubles with her ex-husband and son, and I opened up to her too. She was kind of like a big sister, even if she wasn't exactly the perfect role model.

As our friendship grew, my relationship with Ádám continued to deteriorate. Every day was filled with arguments, and he constantly put me down. My self-confidence began to crumble and I didn't feel the same in front of the camera, or behind it. I questioned myself and my abilities, and began seeing things for what they were. How had I ended up in a relationship filled with such anger and criticism? Maybe I wasn't really a *somebody* after all.

Being at home with Zoli was just as stressful, although now it wasn't because we were arguing but because we were hungry. His hours at work were also being cut back, and we couldn't seem to make ends meet, even with the cheaper rent. We would wander into the kitchen and open and close the fridge as if that would make food appear. It never did.

Asking our mother for help was simply out of the question. We knew she'd be disappointed in us, that she didn't have enough money herself, and we couldn't risk disrupting her new life. Finding me in this situation would be just what she'd expected, and she would finally be right in her accusations: everything was my fault. I was terrified of her finding out.

By spring, I was in a deep depression. Zoli and I were six months behind on our rent and other household bills, and we would fight over the last piece of bread. There was no money in Independent Movie Makers, and I owed a lot of money to the friend at the TV station who I'd borrowed from. One day, an eviction warning arrived at the apartment, giving us thirty days to pay the rent we owed. I was on the verge of a nervous breakdown.

The only good thing in my life was my friendship with Bianka. The way she made money bothered me, but she was fun and exciting, and she made everything look easy and possible. She would take me out for a burger and assure me everything was going to be okay. She drove me around in her car. She taught me how to pluck and shape my eyebrows, and tried to get me to grow my hair out of the little bob I'd sported for years. She filled the big sister void I had in my life. But it all came with a shadowy feeling. She lived on the edge—what did she see in me, a "good girl," a tomboy? There was nothing on the edge about me at all, but the fact that she had chosen me made me feel cool, and cared for.

Eventually, I confided in her about exactly how much money I owed for rent, utilities, bills and the taxes for our business. Saying it aloud made me literally sick to my stomach. I vomited in her bathroom, and she laid a wet facecloth on the back of my neck.

"Timi, if you lose your apartment you can come and stay in mine while I'm away working this summer," she said reassuringly. It was a generous offer that brought some relief, but it was also a reminder of what she would be away doing.

"What exactly do you do when you're in Sweden, Bianka?" I asked, almost afraid of the answer. "Like, how many . . . um, clients . . . do you see in a night?"

She flipped her long, blonde hair back. "About ten," she said casually.

What? Ten? It seemed crazy to me, unimaginable. But I needed to know more. "How much money do you make?"

"About a thousand kronor per day." Converted to Hungarian forint, the amount was astounding. No wonder she only had to work two months a year. But why were her cupboards so empty? Why didn't she just work another month or two, actually get ahead, and then get out of the whole business altogether?

"But how do you *feel*?" I asked. The income was one thing, but what about the cost—the emotional toll?

"You don't feel anything," she said flatly, the same way she had before. "You just close your eyes and turn your head and it's usually over pretty fast."

"It's really that easy?" I asked skeptically.

"I don't care. I just do what I have to do for my kid." It was that simple for her. "Do you want to try it?" she asked me.

"No way," I said. "I can't do that." No matter how desperate I was, I couldn't sell myself.

"It's not for everybody," she agreed. "If you can't do it, you can't do it."

I wanted to ask Bianka how she *really* felt about herself, but instead I asked her logistical questions about her life in Sweden. Was she a hooker, on a street corner? No, it was all very organized, she explained.

There was a big apartment with a beautiful, white kitchen and many rooms—a high-end, modern-day brothel. She and a few other call girls—all women like her, from other countries, with kids to support—rented the rooms from the manager, and the clients came there. There was a big swimming pool to relax in at the end of the day, or in the morning if it had been a night shift, and they all had their own apartments to go home to when they weren't working, rented from the same guy. If you were sick, you took a day off. She said she'd never been hurt, and she really didn't look any worse for the wear to me, although I didn't know what was underneath all the makeup. As bizarre as it all was, there was no reason to think she wasn't telling me the truth or that her clients weren't all like Richard Gere in *Pretty Woman*, or some Swedish version of Prince Charming.

All this talk with Bianka about her work made me really think about my own. I decided I had to give up on the TV station and find something that was more stable and paid better. Time was ticking, and if I didn't get a new job within the next twenty days, I would have to move away from Hungary to a richer European country where wages were higher, somewhere I could get paid right away. Moving appealed to me. I could pay back all my debts, get out of my relationship with Ádám, make some new friends and get my life back on track. I could learn English and become more Western. Maybe I could even save enough to further my education. I loved working in the music industry, but there was still a part of me deep down that wanted to help people, especially kids. I'd heard of girls going to be babysitters or nannies in other countries. I felt a surge of hope I hadn't felt in a long time. I asked Bianka for help conducting a proper job hunt, since I'd always created all my jobs for myself. She suggested we start by looking at classified ads in the newspaper.

And that's when she pointed it out:

YOUNG FEMALES NEEDED TO WORK
IN CANADA, NO ENGLISH NECESSARY.

———

That was the ad that had brought me here, to the Toronto airport, where I waited to be interviewed by a customs officer and for my fate to be determined.

Another hour passed before an older man with grey hair came over to me. "Are you Timea Nagy?" he asked in Hungarian.

I nodded.

"You are going to be interrogated in interview room three. Your friend will be interrogated separately. Just wait here until the officer is free. I will be your translator."

"Interrogated?" I repeated, the word catching in my throat. Interrogation was for criminals. I was a good girl. I'd never broken the law, never stolen anything—not even a candy—in my entire life. I'd gotten myself into a bad situation at home, but not on purpose. Now I was trying to fix it.

I asked the translator if I could go to the bathroom, and he showed me where it was. Inside, I started crying. Frantic, loud sobbing. What if this whole plan fell apart? What if I had to go back home?

4 | Interrogation

I WAS CRYING MY HARDEST when Bianka came into the bathroom and grabbed me by my shoulders. "Get yourself together. You have to stop crying! Now."

I couldn't tell if she was annoyed or scared. I splashed some water on my face and collected myself. We went back out and sat down a few seats apart on the same side of the corridor. I glanced at her and felt my stomach drop. It was as though I was seeing her for the first time. Maybe it was the situation we were in, or the intimidating setting, or simply all the uniforms around us, but suddenly I realized that not only was Bianka a prostitute, she *looked like* a prostitute. I might be a good girl, but I was travelling with a bad girl. Maybe the visa problem had to do with her work in Sweden, and the officers had assumed I was also a prostitute. I thought about how the woman on the plane had reacted to finding out Bianka and I were travelling together, and now I felt stupid instead of indignant. Bianka drew attention and suspicion because of her appearance, and I wanted to hide my connection to her from the customs officers, like I'd hidden it from my family and friends back home. I felt a pang of guilt for thinking this. She'd been a good friend to me, helping me get this job. She was the only person I had here and she was trying to make a better life too. *There's just been a mix up*, I told myself. I could explain everything.

A few minutes later, I was finally called to the interview room. The officer behind the desk inside had black hair, black eyes, a black goatee and a very serious look on his face. Next to him sat the translator.

"Why are you coming to Canada?" the translator asked me.

"I'm here for a job as a babysitter," I told them, wondering why there was confusion. They had my contract in front of them.

"Are you sure?" the officer asked.

"Yes, I'm sure. I'm here to babysit." My heart began to beat faster and I felt hot again.

"Are you sure?" he asked again, more sternly.

"Yes. Absolutely."

"I'm going to ask you again. Why are you coming to Canada?"

"To babysit." The more I was asked to answer this question, the more it seemed like I was lying. I felt faint and was glad I was sitting down.

"Where did you get this babysitting job?"

"Through an agency."

"How did you meet the agency?"

"I answered an ad in the newspaper." I avoided going into a deeper explanation, or telling the story of my debt or meeting Bianka. I remember Mom saying that people usually got in trouble when they said too much to the police. Asking the same question over and over was a strategy she and her colleagues used to elicit admissions of guilt. What did this officer think I was guilty of?

"Did you meet anyone from the agency when you were in Hungary?"

"Yes, I went for an interview with Natasa, from human resources." My mind flashed back to just two weeks ago. It was a springy morning in early April and I'd worn jeans and a nice T-shirt—something clean, casual and appropriate for a babysitter, but also what I usually wore. I was nervous and excited as Bianka and I boarded the train for downtown. When we arrived at McDonald's to meet Natasa, I was surprised that Bianka recognized her, but they didn't seem to know each other well. I figured it was just a "small world" thing. Natasa looked to be in her late twenties or early thirties. She had green eyes, tanned skin, fake nails and over-processed hair, and she was very well-spoken. She told me all about working in Canada. She'd worked there herself in many different jobs—babysitting, housekeeping, even some sort of dancing—and now she worked for the agency as a recruiter, helping Hungarian girls who needed jobs. A team of agents in Canada matched girls up with families and companies needing workers, mainly in a big city called Toronto. There was endless work available in Canada, she told us, and masses of money to be made in such a rich country.

"What is the name of the agency?" the officer asked sternly.

"I don't know," I admitted, feeling like an idiot. "Isn't it in the contract?" The officer didn't look down at my contract, only at me.

"Who's picking you up?" he continued without missing a beat.

"The agents from the agency."

"Do you know Tony Verudi?" The officer leaned in a little closer with this question.

"No—who's Tony Verudi?" I couldn't pronounce the name properly. I just repeated it as best I could. I was confused.

"Do you know Elek Pécsi?"

I *did* know an Elek Pécsi. He was a friend of one of the detectives on my mom's police force—they'd done their army service together. The detectives were a great group of men, and took care of me like big brothers. A few years ago, the summer I was fifteen, they invited me to go to the beach with them. It was there that we ran into Elek, who had also become a detective after his army service. He joined us in a game of soccer, but I hadn't seen him since. Why was his name coming up? It couldn't be the same person.

"I know an Elek Pécsi, but it must be a different one." The officer made a note on the paper in front of him. Then he showed me what looked like a driver's licence or some form of Canadian ID with a photo of an overweight, tough-looking bald guy on it, at least forty years old.

"Do you recognize this man?" the officer asked.

"No, I've never seen him before," I answered, baffled. It definitely wasn't Elek Pécsi. The Elek I knew was slender, fair-haired, had blue eyes and would be much younger.

"Where are you staying in Toronto?"

"I don't know exactly—the agents have made all the arrange-ments."

"So." The officer was now closer to my face than ever. "You're not here to dance?"

"Dance? No, I'm here to babysit," I said as firmly as I could.

I thought back to my interview with Natasa. She had said that work visas for dancers were the easiest kind to get, but I'd said that I didn't want to be a dancer of any kind. She'd tried hard to convince me to change my mind. "You can have your pick of jobs, Timea," she said, "but dancing pays the best."

"What exactly do you mean by 'dancing'?" I'd asked, curious but not interested. I was picturing the sleazy nightclubs I'd driven past in the not-so-nice areas of Budapest. The kind with the neon signs advertising hot girls, where even someone as naive as me knew there was more than just dancing going on.

"It's nothing like you think," Natasa explained. "In Canada, you just walk around in your bikini and guys put money in the straps. Have you seen the movie *Striptease* with Demi Moore? It's like that— but not stripping, just teasing." She laughed at her own little joke, and I smiled. I had seen that movie and it wasn't that bad, but I still knew dancing wasn't for me.

Bianka had wanted to know more. "Maybe I could do that in Canada. Is it really that easy?" she asked.

"Sure—fill out an application," Natasa said, smiling warmly. For Bianka, it was a much better choice than her real line of work.

"Let's get back to the other work," I told Natasa. "I prefer babysitting, with cleaning as my second choice." She nodded. Then I asked a question I'd had since seeing the ad. "Why isn't English necessary?"

"Well," Natasa explained, "there is a big Hungarian community in Toronto—if you need a dentist, you go to a Hungarian dentist. If you need a doctor, you go to a Hungarian doctor. There are even Hungarian grocery stores and shops. Toronto is very multicultural and there is a neighbourhood for every country." I had to admit, it sounded good.

"But how will we get around?" I asked.

"Easy," Natasa said. "Our agency has drivers so you don't have to use public transit."

"How much money do you actually make, and how long does it take?" Bianka inquired. We both needed to do the math.

"How much do you need?" Natasa asked.

"At least as much as I make in Sweden," Bianka said, and then shared the amount. Natasa nodded, and then turned to me.

"What's your situation, Timea?"

I explained that Zoli and I had fallen far behind on our rent and other bills, and that I had a business debt as well. I needed about 500,000 forint, which Natasa said was $3,500 Canadian.

"Well, with babysitting you make about $500 a month per kid, and out of that you have to pay us an agency fee. So that would leave you about $400 per month if you were taking care of one child, but if you look after two or three kids it can really add up." I began calculating the numbers in my head for a family of three or four children. It was a sizeable amount. Maybe I'd found a solution to my problems. Then Natasa laid out the math for dancing, which added up to three times as much.

"But I'm not interested in dancing," I reiterated. "My mom is a police officer here, and she would kill me."

She understood. "In Canada you can do whatever you want. You try babysitting, and if you need a little extra money on a Friday night, you can always try dancing. But it's up to you. When you get to Canada, our agency picks you up and takes you to your accommodation, and then we look at all the jobs that are available and pick the best match."

"How do I get into Canada?" I asked.

"They give out work visas for three months at the border when you present a signed contract from our agency. Once you're in, you just work at whatever job you choose and pay us our agency fee every week. If you want to stay longer than three months, we apply for an extension." It all made sense, but I still had a few more questions.

"But how do I get there? I don't have money for the plane ticket and it's probably really expensive."

"Yes, it is, so we loan you the money for your ticket, and then you pay us back out of your first few paycheques. We also add a $200 service charge."

"What about other countries that are maybe not so far away?" I asked. Maybe there was somewhere I could travel to by train so it wouldn't be so expensive.

"We have worked in England, Germany, Turkey and other countries before, but the market in Canada is the best right now. The most opportunities are there, so that's where we're focusing our agency development." She paused. "The dancing is exploding in Canada, and we've been able to help a lot of Hungarian girls find work—many who have a child or parents to provide for—because Canada has a special work visa for dancers."

This surprised me, but it was irrelevant since I wasn't going to be dancing. "But do they give visas for babysitting?"

"Yes, but it is much easier to get a dancing visa these days." She pulled papers out of her bag and passed them to Bianka and me. "Start by filling out this general application. Then I'll take it from here."

"What do I have to lose?" Bianka said, fishing in her bag for a pen.

It took several minutes for us to complete the forms since they were all in English. Natasa told us what to write in each of the boxes, and I filled in my personal information, and my emergency contact information—my mom's name and address, my brother's, and Ádám's. I hadn't told any of them yet about my plan to work abroad, but I hoped they'd support me. I'd have to call Natasa with my passport number since I didn't know it by heart. I had one from when I went to communist summer camp in Poland several years ago. I hoped it hadn't expired.

That night, Ádám came over and demanded to know where I'd been all day and with whom. I was nervous to tell him my news, but also excited. When I told him, he was upset that I'd been with Bianka. If going to Canada had anything to do with her, he wasn't going to support it.

"She's going to get you into trouble," he warned.

"You're just jealous—why can't you just be happy for me?" I retorted, angry. "I'm doing what I have to do."

"Are you going to break up with me?" he demanded, suddenly sounding worried. His hurt expression reminded me that he did care about me, and that I cared about him too. But I didn't have the answer to his question—I just wanted everything in my life to be better.

"It's just for three months," I said, reassuringly. "It could be good for us." He relaxed but still wasn't enthusiastic about my leaving.

From there, I managed to convince my mom and Zoli that going to Canada for a few months was a great opportunity. I had to fib a bit to my mom, to keep her policing instincts at bay. I told her that a friend of mine from trade school had been in Canada working as a babysitter, but that her visa had run out and she needed to spend some time in Hungary before she could renew it and go back. She needed someone to fill in for her while she was gone, and had offered the position to me. I'd be gone for three months; I'd make lots of money, gain experience, see a new part of the world and learn some English. My mom accepted this fairly easily, asking me to be sure to call her as soon as I was settled with the family I'd be working for. I was relieved. She even said she would come to the airport to see me off. That's when I decided to tell everyone that Bianka wasn't going with me; that she was going somewhere else. It would just make everything easier.

Next, I had to ask my manager at the TV station for a leave of absence. He was surprised because I'd never mentioned wanting to travel before, let alone to Canada, but supported me nonetheless. Then I told Zoli, and promised I'd send him money as soon as I could. I could see the relief on his face. Endre and other friends at the TV station started making me a cute pocket English dictionary, putting together the few phrases they knew with others they'd had to look up, like, "Excuse me, please, can you tell me where the bathroom is?" It was sweet. Ádám had joined them in making the little book to show that he'd decided to be supportive, and this—along with the knowledge that we were going to be apart—brought a little romance back into our relationship. It felt good. My heart warmed, I wrote him inspirational quotes on little cards for every one of the nights I'd be gone. *Maybe distance will do us some good, and we can start over when I come back.* But I couldn't think too far into the future. I needed to pack and get going.

I had one suitcase and I filled it with jeans, T-shirts, shorts and a little bit of makeup—all things suitable for my new job as a babysitter. Natasa had explained that Canada wasn't cold year-round and that in fact it would be spring and summer when I was there, so I didn't need to worry about the infamous Canadian winter. Ádám gave me a little stuffed Simba for good luck, since *The Lion King* was my favourite movie, so I tucked that in along with a new journal I'd bought for my adventure. Then I chose my favourite mug from my collection and wrapped it up in my coziest pyjamas. I imagined chatting with my new roommates over coffee. They'd be just like Monica, Rachel and Phoebe on *Friends*.

I met with Natasa one more time to go over my travel instructions and sign my contract. Natasa explained that I would have to pay a $150 fee at the border for my visa, and she gave it to me in Canadian dollars, noting that it would be added to the amount I owed the agency. It was the first time I'd held something Canadian in my hands, and I felt a small thrill as I thought about all the Canadian money I would soon be piling up. I also loved that it was so colourful, with images of birds, trees, lakes and, to my surprise, the Queen of England.

"Babysitting. Really?" The officer's sarcastic tone snapped me back to the present. I didn't know why he doubted me so strongly. Maybe I hadn't been clear enough. Maybe there was a problem with the translator.

"Yes, babysitting." I was emphatic.

"You're not going to be an exotic dancer? You're not a stripper?"

"No!" I insisted, almost laughing. The idea of me stripping was ridiculous, but I was starting to worry about what Natasa might have written on the contract, and the fact that Bianka was here to dance.

"So you're not here to make $20 a song?"

"What? No way."

"And you're not going to work for Tony Verudi? He's not going to be your agent for $140 per week?"

Who the hell was this guy Tony?

"No, no, no." It was all I could say, over and over.

The interrogation went on for six hours. As soon as the officer finished a set of questions, he went back to the beginning and started over. I was exhausted, scared and on the verge of tears. I looked to the translator for comfort, but he didn't offer any words or even a sympathetic look. I could only guess the same thing was happening to Bianka, only maybe it was worse. Maybe they were asking what she did for a living in Europe. On the other hand, she was fine with dancing, so they should let her in. Finally, I asked a question of my own.

"Can you please just tell me what's going on? Maybe that way we can move forward." I was confused, scared, hungry and exhausted.

The officer sighed. "This contract says that you will be working here as an exotic dancer, with Tony Verudi as your agent. You will pay him $140 per week and you will be employed at Temptations, a strip club not far from here, and you'll be making $20 a song."

"What?" I was shocked. My stomach dropped to the floor. Something was wrong. Very wrong. Why had Natasa written that on my contract? Had she mixed me up with Bianka?

"You signed it, so you must know." He turned the paper around so I could see it. "Is that your signature there?" He pointed to my signature. I swallowed hard.

"Yes, that's my signature, but . . ." I didn't know what to say. This didn't look good. "The contract is in English and I don't speak English. The recruiter told me what the contract said, but what you just read isn't what she translated to me."

"So," the officer said, "you're not coming as a dancer?"

"No," I said for what felt like the hundredth time.

"Then I have no choice but to return you to Hungary for trying to enter Canada unlawfully. You cannot stay if you are not going to be a dancer, because what you have here is an application for an exotic dancing visa."

I was now more confused than ever. Was he saying he would let me in if I *was* a stripper? Why would Canada allow exotic dancers across its borders but not babysitters? I couldn't believe what I was hearing.

"So." He posed his question one last time. "You don't want to be a dancer—right?"

"That's right," I said, weakly.

"Okay. We will not charge you, but we will send you back to Hungary on the condition that you not try to re-enter Canada for eighteen months. If you try to re-enter Canada, you will be criminally charged. Do you understand?"

I felt like I'd been kicked. I was in worse trouble than ever. All I could picture was my mom's face when she found out what I'd done:

racked up a huge debt, signed up with an agency I didn't even know the name of, accidentally put my name on a contract that said I was a stripper, and then gotten in trouble with the authorities. Imagining her rage and disappointment was overwhelming. Then there was the matter of my debt.

I told the officer I understood, and he passed me some formal-looking papers.

"There's just one problem," the officer said. "There are no flights back to Hungary until tomorrow night. Your people from the agency are here waiting for you, so we're going to release you on the promise that you return to the airport at 3 p.m. tomorrow. We'll keep your passport here, and it will be returned to you once you board the aircraft." The translator motioned for me to stand up, and then back to the corridor, where Bianka was standing by the exit door, looking upset and holding the same papers. She must be going home too. Both of us followed the translator to the exit, where we headed down an escalator to baggage claim.

"This is so bad, this is so bad!" she was muttering, repeatedly and angrily, not even looking at me. "I've lost a lot of money now. I never should have come with you." Our suitcases had long been removed from the carousel and placed by a wall with other unclaimed bags. After collecting them, we walked toward another set of doors where a guard checked to make sure they were ours, and then through automatic doors that opened into the terminal. That's when I saw him for the first time—the scary-looking man in the driver's licence photo the officer had shown me. *Tony Verudi*. It was a name I'd heard over and over again for the last several hours, and here he was in the flesh, even more intimidating than in his photo. He stood about twenty feet away from us, arms crossed, unsmiling. He was tall—over six feet—and heavyset, with a protruding stomach. His skin was pasty white, and his eyes small and dark. He was bald on top, but wore his hair in a long ponytail. Behind him were two guys speaking in Hungarian. I recognized one of them.

"Elek Pécsi?" I asked, scarcely believing my eyes. It *was* the Elek Pécsi I knew!

He recognized me, but didn't smile. "Timea Nagy—it's been a long time."

"What are you doing here?" I asked.

"Natasa is my girlfriend," he said. "We both work for this agency."

I was relieved to see a familiar face, but also confused. "But you became a detective after the army," I said.

"Things changed," he said simply, without explanation. I thought I could detect regret in his voice, but I didn't press to find out what happened in Hungary. I could ask that later, if there was time, or assume he'd lost his job because of the failing economy, like my mom. Right now I needed to reassure Bianka.

I turned to her. "It's good. Everything's okay. I know him."

The look on her face didn't change from anger to relief, as I'd hoped. She was still very mad at me.

"You guys fucked up bad," Elek said sternly. "You must have said something wrong, because the immigration officer was all over us. It was supposed to be easy! We've had twelve girls come over in the last couple of months. Easy." He snapped his fingers to demonstrate how simple it had all been. "What did you tell them?"

I was indignant. "What do you mean, 'What did I tell them'? They asked me what I came here to do and I said babysitting."

Elek and the other man looked exasperated at my answer and translated it to Tony, who evidently didn't understand Hungarian. He didn't look too pleased either.

Elek sighed heavily. "You have to get a dancing visa, otherwise you can't stay in the country. Getting you a babysitting job would have come *after* you entered the country. How the hell did you mess this up?"

"No one explained this to me!" Now I was the one who was angry.

"Well, Natasa should have explained it to you better in Budapest.

You can only get into Canada on an exotic dancing visa. Once you're here, you can do whatever you want, but you can only get in on a dancer's work permit." He pointed to Tony. "Tony is the manager who will sign your work permit."

As crazy as all this was, it was starting to make sense again. There had been a miscommunication, and for whatever strange reason, Canada only let in exotic dancers, not babysitters. I felt horrible about my mistake and all the trouble I'd caused. By not lying at customs, I'd made a mess of everything. I'd come to Canada to fix my problems, and now I was in more trouble than ever.

Elek picked up my bag, and the other Hungarian guy—who was introduced as József, a driver—picked up Bianka's, and the five of us headed to the parking lot.

Fear was rising, so I tried to push it down with wishful thinking. Maybe I would go to sleep and wake up to discover this was all just a bad dream. I would have breakfast, get dressed and go to the agency office. There I'd choose the best babysitting job, just like Natasa had promised. Bianka could dance, strip or do whatever she wanted; all I cared about was that we were both making money and paying off our debts. But with no passports and orders to leave the country the following day, none of that seemed likely at all.

5 | First Night

THE BIGGEST CAR I'D EVER SEEN was waiting for us when we walked out of the airport and to the parking lot: a fancy, black SUV with shaded windows and leather seats. *The agency must be a really successful one to afford this kind of car.* We drove out onto a fast, multi-lane highway like I'd only seen in the movies. It was now late afternoon, the sky was blue, and out my window I saw a little bit of snow still on the ground. There were many tall buildings that looked much newer than those in Budapest. From the backseat, I watched the speedometer reach and then pass one hundred kilometres an hour. If things had gone as they were supposed to at immigration, I'd be enjoying this experience. Instead, the speed only heightened my fear.

It was a tense, fifteen-minute drive to the motel. No one said much, except for Tony, who put on a CD and asked me if I liked the band Modern Talking, which I did. At least, that's what I assumed he said because he was nodding with eyebrows up, and I recognized the English name of the band. My thoughts raced as I tried to sort out my situation. *I'm going back to Budapest. I have to pay the agency back for my plane ticket, so now I have more debt than ever. I am in so much trouble! But I can't go back. I need the money. Where am I going to go in Hungary to make this kind of money?* I didn't have any answers to these questions. I looked over at Bianka, who was looking out the window.

I bit my nails and tried to focus on the positive. Other than the money I owed, I didn't seem to be in any danger. I was with my friend, although she was mad at me, and Elek, who I at least sort of knew from home. I didn't know Tony or József, but never mind. *I'm okay.*

We pulled off the highway and into the parking lot of a two-storey building with a sign that said Motel 27. *Hotel* was one of the very few English words I knew, mainly from American movies. I figured that *motel* must be just the Canadian dialect. At any rate, I'd never stayed in a motel or hotel of any kind in my life. I felt a flash of excitement, but it left as soon as it came. This was no vacation. I was supposed to be here to work; now I would only be staying the night and then heading back home.

József stayed in the car while the rest of us got out and walked into the motel. What hit me first was the smell, like it had in the airport. The lobby smelled of very strong cleaning detergents mixed with coffee. I looked around and saw a coffee maker on a table. Next to it was a vending machine with the biggest Coke cans and water bottles I'd ever seen. Everything here was bigger than life. I felt excited again. *I'm in North America! So cool!* Then reality immediately set back in; I wouldn't be staying.

With Elek translating, Tony let Bianka and me know that he'd gotten the two of us a room. We took an elevator to the second floor and walked down the hall. Instead of a key, he used a plastic card to open the door, and then put it in his pocket. Everything was so modern. As we entered, I observed the room. There were two big beds with floral spreads, a TV and a dresser in the main room. There was an ensuite bathroom with towels and little soaps. There was even a little coffee maker with packets of coffee, sugar and powdered cream on a desk next to the dresser. With nothing to compare it to, I was impressed. *Wow, I'm in a real five-star hotel. Look at me!* I *had* to figure out how to stay in this crazy-rich country.

I walked to the window and looked out. I didn't know what time it was, but there was still light in the sky, and I could see the highway. There was a big shopping mall on the other side of the highway with an enormous parking lot, packed with huge cars. One day, once I paid back all this money, maybe I could come back and go shopping there. I exhaled slowly and tried to reassure myself with positive thoughts, as I'd learned to do back in my camp days. *Everything is going to be fine.* I turned around to look at the men and saw two serious faces staring back at me. Bianka still wouldn't even look at me. There was no reassurance to draw from any of them.

Tony motioned for Bianka and me to sit down on the bed.

"So what now?" he asked, with Elek translating for him. I stared at him blankly. "How could you be so stupid?" he demanded. "What are you doing here anyway?"

"I came to make money." My truthful answer sounded flimsy. On the heels of my airport interrogation, scared, hungry and exhausted, nothing sounded like the truth anymore. I looked at Elek. "My mom moved out," I began, scrambling to explain my circumstances.

"I know," Elek said.

"You do?" I asked, confused. *How?*

"What about the TV station?" he continued. *He knew about that too?* I didn't think I'd mentioned either of these points to Natasa.

"I couldn't make enough money there," I explained, dumbfounded. Tony looked at me sternly, and then looked back at Elek, waiting for the translation. "I owe a lot of taxes and I was going to lose my apartment," I continued, "so I came here to make the money to pay off my bills and keep my apartment. You know how the economy is in Hungary." Maybe that's why he'd moved to Canada.

"Why did *you* come here?" I asked, turning the attention back to him.

"I make so much more money here—this corporation, this agency, it's booming. We have girls working all over, and branches across Western Europe. I could never be this successful back in Hungary," Elek explained. He noticed Tony looking impatient, so he changed the subject back to me. "I'm really concerned now, Timea. You've put us in a really bad spot." He didn't direct any of his questions to Bianka. I seemed to be the target of blame. Why wasn't everyone mad at Natasa the recruiter?

"How?" I asked, genuinely confused. I was the one in the mess.

"Well, Tony is the manager. He paid $1,500 at the airport to get you guys out. Our agency also paid for your plane tickets, which were $1,000 each, and this room for tonight. So right now, each of you owes us about $2,000." He glanced over at Bianka, who looked sick, but continued to speak mainly to me. "And we have a boss, Sasha. He's the agency owner and we report to him—he's a Ukrainian guy. And you know Ukrainians—you don't mess with them." The way he said this gave me chills. "So I need to get the money to Sasha as soon as possible," he continued. "How much money do you have on you?"

"Just a few thousand forint," I said, feeling really stupid, wishing I had more, "and the $150 Canadian that Natasa gave me for the work permit fee." I looked over to Bianka to see if she could help out.

"Same here," she said, still avoiding eye contact with me.

"Well, then we have a real problem." His words chilled me. "Not only do you owe us a lot of money, but you put our whole business at risk at the airport by calling attention to us. Now you're going to be sent back, which looks very bad for our reputation." Elek paused, glanced again at Bianka, and then returned his attention to me. "So what are you going to do?"

I didn't have a clue. All I could picture was the grand total of what I now owed—about $5,500—and how it would be impossible to pay back if I couldn't work in Canada like I'd planned.

"I don't know," was my simple answer. I turned to Bianka to see if she had any ideas.

"Well, I'm going back," she said angrily. "I'll go to my job in Sweden right away. It will take me longer than working here, but I can pay it back." I shuddered, thinking about her going back to what she'd been doing there.

"Okay, let's not panic." Elek's tone suddenly changed to reassurance. "We're going to figure this out. Timike," he said, calling me by a nickname no one had used for years, "I'll take care of you, don't worry. Bianka, you'll figure it out. If you guys just want to freshen up a little, we'll take you to the place where we usually hang out at night and you can work there for a few hours and make a bit of cash. Now it won't be what you wanted, but you're in a tough spot. There are a lot of ways to make a lot of money quick, so just get ready and we'll go."

"Where are we going?" I asked. All I wanted to do was crawl into bed and wake up to a solution.

"Just shut up, Timea!" Bianka spat out, finally addressing me. "You've done enough already. Just do what they say." Hearing her words and tone filled me with hurt and shame. She was my friend— the closest thing I had to an older sister—and I'd let her down without intending to.

I asked Elek if I could take a shower and put on clean clothes, but he said there wasn't time. We needed to get going to wherever he was taking us. I hoped we would be back soon so I could have an early night. I noticed the clock radio on the nightstand, and it read 7:30 p.m., which was 1:30 a.m. to me. I went to the bathroom and splashed some cold water on my face.

Fifteen minutes later we pulled up to a low, windowless building with a neon sign of naked women dancing. A knot began to form in my stomach, but I didn't have too much time to think before we were ushered in the door. A man dressed in a tuxedo stood at the top of a set of stairs leading down, and Tony said something to him in English. The guard nodded and motioned for us to go down the stairs. I'd never set foot in a place like this. What was I going to see? What was I going to do? I said a silent prayer that it would be cleaning toilets.

Walking into the basement of the club, it was once again the smell that hit me first. I was reminded of my mouldy childhood apartment, and I felt sick. It brought back a very bad feeling. But it was more than just mould—beer-soaked carpet, cigarette smoke, cheap perfume, sweat and fried food. It all smelled utterly filthy, in every aspect of the word. There was another dank smell too, but I couldn't place it.

I looked around in the dim light and saw a lot of young women, maybe twenty of them, in bikinis, walking around. Music was blaring. Several more were dancing on a stage at the front of the room, some naked. There was a bar along one side, and a few men sitting at it, as well as at the tables around the room. I figured this must be the exotic dancing that Natasa had described, and that Canada was apparently giving work permits for. Were they going to ask me to do this? The knot in my stomach tightened.

The five of us—Tony, József the driver, Elek, Bianka and me—sat down at one of the small tables. József asked if I wanted something to drink. I asked for a Coke, since I didn't drink alcohol. Even though I was twenty, I'd never had a drop. My father's alcoholism had made it unappealing.

"Come on," József insisted. "Have a drink!"

I declined again.

"Do you want a line?" he asked, trying something different.

"A line of what?" Now I was really confused.

"You know, a line." He pressed his finger to one nostril and snorted, and I realized he was talking about cocaine. I'd only ever seen it in the movies.

"No, no, I don't do that," I said firmly, shaking my head.

"Oh, we have a good girl here!" he teased, not in a friendly way. Elek motioned for him to stop bothering me, saying, "No, forget it. I know her. She doesn't do that stuff." He looked serious and almost worried.

"So what are you going to do?" Elek asked me again. I stared at him blankly. "Look around the room, Timike. All these girls are making a ton of money just by dancing. That girl right there"—he pointed to a girl in a bikini on the stage—"she makes $300 or $400 a day. That's 50,000 forint."

I looked at her, and then back at him in disbelief. "Just for dancing like that?" I asked. "She doesn't have to take her clothes off?" I almost had to shout over the music.

"Well, she does have to take them off by the third song to make that kind of money. That's how it works."

In that moment I realized that *exotic dancer* was just a fancy term for "stripper."

"You need to do that, Timike," Elek said. József nodded in agreement, and Tony just looked me up and down, making me uncomfortable. "It's the only way you're going to make any money, and you need to start now. You can't just sit here taking up space." He said the same thing to Bianka. She wasn't at all fazed.

József spoke up. "You actually can't even be in a place like this without having a form signed. The police can come in at any time and ask for your papers, so you need to go with Tony to his office and fill out the form."

Tony stood up and motioned for me to go with him, and for Bianka to stay put. *Didn't she need to fill out the form too?* I looked at Elek and József, who both nodded. "Just go sign the papers, Timea," Elek said, "and then come back and we'll make a plan to bring you guys back to Canada, because this is the only way you're going to make any real money." I trusted Elek; he was a comrade from home. I stood up and followed Tony. He led me past the bar, away from the music, smoke and people, and into a dimly lit hallway. We walked past what looked like a change room for the dancers. A heavy scent of perfume wafted out, barely masking the smell of sweat and other bodily fluids. I almost gagged as we continued down the hall to a closed door. Tony opened it and I entered a dark and messy room—his office. A large desk in the centre was covered in paperwork, and behind it were piles of more paper and files. The walls were white but dirty, and a poster of a naked woman was the only decor. By the door was a clothing rack full of bikinis and shiny, sexy dancer's outfits, and underneath it, a row of high-heeled shoes in all sizes. Tony pointed to the clothing rack, and I understood I was to change into something else. Terrified, with dread in the pit of my stomach, I found the least revealing top and skirt I could and ducked behind the rack so I could hide from his eyes. I left my jeans and Pink Panther sweatshirt folded on the floor.

Then Tony called me over to his desk. He pulled out an official-looking form and told me to write down my name, address and phone number by pointing to the words and saying them over and over in English until I understood. As I wrote, I could smell his sweat. I could feel his small, close-set eyes on me. We call these "fox eyes" in Hungary. "Never trust anyone with fox eyes," my mom always said. "They are really sneaky."

Tony sat down heavily in the big, black leather chair at his desk and began sorting through some papers. I finished filling in the form and then handed it to him. He put his hand on my hand and patted it like I was a child. I wanted to yank my hand back, but I tried to smile politely instead. I didn't know what else to do. He was my new boss and he'd just paid a giant fine at immigration for me. Maybe he could help me stay in Canada. I had to be nice to him. Maybe he was being nice too.

But then he took my hand and pulled me close to him, bringing us face to face. I could see straight into his fox eyes. I immediately had flashbacks to the guy at the TV station, and to the time my mom's colleague grabbed me while I waited for her to finish her shift. Those times, I'd been able to get away, but where could I run to now? I didn't know where I was, and I didn't know anyone here but Bianka, who wasn't even speaking to me. If I screamed, no one would hear me over the loud music. I couldn't move, so I silently began to pray. *Please don't hurt me.*

Tony put his hand around my waist, and then moved it down over my butt. I didn't fight or try to move his hand; I didn't question; I didn't say anything. I just stood there, frozen. Then he stood up and pushed everything off his desk and onto the ground before reaching for my top and pulling it off over my head. He lifted up the miniskirt I'd just put on and took off my underwear, discarding them on the floor. He was sweating now and moaning, grinding against me. It was disgusting. He lifted me up and sat me on the desk. All I could do was hope that whatever was going to happen would be over quickly.

Tony began kissing my face, ears, neck and breasts while breathing heavily and sweating like a pig. Then, without any warning, he shoved his finger in me. It hurt like hell. He pulled out his penis with his other hand and played with himself while still fingering me. His nail was sharp and it scratched and cut into the walls of my vagina, like a knife going in and out. My thoughts were a cloud of confusing and conflicting ideas. *Is he going to rape me? Is this how guys in Canada are? Does this mean he's my boyfriend?* I had the crushing thought that I was cheating on Ádám, and that if my mom ever found out about this she would kill me. I hoped he'd washed his hands; I didn't want to get sick down there.

I had to get to safety somehow, so I mentally and emotionally left my own body and floated to the other side of the room like a ghost. I'm not even sure how. I watched everything happen to me from that distance. I watched him kiss me on the forehead like I was a child. I watched myself stay utterly still on the desk, naked and vulnerable. I saw that I was in pain. Then, suddenly, I felt the pain, and I came back into my body as quickly as I'd left it.

I didn't know what had happened, what to call it. Rape, as I understood it, was violent and mean, and other than the scratching, this hadn't been either of those things. Tony wasn't mean. He wasn't holding me down and calling me names and forcing sex. He was causing pain, yet it didn't seem like that was the point—he wasn't trying to hurt me; he was trying to satisfy himself. I didn't know what to think, so I began running through ideas in my head. *Okay, this isn't rape. I don't think I'm cheating because I'm not kissing him back, and I don't want this to be happening. So what is this? Did I invite it?* He tried to kiss me on the mouth while still fingering me, and I turned my face away. I just wanted to stay frozen and emotionless, like a mannequin.

He sped up his hand movements on himself, made a final, loud groan and then stopped. I could smell his semen, and felt sick. Then I felt something wet between my legs. At first I thought I was somehow turned on by what had just happened, which made me feel even more confused and guilty, but then I looked down and saw a trickle of blood; that's how rough the scratching had been.

What had I gotten myself into? My stomach shrank into a tight knot and I started shaking and sweating. I wanted to cry, but I knew I couldn't fall apart. Not here, not now. *Don't think about how bad this is. Just stand up and pretend everything is okay.*

Tony took out a clean pair of jeans from his drawer and slowly put them on. I was still sitting on the desk, not sure if I was allowed to get up. Then he lifted me off the desk and guided me a few steps toward the rack of clothing. I reached for my jeans and my sweatshirt, but he handed me the miniskirt, bikini top, and six-inch stilettos he'd taken off me just minutes before, and some tissues to wipe off the blood. Then he handed me a plastic bag, gesturing that I should put my jeans and shirt in it. As I stuffed in my babysitter clothes, I stuffed in my Hungarian self—my upbringing, my values, my memories of summer camp, my ribbons and awards, my family name. I put on the stripper clothes and shoes and walked toward the office door, trying not to fall. I'd never worn heels this high—I'd barely worn heels at all. Tony playfully spanked my butt before pushing me out the door and back into the club.

6 | Orientation

WALKING BACK TOWARD THE main room, I passed several girls in the hall. They looked at me like they knew what had just happened, but they didn't say anything.

I went over to the table where Elek and József sat. I didn't know how long I'd been gone, but I felt like a completely different person than the one who'd left the table. I looked around for a clock but couldn't see one. I hadn't eaten since the plane, but I didn't feel hunger—only thirst. And I desperately wanted a shower. More than anything, I needed to lie down and rest, and figure out what to do next. I knew I couldn't go back to Hungary now. *You're a whore. Everyone is going to know you're a whore. You're done.*

"Your turn for the paperwork, Bianka," Elek said, motioning for her to get up and go over to Tony, who was standing at the doorway to the hall. *Is he going to do the same thing to her?* I didn't have time to think or feel before Elek pulled me down into the chair next to him and began talking.

"So, was he nice to you?" he asked cheerfully. Both he and József smiled as they waited for my response. They'd known what Tony was going to do to me.

"Yeah," I said, playing it cool. I couldn't understand why they weren't bothered by what had just happened to me. They knew I had a boyfriend.

"I think Tony really likes you," József said. "I think he wants to be your . . . close friend."

"What do you mean?"

"You know; he'll take care of you. He can get you stuff you need. When you come back, he'll make sure you can work in Canada." I didn't feel comforted at all.

"So you wanna try the stage?" Elek asked. "You're all ready for it." He looked me up and down, approving my outfit.

"No," I said. "I don't."

"Look, Timea, the only way we can get you back into Canada is as a dancer. You heard what they said at immigration. Just give it a try and we'll see what you can do. You can make a lot of money, pay us back quickly, and then we can look at the rest of your schedule and see what we can figure out." Elek's tone was light but serious. "Go talk to those girls over there, Sylvia and Adina. They work for our agency too. They can show you what to do."

I looked at the two girls in the corner. One was skinny and blonde, wearing a little bit of makeup, and looked about twenty-five or -six. The other looked much younger, even younger than me; she had a cute face, dark hair and a knockout figure. They looked at me and smiled.

"Just go and say hello, Timike." Elek was insistent, so I got up and walked over.

The girls greeted me in Hungarian. They weren't rough and tough; they were friendly. "Good to meet you," Sylvia said. "We heard you had a rough time at the border. Glad you made it through." Word spread quickly in whatever world this was.

"So you guys work for Elek?" I asked, trying to act normal while images of what had just happened to me circled through my mind; I pushed them away as best as I could. "How's that going?"

"Oh good, good," they answered, almost in unison. "He's awesome. He really takes care of us."

"Are there more girls, or just you two?" I felt almost robotic, interviewing them like I was interviewing a band for my TV show. Talking would distract me from the pain between my legs.

"There are lots of us." Sylvia began pointing out girls in the room. "One there, two there, a few more over there. There are also some at other clubs we go to."

"Other clubs?"

"Yeah, we switch around so it doesn't get boring," Adina explained. I took this all in, piece by jagged puzzle piece.

"What about other jobs?" I asked. "Like babysitting. That's what I was supposed to do here."

"Babysitting? Ha! Forget about that. All the money is in this work," Adina said.

"How much do you want to make?" Sylvia asked.

I explained my debts at home, plus the cost of my plane ticket.

"You're gonna make that much here in a week."

"What do you have to do?" I asked. I was nervous, but I needed as much information as I could get.

"Come on, we'll show you."

Adina and Sylvia walked me across the room and past the stage where a girl was dancing in a bikini then back down the hall toward Tony's office and into the change room I'd passed before. The air was even thicker with perfume inside than it was in the hallway. There were more racks of lingerie and bikinis, as well as some skimpy costumes, and tons of high-heeled shoes. On one side of the room was a long table stacked with makeup and several aerosol cans of hair and body spray. In the corner was a pile of T-shirts and jeans—probably the clothes the girls came in. None of it was very organized, and the room was dirty. There was a small bathroom, which I couldn't really see into, but I figured it was probably dirty too. A few chairs were scattered around, and Sylvia and Adina pulled them together in a little triangle and told me to sit down, which I gratefully did. The stilettos hurt.

"If you want to make a lot of money," Adina said, "the only way to do it is by dancing."

"How much do you make?" I asked.

"You can make as much as you want, but you only have to work for a few hours to make $500. It's easy," she said.

"But what do you *do*?"

Sylvia began laying out the protocol. "You choose three songs—the first one should have a fast beat, the second one slower and the third one really slow, like a ballad. You stay dressed through most of the first song. You can wear whatever—a T-shirt and skirt, a costume, a bikini." I listened carefully, holding my breath and clasping my hands. I was cold but my hands were sweaty. "By the end of the first song, you take something off. During the second one, you take more off, and by the end of the third song—even if it's just in the last five seconds—you have to be completely naked."

"Completely naked?" I asked.

"It's no big deal. Did you see how dark it is in the club?" Adina dismissed my concerns. "Besides, no one gives a damn about what's happening on the stage. That's not where the real money is made." I didn't want to ask what she meant, but I felt compelled.

"Where is the real money made?"

"The VIP room. Come on, we'll show you."

We'd only been sitting for a few minutes and now we were on the move again, to somewhere I really didn't want to go. I didn't want to see what was going on wherever they were taking me. They led me back into the club, through the tables where girls were sitting on guys' laps and toward a door that had a bright neon sign above it with the letters *VIP*. Red strobe lights flashed around the door frame. As I stepped through the threshold, I felt like I was entering one of the caves I'd been trained to get out of back in my summer camp days. My heart was pounding, and I tried to get my bearings and stay calm. The room was so dark, dank and smoky that at first I could hardly see anything except for the bright bikinis illuminated by black lights. There were also towels—lots of white hand towels—glowing like the bikinis. The music was the same pop music blaring in the main club. As my eyes adjusted I could see there were couches in the centre of the room and restaurant-style booths around the perimeter, maybe twenty of them. In the booths, the girls were completely naked, performing hand jobs and oral sex. The men were clothed, but all of them had their pants open.

"This area is for private dancing," Sylvia explained in a loud whisper right in my ear. The music was so loud. "To come in here, you pay the cashier $5 at the door. She'll give you a towel, and then you lead your client to a booth. He sits down and you do a private dance just for him. It's simple. There's one rule: no touching. If an undercover cop comes in here and sees touching, he can shut the whole club down."

"But everyone is touching," I said, pointing out the obvious.

"You just need to know the rule," Sylvia said. "If someone tells you an undercover cop is here, or you see cops in uniform, stop touching immediately or you'll be arrested."

At the mention of police, I thought of my mother, and I felt shame wash over me again. I quickly pushed the image out of my mind. I had to focus on how I was going to get out of this mess. Maybe it was a good thing that there could be police here—some protection. As if on cue, Adina pointed out a security guard in a far corner. If I ever had a problem with a client, she said, the security guard would quickly remove him.

Okay, I thought, slightly comforted. *This is nasty. This is disgusting. But it could be worse.* I was with other Hungarian girls who seemed fine. Aside from the fact that they were wearing bikinis, they looked completely normal. Still, I wasn't ready to take the stage, nor was I convinced that it would be easy or that I would be safe. My reluctance must have been written all over my face, because the girls turned our conversation back to all the money they were making.

"We know what it's like, Timea," one of them said. "We came from Hungary too. This is the only way to get out of debt." I wondered how long they'd been here, but there was no chance to ask, because Adina and Sylvia turned and began walking toward the door of the VIP room, back to the main club. I followed, but stopped in my tracks when I noticed a girl sitting on a guy in one of the booths, totally naked. She had her knees up around his hips and was dancing with her upper body. His hands were all over her. I was almost certain they were having sex.

Sylvia glanced over her shoulder at me, and I didn't even need to ask the question.

"Some girls are dirty girls," she explained. "And they can do whatever their customer asks if they want to make more money."

"But what about the undercover cops?" I asked.

"She's a Canadian girl, so she doesn't have to worry," Sylvia said. "They can give her a warning or a ticket or whatever, but she's a citizen. She can't get deported. We have to be more careful."

"You can make a lot just giving hand jobs," Adina pointed out. She said the term in English, then gestured what she meant. I almost gagged. Then she carefully pronounced the word "towel" so I could add it to my necessary vocabulary. In my first twelve hours in Canada, I'd learned the words *interrogation, motel, club, hand job* and *towel*.

"It's the easiest thing to do, it's super-quick, and you can charge an extra $15 or $20. All you have to do is wash your hands after." Sylvia explained the details in such a nonchalant, matter-of-fact way that we could have been working in a café and she was explaining how to make the coffee. "Just lay the towel on the guy in case he comes too soon," she went on, "and you can just clean him up when you're done."

I was glad to leave the VIP room and head back to the main club, where Adina and Sylvia led me toward the stage. They stepped up onto it and started dancing around the perimeter while waiting for their names to be called and their songs to play. I stood awkwardly to the side; not having any idea what to do, I just watched. I heard names being called—all English names—and saw girls step up to the front of the stage. They danced to the first song, prowled like animals on the floor or twisted themselves around poles for their second song, and stripped off their outfits slowly and provocatively during the third song. Once it was over, they left the stage and walked around the tables until they were called for lap dances or into the VIP room by men with green bills in their hands, which I soon learned were twenties. I saw Adina and Sylvia answer to English names and take their turns. *This is what was expected of me?*

I went into survival mode, shutting off my emotions one by one, as if they were breakers on an electrical panel. I sent the good girl I'd been when I arrived in Canada as far away as I could so she didn't have to see any more of this disgusting underworld. The faces of all the people in my life flashed before me: my mom, my godparents, Zoli, Ádám, people at the TV station. Each one I shut down and pushed out of my mind. If I couldn't picture them, they couldn't see me like this. Feelings of shame, guilt, disgust: I switched them all off. I shut down panic, I shut down pain and I shut down fear until there was nothing. I felt more blood between my legs, so I calmly asked another girl for a towel and quickly wiped myself as though I'd spilled some coffee in the café where I was working. I wasn't here. This wasn't happening.

7 | Accounting

THE CLUB WAS WINDOWLESS, and with no clocks, there was no way to tell what time it was. The hours went on and on, measured out in songs and $20 bills. Exhausted, hungry, jet-lagged and in shock, survival-mode adrenaline was all that kept my heart beating. Customers kept arriving until the club was quite full. At one point, one of them—a middle-aged white man wearing jeans and a black T-shirt—motioned for me to come over to his table from where I stood in the shadows, but I didn't go. I just stood there in my stilettos, trying not to feel anything. After a while, Sylvia took my hand and walked me among the tables and clients, trying to help me earn some money.

"Smile, Timea," she encouraged. "Be flirty. Stick out your boobs and shake your butt when you walk." I straightened up a little and plastered on a grin but couldn't bring myself to do as she instructed. She was a pro and I was an utter amateur. I didn't dance, but neither did I make any money.

Finally, Elek told Sylvia, Adina and me that it was 2:30 a.m. and time to go. The club was closing. My feet were killing me, and I couldn't wait to take off my shoes and get some sleep. Ilona and Ezster, two other Hungarian girls, appeared with Bianka, who I hadn't seen for hours. We made eye contact but didn't exchange any words. I didn't know what had happened to her, but figured it must have been the same or something similar to what I'd gone through with Tony. Maybe she'd been in the VIP room.

We went to the change room and got back into our regular clothes. Everyone else was chatty, but Bianka and I were silent. Finally, we left. Two of the girls went with Tony and another driver while the rest of us crammed into the back of József's SUV, with Elek in the passenger seat. We drove to a fast food restaurant where Elek placed an order. He handed every girl but me a hamburger and French fries. I got nothing except for a few fries from one of the girls. Back at the motel, Elek announced it was time for a family meeting, and we all shuffled into a room.

We sat on the bed in a row like children, while he pulled out a notebook and pen. He called Ilona first, and asked how much she'd made. She pulled out a wad of cash and counted out $800. I'd never seen so much money in my life! Even though the numbers on the bills were much smaller than what I was used to seeing on our forint, I knew how much Canadian dollars were worth. The amount was astounding—thousands and thousands of forint. So far the only thing that was true about this experience was that you really could earn a lot of money in a day in Canada.

Elek opened his notebook to Ilona's page.

"Now, you owe Tony $140 for his weekly manager's fee, you owe me $140 for my agent's fee, plus your accommodation and transport, and I also bought you some food, so that's . . . $350 total." He scribbled some notes as she handed him the money. "Okay, good job," he said. "Now you keep $20 for your living allowance, give me $300 for Sasha's cut, and the rest goes toward your debt." She pulled a twenty from the wad and passed the rest over to him. He counted it, then subtracted the $130 from her debt to the agency. The fees were high, but I figured she must be pretty new, and was still paying back her airfare. At this rate, it still shouldn't take too long.

Elek turned to Adina and ran through the same basic accounting. She'd earned $860 but she had to pay $50 more because it was her turn to buy cigarettes for everyone; plus she'd used some little bottles of shampoo at the motel. They seemed pretty expensive, but what did I know? I also noticed in the bright light of the motel room that Adina was even younger than I'd thought, maybe fourteen—barely old enough to even be a babysitter, which must be what she had come to Canada for too. How had she gotten into this country? Did she have anyone at home worrying about her? My questions would have to wait. Next was Sylvia, then the other two girls. There was a lot of money changing hands and scribbling of notes. There was so much going back and forth that all I really gathered was the total amount that had been earned—somewhere in the thousands—not who was ending up with all of it.

"Well done, girls!" Elek said enthusiastically. "You're getting there! In just another week or so you'll have paid me off. Then in a couple of months you'll have enough for your apartment. You see, Timike?" He looked at me, and then pointed at Ezster. "She's saving for a house for her parents." I looked at her—a nice, regular girl who didn't look like a stripper—and then back at Elek, who'd been a cop, who'd been in the army, who knew my mom, and who was from my hometown. Everyone seemed normal, but this whole situation was absurd. None of it made any sense.

"Now, let's see how you did, Timea and Bianka," Elek continued. I shook my head. My pockets were empty. Bianka had made $700.

Elek motioned for me to stand up, and he said goodnight to the other girls before walking us down the hall to our room. Tony followed and stood blocking the door and I sat down on the bed, with Elek opposite me, in a chair.

"Okay, Timike," Elek began, focusing on me. "I know that you're a good girl and this is all new to you, but you're in big trouble. You owe us a lot of money, and we have to take you back to the airport in a few hours, but you're going to have to come back here to work and pay it off."

"How am I going to do that?" I asked. I couldn't even try to re-enter Canada for eighteen months because of how I'd botched my work visa at immigration.

"We're going to get you a different passport. You won't be coming back as Timea Nagy." I was going to be travelling on a fake passport? I would be a criminal. I couldn't do that. I shook my head.

"Don't worry, Timea, you can pay us back in a week or so—you see how much these girls made tonight? You'll go back to Hungary for a couple of weeks until we get your paperwork organized, and then you'll be back here and everything will be fine." His tone was firm, but reassuring. Like the girls who'd shown me around the club and told me what to do, everything he said was matter-of-fact, even though he'd just told me that I'd be breaking international immigration laws and be working as a stripper. I was overwhelmed.

"To make sure you're okay back in Hungary," Elek continued, "we're going to have someone there checking on you. Nothing to worry about, but one of our agents will be around your apartment and mother's house, because we don't want to lose a good girl like you."

Lose me? What did he mean? Before I could ask him, he carried on.

"And also, Timea, we need our money soon. If we don't get it, we won't be able to protect your brother."

My brother? What did Zoli have to do with anything? And "protect"? I must be hallucinating. It sounded like I was in a mafia movie.

"What do you mean?" I asked weakly.

"Well, Timea, in this kind of business it's all about who you know and your connections, and keeping people happy. Our boss, Sasha—the Ukrainian—isn't going to be too happy about all this. We owe him a lot of money because of you, and we can't give it to him until you earn it and pay us back." He paused and exhaled slowly before continuing. "Unfortunately, Sasha is not an understanding guy. After all, this is his business, and he's at the top. I can't say what he'll do, but he will get his money any way he can, and he'll start by sending some agents to see your brother in Budapest."

I had no words. My survival adrenaline drained away and my panic switch flipped back on. I imagined my brother finding out about me and what I'd done, and then being asked for hundreds of dollars he would never have. I couldn't let my thoughts go any further. What might happen to him?

"Your brother still works at that grocery store, right?" he asked casually, not waiting for an answer. "I know that area well. It's pretty dark at night there, not a lot of streetlights from what I remember. Anything could happen on his walk home, Timike."

I began to shake and I could feel my heart beating quickly. *I need to fix this.*

"And just imagine how people will talk—you know how they are on Csepel Island. If they find out what you're doing here, and what you've already done, it will be very hard for you to ever go back. Your poor boyfriend—that camera guy, right? He'll be devastated."

I kept my face impassive, but I couldn't stop my body from shaking. Inside I was screaming in terror. *He knows everything about me.* But at the same time, I also knew Elek was trying to protect me. *He's thought of everything and he's really trying to help. I need the money. I have to get the money.* Elek calling me *Timike* in the same breath that he seemed to be threatening me was crazy-making. I couldn't tell if he was my friend or my enemy. All I could picture was everyone at home finding out about what I had done, and that was devastating. Ádám finding out was a nightmare. The TV station—my career would be finished. My mom—that was a whole other story. I would be dead.

Elek was still talking. "So we're going to put you and Bianka back on the plane today, and we'll have one of our agents go with you. You won't recognize him, but he'll be there, just to make sure nothing happens to you and that you get home. Then you get some rest, and someone will come and find you and let you know the plan, okay?" He laid out these next steps carefully.

"How is it going to work with the passport?" I asked, scrambling for more information so I could understand what I was being pulled into.

"You don't need to worry about that, Timea," Elek reassured me. "We've done this before. It's going to cost more money to get you a new one, but as you can see, you'll be able to pay that off too, as soon as you're back here working. It might take an extra few days, but you saw what you can earn dancing. Your debt will be cleared with us in a couple of weeks, and after that we can get you the babysitting job if you don't want to dance anymore. In a couple of months, you'll have your debts paid off in Hungary too. Then you can do whatever you want."

There really was no other option, I realized. I could handle the dancing. What I couldn't handle was anything that went on in the VIP room—but I could dance for a couple weeks. I had to. I'd gotten myself into this situation. I had no one to blame but myself, and I had to pay the price for my mistakes. Elek could probably tell by the expression on my face that he had me convinced, but he kept going.

"I just don't want you to forget, Timea, that you signed a contract with us, and Sasha has the original copy. And this is a real business. If it were up to me, I'd just let you go now. But I can't do that without the money. Sasha will come and find you, your brother and your mother. And there is nothing I can do to stop him. So I'm going to help you. I'm going to help you be like these other girls and make your dreams come true, get you a new life." He smiled a little, and then asked, "Do you want something to happen to your brother?"

"Like what?" I asked, somehow needing to know *exactly* how bad this was.

"I don't know for sure, Timea, but I've heard some stories. These guys of Sasha's can be fucking crazy."

I shook my head. *No, I don't want something to happen to my brother.*

"Good girl. You're doing the right thing. So, you and Bianka just go back to Hungary, get some sleep, and within a couple of weeks you'll be back here and back on track."

"What about my flight? How will I pay for my flight?"

"We'll take care of all that. Don't worry."

A few hours later, Bianka and I found ourselves on a plane headed to London, and then on to Budapest. We barely spoke other than to try to figure out what to do. She was still angry with me, but by the end of our flight we'd managed to figure a few things out. She was going to stay in Europe and go back to her work as a high-end prostitute in Sweden, and she would pay the agency back from that money, but ultimately I would have to pay her back for her flight. After all, I'd screwed everything up at the border and it was only fair that I at least pay back her costs. So now I owed money for my apartment and bills in Budapest, to my friend at the TV station who'd given me a loan, to the agency in Canada, and to Bianka, who had been my only friend over the last few months. She didn't share my fear of Sasha following her; as she reminded me, her ex-husband was in the mafia. She had connections she could call on for protection if she needed them. She didn't offer them to me. I felt our friendship fracture further.

As I got up to go to the bathroom I scanned all the passengers to see if I could tell who the agent was, but I couldn't. Everyone seemed to be minding their own business. There were families heading to London for holidays, or back home from a trip to Canada, and single travellers with briefcases, books and portable CD players to pass the time. I couldn't believe everything that had happened over the last two days, or that I was going back home. A home that offered no hope for me. Despite all the ugliness I'd seen in Canada in those brief twenty-four hours, I still had the sense that it was a hopeful place—a rich, modern country where people could do anything. Hungary was none of those things, especially for me.

8 | Girl for Sale

THIRTEEN HOURS AFTER LEAVING the club, I was back at my apartment on Csepel Island in Budapest. I sat down on the floor of my bedroom because I didn't want to sit on my bed or furniture. I felt so dirty, inside and out. I couldn't even cry—I was too tired and too scared. Zoli came out of his room and was shocked to see me.

"What are you doing here?" he asked. "What happened?"

"Things didn't go well at the airport in Toronto and I had to come back." I had practised a simple explanation during my hours on the plane.

"You know we only have twenty-one days left before we get kicked out, right? Twenty-one days to pay our bills." He was angry. I was supposed to be away for three months, sending money as often as I could.

"I know, I know. Don't worry, I'm going back really soon. And I'm going to make the money. I saw that you can really make a lot of money there—you wouldn't believe it." I tried to reassure him but also to not raise any questions. "Have you found a job yet?" I changed the subject.

"I'm looking—I'm looking in Germany, in England, everywhere!" I could tell he was scared too.

But Zoli gave me an idea. Maybe I could look for a job in a different country. Maybe there were actual babysitting jobs in Germany or England. Maybe there was a way for me to avoid going back to Canada and dancing. I didn't ever want to see Tony again. *Maybe no one is going to come for me.* Maybe Elek was just trying to scare me.

I waited a few days, and tried to rest and recover a little bit from my ordeal. I went to see Ádám, who didn't react well.

"You're a liar," he said angrily. "Was this just a little vacation you took? What are you not telling me?"

"Nothing!" I insisted. "There was a problem with my paperwork, but the agency is going to fix it and I'm going back in a couple of weeks unless I can find a better job here or somewhere else in Europe. I'm going to start looking right away." He didn't believe me. Maybe he could tell something was wrong, that I was different now.

"That can't be," he argued. "You don't just go all that way, stay one night, and then come all the way back!" He paced the floor, looking down, breathing heavily. Then he stopped and looked up at me. "Are you cheating on me?"

"No!" I cried, visions of what had happened with Tony flashing in my mind. "Of course not. I'm just doing my best—I'm doing everything I can to pay our taxes and keep my apartment." I felt extraordinarily guilty.

On my fourth day back at home, there was a knock at my apartment door. Zoli was in his room, so I answered. It was Natasa, from the agency, and a big, tough-looking guy I'd never met. Was it Sasha?

"Timea, we need to talk," she said. "You've been here for four days and you haven't called me. You screwed up at the border, and now you have to go back to Canada and fulfill the terms of your contract. You weren't planning on running away, were you?" She sounded threatening. The man said nothing, but bored holes in me with his eyes. I stepped into the hallway and closed the door behind me so Zoli wouldn't hear anything.

I wanted clarification, and for Natasa to share the blame for the problem at the border. Why hadn't she been clearer about what I was supposed to say to the immigration officer? But I also wanted to confide in her. She was a woman; she would understand. And she should know what "dancing" really meant in Canada before she signed up any other girls to go there. She should also know what kind of work her boyfriend Elek was involved in—if I were her, I'd want to know. Most of all, I wanted Natasa to comfort me, to ease my disappointment over what I'd gotten myself into, and to apologize for not giving me better instructions. Then I wanted her to talk to the agents, and get me a real babysitting job.

"Natasa, something happened there. I'm really confused—"

She cut me off, her voice now slightly raised. "I don't care, Timea. You need to go back. You owe us a lot of money. I will find a way to get you to Canada, but right now, you need to come with us." She was acting completely different from the caring human resources recruiter she'd been just a couple weeks ago.

"Get dressed," Natasa ordered. "Nicely. We're going to meet Bianka at the Canadian consulate because she wants to try again to get a work permit, so you're coming too." Bianka had changed her mind about going back to Sweden? That surprised me.

"I don't think that's a good idea . . ." Surely our passports had been flagged.

"Now," she said firmly, cutting me off. The tough guy cracked his knuckles.

There was no point in arguing. My life and the lives of my family were in danger. I had to do whatever the agency told me to protect them.

———

At the Canadian consulate in Budapest, we were told that we would have to go to the embassy in Vienna to apply for work permits. The Budapest office was really more of a satellite, without the full capabilities of an embassy.

"I'd prefer to look for a job somewhere else," I said to Natasa, glad for this hurdle. It would give me more time to find work as a baby-sitter or housekeeper somewhere else in Europe. "It would be cheaper for me to go to Germany or England, right?"

"You can't make nearly as much money in those countries as Canada—I told you that before. How would you pay back the money you owe us?" Natasa asked. She and Bianka looked at me with question marks in their eyes, and not a flicker of any sympathy or understanding. For the first time, I felt a rush of anger surge through me. *I made a mistake!* I wanted to scream at them. The stupid contract and exotic dancer visa—why hadn't Natasa just explained it to me properly? Why was I being blamed? I asked them pointedly.

"Don't waste your energy being angry, Timea," Natasa warned. "We need to figure this out."

"Fine, let's go to Vienna."

There was no further discussion.

The next morning, Natasa drove us the three hours to Vienna, where Bianka and I filled out the visa application forms, being sure to clearly state that we were applying to enter Canada as exotic dancers. The big tough guy didn't come, to my relief. We were inter-viewed an hour later and both denied work permits. As I'd expected, our passports had been flagged. Natasa was livid, and let me know on the way back to Budapest.

"What are you going to do now? Do you know how much money you owe us? Do you know what's going to happen to you?"

I was asking myself the same questions. Bianka was silent, and I got the feeling that she and Natasa had spoken on their own and worked out some sort of plan. My friendship with Bianka was quickly unravelling, which only added to my worries. We didn't seem to be in this together anymore.

"The only option is going to be for us to get you a fake passport, just as Elek suggested," Natasa said.

"I'm not sure I can do that," I said. If I was caught, I could go to jail. That could not happen.

"You don't have a choice," Natasa hissed.

"Can I still babysit after I pay you back?" I asked, trying to think ahead and grasp onto something hopeful.

"Sure, whatever you want," Natasa's tone was dismissive. "We just have to get you back there as soon as we can. There's nowhere else you can earn the kind of money you need." She dropped me off at my apartment and told me we would meet the following week.

I spent the next few days doing research on working as a nanny somewhere else in Europe. I called agencies listed in the phone book and friends of friends who had travelled abroad. The answer was the same everywhere: English was necessary. On top of that, I worried that even if I did find an agency that would ignore my lack of English, the stamp on my passport from Canada would be an obstacle.

I didn't want to be seen on Csepel too much because I was hiding from my mother (and, by extension, almost every single police officer in the area) and from the TV station. I didn't want to see anyone who thought I was away working as a babysitter in Canada. I didn't know how to explain why I was back home, let alone all that had happened in the twenty-four hours I'd been gone. I hardly even saw my brother. I stayed inside our apartment, passing the time worrying and pacing. Bianka called often.

"Have you found a job yet?" she would ask each time.

"I'm working on it," I assured her. "Trust me."

"I just don't want you to forget about what you owe me," she reminded. "I have my son with me now, and I'm not made of money." I couldn't understand her at all. Why was her son back with her when she'd planned to be in Canada or go back to Sweden? I didn't bother asking. I had too much to figure out on my own.

Ádám came over whenever he wasn't working, acting possessive and suspicious. I did my best to pretend everything was fine and avoided answering the phone when he was there in case Natasa, Bianka or the agents in Canada called. I prayed that no one from the agency would come to the door when he was visiting. He could not find out about any of this.

Natasa showed up a few days later and let me know that my new passport was almost ready, but that I'd need a new passport photo. On the way to the photographer, she explained that she'd thought things through and that she did feel bad for me, knowing I was a good girl who didn't mean to make the mistake I did, and that she'd talked to Bianka about the situation.

"Bianka has agreed to contribute half of your return airfare," Natasa said. "She needs you to pay back what you owe her just as much as we need you to, so she's going to help you out with her savings and get you back to Canada."

"Oh, wow, okay . . . that's generous of her." I felt a tiny bit relieved. Bianka still wanted to help me, and it would be better to owe her more money than the agency. Maybe she'd give me extra time to pay it back, and I could earn the money babysitting and not dancing.

"We'll pay the rest, plus your passport fee," she continued. "Fake passports, unfortunately, aren't cheap."

"How much are they?" I asked, although it almost didn't matter anymore. What was another few hundred dollars to owe?

"Five hundred dollars," she responded. "Seventy thousand forint."

I was stunned. "Can't I just find a job somewhere else in Europe? Elek said the agency has branches everywhere. Why do I have to go back to Canada?"

"Right now our focus is Canada," Natasa reiterated. "Sure there's work in Europe—Germany, Austria, even the UK—but they don't pay nearly as much, and there it's not just dancing—you have to have sex. And you said, Timea, that you don't want to do that. Plus, we are Hungarian and we don't want our nice, good Hungarian girls to become prostitutes, so that's why we're working with Canada. You can see that even the Canadian government is on board with the dancing."

I had my picture taken, and then Natasa sent me home on public transit, telling me she'd come to my apartment in a few days with my new passport and new paperwork for me to present at immigration in Toronto, including two reference letters from well-known nightclubs in Budapest that said I'd worked as a go-go dancer. The agency had connections—that much was clear. In the meantime, she suggested I go and see Bianka to get the money she was going to lend me.

When I got home, I went up to Bianka's apartment. Though we'd spoken on the phone, I hadn't seen her since our trip to Vienna, and I wanted to talk to her about the loan she was giving me. I found her in the kitchen preparing dinner for herself and her son, who was lying on the couch playing on his Game Boy. She was wearing a swim cap and goggles over her eyes as she chopped onions. Now she didn't look like a prostitute or a mother. She just looked ridiculous. I wanted to laugh, but I was so filled with anxiety that I knew if I started, it would turn into hysterics.

"So, you're going back?" She put the knife down on the cutting board and looked at me directly, through the goggles.

"I have to," I said, looking down at the onions.

"It's a good decision for you, because you really screwed things up and you need to fix everything and pay us all back."

How many times did I need to be told this? I wanted to ask her what she said at the border, and why she had been sent home, too, but I could see she was in no mood to open up. She seemed to only want to blame me, and I didn't want to question someone who was about to help me with a loan.

"I never should have gone with you," she lamented. "You made us both look suspicious and now I've spent money I needed to get me through until August when I go back to Sweden—money I needed for my son. So you have to send me $500 each month as soon as you get back." These weren't the terms I'd been hoping for, but I just nodded. *Okay.*

"I know you have to pay the agency when you get to Canada," she went on, "so what I'm going to do is set something up here for you to make your first payment to me before you go."

"What is it?" I asked, hesitantly.

"I have two friends—guys," she said, "and they like to do coke on Friday nights, and all you have to do is entertain them and they'll pay you."

"Alone?" It sounded dangerous. I shuddered, remembering my tour of the VIP room at the club back in Toronto.

"Don't worry about it. Look, they're going to be really, really high—nothing can happen. Just tell your boyfriend not to come over, tell your brother not to come home, and tell the neighbours you're having a little party and there is going to be music. I'll send the guys over—they're nice. They have wives and kids and they just want to have some fun and do coke somewhere they won't be seen." Her tone reassured me a little, but not much. I hated the whole idea, but I asked her what, exactly, I'd have to do.

"Just take off your clothes and walk around naked for a few hours. You saw how the girls did it at the club. You'll make $500 Canadian."

I was speechless, but I knew I didn't really have a choice. Less than two weeks ago, on the plane going to Toronto, I'd felt able to breathe for the first time in so long. Now, almost all the air had been pressed out of my lungs. How had I become so powerless?

"If I do this, can you help make sure no one finds out about it?" I asked. There was no point in taking this risk if I was only going to end up dead, at my brother's or mother's hands.

"It's all confidential, Timea. Come on, do you think these guys want their wives to know what they do on their nights off?"

Bianka had a point.

"Fine, I'll do it," I said. She smiled at me for the first time since we'd been on the plane together, which made me feel better. She was my friend, after all. I felt my lungs expand just a tiny bit.

Bianka said she'd set it up for the next night, so I went home and, as casually as I could, asked Zoli what his plans were for the following evening. He told me he was going to a party and asked if Ádám and I wanted to go. I said yes, but when Ádám arrived the next night, I pretended to be sick and sent the two of them on their way without me. All I wanted was a peaceful night's sleep, I told them, so it would be best if they went back to Ádám's place after the party. They easily bought my story, and once they were gone, I prepared by putting away photographs, my *Friends* mugs, and other personal items. Then I put on a T-shirt and one of the few skirts I owned, but changed my mind and put on jeans. I dabbed on some lipstick, which I rarely wore. Then I locked the cats in my brother's room. I didn't want any witnesses.

The two men showed up around 10 p.m. and made themselves comfortable in my bedroom, walking in like they owned the place and looking around as they introduced themselves. They looked like regular dads of young kids—midthirties, clean-shaven, dressed in jeans and T-shirts. They were friendly. They asked if they could put on some music. I nodded, and one of them popped a techno CD into the stereo on my dresser and turned the volume way up. I turned it down a little—"Because of the neighbours"—and then watched as they laid out lines of coke and snorted them. They offered me one but I declined and they didn't pressure me. Then they put a porn tape in my VCR, turned on my TV and lay down on my bed to watch it. I felt shame cloud my room, but instead of prolonging the inevitable, I took off my clothes.

The high hit them as I "just walked around, naked" like Bianka had told me to. They reached for me and tried to touch me but I sidestepped them, which made them think I was teasing them. They asked me to touch them, but because they were so high, there was nothing really to touch. Instead, they masturbated for hours, snorted more coke, watched more porn, drank beer and vodka, and listened to music. All the while, I either walked around or stood in the corner, leaning against the wall for a break. To push out the sound of their techno music, and the words my mother would say to me if she knew what I was doing, I ran through the lyrics of some of my favourite songs in my head. Finally, at 4 a.m., I said it was time for them to go. They put the money on my bedside table, got dressed, picked up their drug stuff and videotapes, and left.

I breathed a huge sigh of relief as I closed the door behind them. I let the cats out of Zoli's room but I couldn't even pet them. I fell to the floor in tears. Just ten days ago I'd been so excited to head off on my adventure to Canada. Stressed about all the money I owed, sure, but confident in my plan to earn it as a babysitter for a nice Hungarian-Canadian family. Now here I was, back in Budapest, owing more money than before, and taking my clothes off to earn it. The shame that had infected my room flooded me until I was drowning in it. It silenced me, and stopped me from asking anyone for help—and it made me feel like I didn't deserve it anyway.

A couple of days later Bianka called and told me that I'd done well, and that one of the guys really liked me.

"He wants to see you before you leave," she said.

"What do you mean, 'see me'?" I asked, screwing my face up in disgust. "I have no desire to see him."

"You know, just to say goodbye before you go. Maybe have a drink, or a coffee. Didn't you like him?"

"Bianka, I have a boyfriend." I was getting frustrated with her and how she didn't seem to understand this fact.

"Your boyfriend is a loser, Timea. This is a nice guy, a good-looking guy, and he really likes you. Wasn't he nice to you? Anyway, I told him you'd been through some hard times lately, and that you are moving to Canada. He wants to give you a little gift before your trip, so I'm going to arrange for you to meet up." She told me I could go to his parents' house, which was in our neighbourhood, and because I was indebted to her, I agreed. I didn't have the upper hand here.

Ádám usually worked on Monday nights, so Bianka made the arrangements and I went to the address she gave me. The guy introduced me to his parents as his friend, we made small talk, and then he led me to his childhood room, which was still set up as if he was a teenager, even though he was at least thirty and had a house, a wife and kids. He put on some loud music and began kissing me. He told me how much he liked me. Then he began to take off my clothes.

I froze. *I don't want this. I don't want this.* My vocal cords seemed to swell and my throat felt like it was closing. I couldn't speak.

He continued, enjoying himself, without seeming to have any awareness—or care—that I hadn't said yes or given any indication that I was interested in sex.

Just get this over with, I thought, simply too weak to do anything to try to stop him. *Whatever.* Whatever, whatever. *It's no big deal.* I felt myself detach and float away like I had with Tony. I looked down at mannequin me. I watched as the guy laid me down on his bed and had sex with me. *Is this rape? No. It wasn't mean or violent, just like it hadn't been with Tony. Did I want it? No. What was this, then?* I wanted to pick myself up out of this guy's arms and fly away.

Afterwards, he cuddled with me. Then he got up, snorted a line of coke and lay back down, pulling me in close. *I need to get out of here. Ádám is going to be coming home any minute and I need to be there. I need to have a shower. I need to get* him *off me.*

He started to drift off to sleep, and I said I had to go.

"Mmm," he said softly, "here's a little gift for your trip." He pulled a 10,000-forint bill out of his pocket and passed it to me. It was a lot of money—about $60 Canadian—but I didn't want it. Taking it would make me a prostitute. Not a dancer, not a stripper, but a full-blown prostitute. I said I didn't need it.

He insisted, sitting up and shoving it into my jeans pocket as I got dressed. I decided I could leave it with Zoli, or just give it to Bianka toward my next payment. She wouldn't care that it was dirty money.

"Listen, Timea," he began seriously, despite being high. "If you get into any trouble while you're gone, you call me. Bianka told me about who you're working for, and I don't like these guys. You're a good girl, and you shouldn't be involved with them."

"Sure," I said. "Okay." As if I would call him. As if I ever wanted to see him again in my life.

I walked the two blocks home. As I got close to my building, I saw Ádám's car waiting in front, him leaning against it, and my heart began to race. He'd finished work early, found that I wasn't home, and had been waiting for me for who knows how long. I thought about turning around and walking away but he'd already seen me, so I kept walking toward him, stopping when we were three feet apart.

"Where were you?" he demanded.

"At a friend's," I said, scrambling to think of what to say next. I was completely caught off guard. I'd thought I'd have time to compose myself, to come up with a story to tell Ádám if I needed to.

"You're lying to me! I know you've been cheating on me. You're disgusting, Timea." He was right. I *was* disgusting. "Do you know what you're doing to us, to our reputation on the island?" His questions came one after the other, without pause. "Everyone at the TV station is asking about you, and what happened—why they never see you when they've heard you're back. And I don't have any answers. I don't have any answers about my own girlfriend!"

I shrugged, neither confirming nor denying. I didn't have the energy for an argument so I played it cool. "I guess you'd better not come upstairs, then," I said simply.

"You know what, Timea—screw you! I've had it with you." He got into the car and drove off. After all this time, our relationship was finally over. I don't remember feeling relieved, or sad or anything other than numb.

Natasa delivered my new passport to me a couple of days later, just before I left, and I memorized my new name and birthdate. I was twenty-four-year-old Andrea Hernuss, a young woman who, based on all the stamps in her passport, had travelled extensively throughout Europe. It was a real passport—with my photo swapped in for Andrea's. Natasa told me Andrea had sold it to Elek in Canada and he'd sent it here. She must have needed the money, just like me.

Boarding the plane in Budapest was easy, but going through customs on my stopover in Frankfurt made me a nervous wreck. I did my best to act like the twenty-four-year-old experienced traveller my passport said I was, but my palms were sweating, my pulse was racing, and the more I tried to look normal the more I was certain I looked guilty.

A German official walked down the customs line, pre-checking everyone's passports. He directed anyone from a European Union country to one queue, and everyone else to another, including Hungarians, since we hadn't yet joined the EU. Every so often he pulled someone from the line and sent them to some other area, probably for questioning. As he came closer to me, I tried to look at him directly, but without being bold, coy or suspicious. I couldn't quite believe it when he glanced at my passport and then waved me into the "everyone else" line. I was so relieved.

At the booth, the German customs officer opened my passport, and then asked me my name and why I was going to Canada. He spoke to me in German, and then English. When I couldn't understand either language, he called over a translator.

"To work for the summer," I answered simply, as Natasa had instructed. She'd said not to answer more than I was asked.

"Have a nice time," the officer said as he stamped my passport. It couldn't have been easier. Next stop, Canada. My relief over having gotten this far lasted only for a moment, and then I began to think about what would happen when I arrived in Toronto.

I was too nervous to eat on the plane, and I barely slept. I wondered if the agency had anyone on the plane with me—maybe the same person they said they'd had watching Bianka and me on the flight over, but there was no one who looked familiar. Natasa had explained that I would be landing at a different terminal this time. She had booked me on another airline to minimize the chance of me encountering the same customs officer who had denied me entry as Timea Nagy. If I were caught, I'd be jailed. Everything was at stake.

I arrived at Pearson Airport twelve hours after I'd left Budapest, and it was as clean-smelling as it had been before, but I didn't have time to think too much about it. I headed straight for customs.

The line moved quickly and before I knew it, I was in front of an officer much younger than the one I'd had before. To calm my nerves, I pretended I was going in front of the camera on my TV show, in a professional role. Fearless, confident Timea Nagy, under a new name.

"English?" he asked.

"*Magyar*," I answered. Hungarian. He picked up a phone and called for a translator who arrived moments later—a woman who was as young as the officer. There was no waiting this time.

"Name and citizenship?" the officer asked through the translator. He glanced at me briefly and then back at my passport. I gave a half smile and relaxed my shoulders. I didn't want him to suspect anything.

"Andrea Hernuss, Hungarian."

"Purpose of your trip?"

"To work for the summer."

"What kind of work will you be doing?" He looked at me again. My stomach tensed and I hoped I wouldn't break into a sweat.

"Dancing." I couldn't believe it. Not only was I actually going to be dancing—something unimaginable two weeks ago—I was telling a customs officer about it and expecting to get a visa. It was preposterous.

"Papers?" I handed him my agency contract and my letters of reference from the Budapest nightclubs.

The officer flipped through my passport and papers quickly. Then he reached for his stamp.

"You have three months." He scribbled the expiry date on top of my permit.

I was in. It was true what they'd said—that you could come to Canada as an exotic dancer but not as a babysitter. I looked at my stamp of approval and could scarcely believe my eyes.

Part II | CAUGHT

9 | Training

TONY, ELEK AND JÓZSEF were waiting for me as I entered the arrivals gate. They were very pleased that I'd made it through.

"Good girl, Timea. We knew you could do it," Elek said, smiling. I was relieved. Finally, I'd done something right.

"Now if only you had done that the first time," Elek lamented, "you'd be ahead by $3,000. But don't worry, you'll be able to make it all back within a few weeks."

We drove the short distance to Motel 27 and checked in. Tony led me into my room—which was a different one than before but looked identical. He motioned for me to put my bag down, and then for me to lie down on the bed where he began taking off my jeans, touching me and kissing me. I knew what was coming, so I instantly went into mannequin mode. I wasn't in my body when he entered me, and it was over very quickly. I remained numb as I put my jeans back on. He hadn't said a word the whole time, and I wouldn't have understood him if he had. The silence added to the feeling that I wasn't real; that

I was just a body. *You feel nothing,* I told myself. *No fear, no fear. You will be fine.*

There was a knock at the door, and then Elek opened it and poked his head in.

"You can use the bathroom to freshen up and then we'll head right to the club," he said.

"Can I take a shower?" I asked, feebly.

"There's no time."

In the car, I tried to think clearly. Did Tony think I was his girl-friend, or was I just some kind of sex toy? Since we couldn't com-municate, I didn't know what he was thinking. Whatever our relationship was, I needed to get out of it.

"Elek," I said. "When can we talk about the babysitting job? I think it would be good to make arrangements and for me to do some interviews with families soon so that I can start in a few weeks, after I finish at the club." I needed something to look forward to.

"Let's just take it one step at a time, Timea. The most important thing is that you earn the money you owe us, plus you have all your debts in Hungary. After that we'll get everything sorted out. Baby-sitting or whatever. I also have a buddy with a restaurant who needs a waitress."

He was right. I had to make the money and get myself out of this mess before I could really ask for anything else. I had Bianka to pay back too. Dancing was the fastest way. I nodded.

We got to Temptations and it was like I'd never left. Everything was exactly the same, only this time I knew my way around a little bit. Tony asked me—using Elek as translator—to sit down and have a drink. I reminded him that I didn't drink, so he suggested a Baileys Irish Cream, since it's sweet.

"We'll fill it up with milk for you, Timi," Elek said, treating me almost like a little sister.

"Fine." I drank it down quickly and immediately felt the effect. The stress of the last few weeks had caused me to lose weight; that, combined with the fact that I had no tolerance for alcohol, made my head spin. The smell of the club was overwhelming, and I felt like vomiting.

"Another?" Elek asked.

"Definitely not," I said.

"Okay then, you better get started. The girls you met before—remember Sylvia and Adina? They're here already." Elek saw them over by the stage and motioned for them to come over. "They'll take you and get you ready. You can talk to them and other girls from our group, but no one else. You never know who someone is. Anyone could be an undercover cop, and you're here on a fake passport." Right. I was now a stripper, a liar and an illegal alien.

Sylvia and Adina led me to the change room where they went over the basics they'd taught me before, plus a few new tips. It was all very simple: I didn't have to put on makeup or fake nails, or do anything "sexy" with my hair. The only thing they said was that we all had to keep tidy and shave our pubic hair. It was preferred by most clients. Adina gave me a pink plastic razor and sent me to the bathroom. Still feeling dizzy from the alcohol, and emotionally shut down from my encounter with Tony, I shaved without thinking or feeling anything.

When I was done, Sylvia had more instructions. "Okay, Timea. This is for real now." I nodded in agreement. "You get dressed and you get out there. You pick your songs and tell the DJ—we'll introduce you to him soon, when you're ready—and you get naked by the third song. If you don't want anyone to touch you, don't let them. If you don't want to touch anyone, don't touch them. Just remember, you'll make a lot more money with touching."

"It's up to you," Adina coached. "You set the rules."

"Just make sure you always have a towel with you, and that the guy is always covered," Sylvia added. "There is no sex or we can get shut down." I thought back to the last time I was in the VIP room. I'd seen dancers breaking all these rules.

The girls showed me a few dance moves. I'd been trained for many jobs in my life, but never by anyone dressed in a bikini and stilettos. It was surreal. I had to focus, though. The faster I learned what to do and how to do it well, the faster I could get out of this situation. My determination hadn't failed me in the past. I could do this. I steeled myself and checked that all my emotional breakers were switched off.

Adina and Sylvia also reviewed the vocabulary I'd learned before— *towel*, *hand job*, and *VIP room*. Then they added some new words and phrases: *Kleenex, baby, sexy, "don't touch," "you want?" boobs, butt* and *pussy*. I repeated all the words as best I could.

Then, dressed in a bright orange bikini and six-inch heels, I followed the girls back into the main room and onto the stage. The music was too loud for us to talk anymore. I stood by the sidelines, watching the other girls to see exactly how they did it. They mainly shook their butts and tried to get the audience of customers interested by running their hands over their breasts and being provocative. I felt incredibly self-conscious, but didn't let myself dwell on that. I imagined I was at one of my old gymnastics performances, warming up for my routine. I had to dance and dance well.

I looked out at the clientele through the bright lights of the stage and tried to see who I had to perform for. It seemed like there were men from all walks of life. Some were in business suits, some in baseball hats; some were kind of tough-looking guys, while others just looked like regular dads or brothers. They were all ages and all types, but I knew the one thing they had in common: they were all there to escape and have a good time.

I'd been walking around the club for about an hour when, suddenly, through the smoke, dim light and loud music, I heard someone excitedly calling out my name. I looked around and saw a tall blonde girl walking toward me from the far corner of the room.

"Timea Nagy! What are you doing here?" she squealed. She was dressed just like me, in a bikini and heels, and she spoke in Hungarian. I squinted my eyes.

"Reka?" I couldn't believe it. Reka was a friend from trade school who I'd often eaten lunch with. I hadn't seen her for a few years. We'd gone our separate ways after graduation—I started my business, and I'd heard that she'd gone to America to become a porn star, which I'd thought was just a rumour. She was always more of a risk-taker than me and had been the first to do a lot of things: smoke, try drugs, have sex. But becoming a porn star in America? That was too far-fetched. Now here she was standing in front of me in a Toronto nightclub, and we were both strippers.

"It's me!" she said, enthusiastically, genuinely happy to see me. "What are *you* doing here?"

"I'm dancing," I said, stating the obvious. "I just really needed the money—you know, the economy is pretty bad in Hungary right now." I tried not to sound as embarrassed as I was.

"I know." She nodded in understanding. "I left a while ago. I'm dancing right now, but not for long. I'll get a different job soon."

"I'm going to be a babysitter," I said. "I just have to do this for a while to pay my agency. This is actually my first real shift."

"Who are you with?" she asked.

"Elek Pécsi and a couple of other guys."

"So am I!"

I was surprised to hear this. "I was here a couple of weeks ago, but I didn't see you."

"I was at another club," Reka explained. "They move us around so the clients don't get bored." Adina had told me about moving clubs, but I'd thought it was so that the dancers didn't get bored.

"Where are you staying?" I asked.

"Motel 27," she said. I could hardly believe it. I had a friend from home with me! This was the best news I'd had in a while. *Thank you, God.*

"Me too!" Had it not been for my heels, I would have jumped for joy.

"How much have you made so far today?" she asked.

"Nothing," I confessed.

"Need some help?"

"Definitely," I said. "Please."

"Come on," she said. "I'll show you how it all works. We need to get you going so you can make your money." She understood.

"Can we get something to eat first?" I asked. I was starving; I'd hardly eaten on the plane.

She shook her head. "We do that at the end of the night, as a group."

I was disappointed. How did everyone manage to dance through their hunger?

"The first thing you need is a stage name," she continued. "Do you have one?"

"A stage name?"

"Yeah, you don't want anyone knowing your real name here." I thought about how I didn't even have my real name anymore, how my passport said I was Andrea.

"Pick an English name."

"I don't really know any English names," I said.

"Then just choose your favourite character from *Melrose Place*," she suggested. I remembered how we'd talk about that American show and another one we loved, *Beverly Hills, 90210*.

"Allison."

"The drunken girl?" Reka smiled. She knew it was funny because I didn't drink.

"Yeah, that one." I smiled back.

"Okay, good. My favourite character is Amanda, so I'll switch to Amanda. I've been using Brenda from *90210*, but it doesn't feel right." It was almost like we were just play-acting in drama class. "Now you need to choose three songs and give them to the DJ so he can call you up when it's your turn. He'll play your songs in a row, and if you don't go up you'll get a penalty."

"A penalty?"

"You have to pay him if you miss your song or don't get naked on the stage. The only exception is if a client calls you over to his table." I memorized the rules like I was going to play a new board game.

"Come, I'll introduce you," Reka said, taking my arm in hers. I really was starting to feel better. There was nothing more reassuring than a familiar face in an unfamiliar place.

We walked over to the DJ and Reka greeted him, introducing me as Allison. I smiled. He nodded, but stayed focused on mixing the music, headphones on.

"You know English?" I whispered to Reka. I was impressed.

"A fair bit," she said. "Maybe you heard back at home, but I went to the States to make porn films and I picked it up there. Then I came to Canada because the money is even better."

I was glad to hear that she'd learned some English because it meant I could too, but I was sad that the rumour about her being in the porn industry was true. How she'd gotten to Canada and started working for Tony and Elek I didn't know, but it did seem like a small world. A small world and a big agency. I'd ask her later. It was too loud at the club for a real conversation.

"Now you have to choose some songs," she said, reaching for a binder of CDs on the DJ's table. "The most important thing here is that there is always someone stripping and someone waiting to go on stage. If there is a gap, everyone gets upset—the customers, the agents, the security guard, the bartender and the DJ. You don't want that."

No, I didn't. I didn't want anyone else to get upset with me.

"It's also for the girls' sake," Reka continued. "If someone has to fill in for you on stage, that means they're not in the VIP room, where they can make more money." I nodded. Maybe the other girls could do the VIP, and I could stick to the stage. "The guys don't want fights between us girls, so that's why they just have a penalty system to keep things fair."

"How much is the penalty?" I asked.

"About $35 or $40."

That was a lot.

"I should mention that you also have to pay the DJ a fee of $40 per half day—we all do. If you stay for the whole night, it's $75. That's how he makes his money. It doesn't come from the agency; it's from us girls." Overhead expenses. Just like any other business.

"And you want to stay on good terms with the DJ," she continued, glancing over at him. "If he likes you and you're good to him, he'll play your songs. If not, well, you can't make any money."

I gingerly flipped open the binder of CDs to look for songs I might be able to dance to, while Reka continued talking.

"You also need to tip the bartender, and the servers. Get your guy to order more drinks and he'll get drunker, which is good because both you and the bartender will make more money."

"My guy?"

"Your customer. You'll see how it all works—if you're not on stage, you have to be walking around the room getting the customers to notice you. You flirt with them, tease them. If they ask you to sit down, that's good. It means they like you and they might give you some more money or ask for a private dance. Sometimes they just want you to sit on their lap, or some light touching. It's up to you if you go into the VIP room or not."

"What do I do if he asks me to go to the VIP room and I don't want to go?" I asked, wanting to avoid ever setting foot in that disgusting room again.

"Just walk him to the door and call another girl over. There's always someone who will do it. But Timea, it's not that big a deal. It's how you make real money."

My stomach churned.

"If you do go into the VIP room," Reka went on, "you get different amounts for what you do. For example, a blow job is $40." She paused in her explanation to carefully and slowly pronounce the words in English so I could add them to my vocabulary. *Blow job.* I repeated the words and couldn't help but shudder.

"A hand job is $20," she continued. "If he wants to touch you, name your price. Just make sure you always cover the guy up with a white towel. It's for your protection in case he gets too excited and comes on you. Otherwise, you'll be the one to pay." Her voice dropped to a loud whisper. "You can get some nasty stuff here." I hadn't been well educated on sexually transmitted diseases, but I knew what she meant in general. My mom had taught me never to sit directly on a toilet seat and I knew about AIDS from the movie *Philadelphia*, with Tom Hanks. Ádám and I used condoms to prevent pregnancy. How would I protect myself from the filth that was around me, and from Tony?

"Just keep yourself in everyone's good books," Reka said, slightly more cheerfully. "That's the only way it all works."

I made mental note after mental note, trying to make sense of this world. My head felt like it was going to explode while my feet throbbed inside my stilettos.

"And tell the bartender that you don't drink," she said finally. "If your guy wants to order you a drink, then the bartender will mix you a virgin version of whatever you order for yourself but he'll still charge the client the full amount for an alcoholic drink. Sometimes the bartender will give you part of the profit."

I chose three songs from the DJ's binder—songs I knew, but not my favourites—and gave them to him with my new name. I had to sign on a piece of paper that I would pay him $40 at the end of the night since I didn't have any money yet. Then we went over to meet the bartender, and he asked me in English what my drink of choice was. With Reka translating, I told him I didn't drink, so he told me to always order a vodka and orange juice and he'd remember and leave out the vodka. Everything was getting organized and I felt a little relieved.

While I waited for my turn on stage, Reka and I walked around together, trying to be sexy and catch the attention of the customers. Soon the DJ called my name and I went up for my first song. I was nervous, but I kept all other emotions switched off. I began dancing, and at the end of the song, I pulled down one shoulder strap of my bikini top. It was enough for one of the customers, who called me off the stage to dance just at his table. I went over and continued dancing, eventually taking my top off by the end of the second song. He put $20 on the table, but motioned for me to take everything off, so I kept dancing when the next song came on. This time I stripped down completely. I tried to do it smoothly and professionally, like all the other girls around me, but I was awkward. The customer was clearly disappointed. He slammed $20 on the table, got up and walked away.

Wow. I picked up the money. *I just made $40 in ten minutes!* It was already enough to pay the DJ. In my head I calculated how quickly I could pay off my entire debt, and it was true—at this rate, it would only take a couple of weeks. I went over to the DJ, paid him the $40, chose three new songs, and went back on stage to wait for my name to be called. *This is okay. I can do this.*

On stage I was just as awkward as I'd been with the guy at the table, so unfortunately I didn't make any more money that night. No one else called me over to their table, and the DJ didn't play any more of my songs. I followed Reka around like a puppy, watching her, watching the whole shady, smelly, smoky scene in the club. It was a slow night, and the bartender looked bored, emptying the dishwasher and wiping the counters. When Reka was busy with a customer, I tried to find the other girls in my group to get information or tips, but most of them were too busy dancing or in the VIP room. I minded what Elek had told me—not to talk to anyone who didn't work for our agency. I tried not to worry about my lack of earning—it was my first night on the job, after all—and I got through the night until last call was announced and we only had to dance a few more songs before we were allowed to go change. The change room was crowded with girls speaking Russian, Polish, Romanian, Ukrainian and English. Some were quite drunk or high, reminding me of the guys Bianka had set me up with at home, while others were sober and subdued, like me. I didn't know if I was more hungry or more tired. I was glad that food and rest were coming.

Once we were all crammed into the car, Elek asked us how we did, and all the girls, except for me, reported their earnings. Elek seemed pleased and said we were going to McDonald's. As we drove, the girls recounted the ups and downs of the evening—which guy was the stupidest, the most pathetic, and what was the biggest transaction. Some were over $100. Elek congratulated everyone, like a proud papa.

"And how did our little Timike do?" he asked.

"She did pretty well!" Reka said enthusiastically. "She listened to everything I said and she danced the whole night."

"And how much did you make?" Elek asked.

"Only $40," I said regretfully, "which I had to give to the DJ." Elek glanced at me in the rear-view mirror.

"Oh, that's not how it works, Timea," he said. "You pay the agency fee of $300 per day first."

"I'm sorry, I didn't know." I hoped he would understand, and he did.

"It's okay, it was your first night. The girls should have told you." I was relieved he wasn't angry.

We went to a drive-through McDonald's, which was new for me. We had McDonald's in Budapest, but no drive-throughs. Just like on my first night, two weeks before, Elek ordered food for everyone but me. I couldn't understand why I wasn't being fed, but I didn't ask. I was too busy thinking. The agency fee was $300 a day? I thought Elek had said $40. Or was it $140 per week? Isn't that what my contract said? $40 per day to Tony, plus accommodation, transport and food. There was also the DJ fee. There was so much to figure out, and a lot of fees to add up and keep track of. No wonder these girls tried to make $600 or $700 per day, since half went to expenses. Still, it was a good wage, and I could pay my debts quickly—as long as I got better at dancing and stripping.

We arrived at the motel at the same time as many other dancers, who'd come with other drivers. There was also another Hungarian agent, named János. We all filed into one room for the family meeting. Elek got out his notebook and scribbled amounts, crossed off debts, tallied up fees and subtracted penalties. I watched as a lot of money went around. He was very proud of one girl, saying, "Great job! You're almost there." I couldn't wait until that was me. When my turn came, Elek already knew that I hadn't made any money, but it didn't stop him from asking, in front of everyone, "Nothing to report?" I shook my head, feeling small, and Elek looked disappointed. I didn't like the feeling of failure.

Next, we divided up into rooms, and I was happy when Elek told me to go with Reka. Our group took up practically a whole floor on one side of the motel—eight rooms, two of us in each. Elek and János had their own rooms at the end of the hall.

"Have a shower and then get into bed, Timike," Reka said. "We have to get up early to be back at the club soon." The clock radio on the bedside table read 3:55 a.m.

It was almost 10 a.m. in Hungary, so I'd been up all night and into the morning. I wanted to sleep for days.

"Why? What time does it open?"

"Eleven in the morning," she said. "And we have to be there when it opens, so we leave here at 10:30 a.m. It's in our contract."

Reka motioned for me to follow her into the bathroom, where she showed me how to work the shower faucet. Everything was different from at home.

In the shower, I let the hot water wash over me and closed my eyes for a moment. Thoughts about everything that had happened in the last several hours—and the last few weeks—began to swirl in and I shut them down by opening my eyes. I couldn't go there or I would be crushed by the weight of it all. I just had to stay focused on learning everything I needed to know and doing a good job. The only way out was to pay off my debts.

Reka set the alarm for 10 a.m. and got into bed. I pulled a T-shirt on. I didn't take out my nice pyjamas, the ones I had packed two weeks ago when I thought I'd be a babysitter in Canada. I would save them for when I was out of this situation, for when I had paid back all my debts and was far away from the club. I got into bed and immediately fell asleep.

It seemed like I'd only been asleep for a few minutes when the alarm went off. Reka crawled out of bed and called to me, urgently, "Timi, I'm having a shower first, then you. We have to get ready!" My stomach was growling like a lion—I hadn't eaten in two days. I hoped there was some breakfast waiting for us downstairs in the lobby with the coffee.

There wasn't. Reka helped herself to a cup of coffee and told me it was free so I followed suit, dumping eight packets of sugar into mine. I'd never liked coffee, but it would keep me awake, and the sugar would give me some energy. Over the next few minutes, all the other girls came down and we divided up into different cars and drove to the club. We changed and then went out into the main area. There were no customers yet, so I just walked around, waiting for men to start coming in. It was a slow morning, so I asked Elek if I could go back to the motel to sleep for a few more hours, just to get over my jet lag.

"I can't let you do that, Timike," he said. "I can't leave you alone. What if something happens to you? You can't call me, and there's no one you can ask for help if you need anything because you don't speak English." It was a good point. If something happened, I wouldn't know what to do. If the police came and arrested me, I would be helpless.

"You also need to work," he went on. "You can't hold back the group. And if I let you take a break, then everyone else will want one too."

Right.

"It works like this," he began to explain. "You work for Tony—he's the one on your contract and on your work permit. Every Sunday, you pay him $140 for his weekly fee, and another $140 to me because I'm your agent." I did the math—$280 per week. That was where the $40 per day came from—it was $20 to each agent. It was reasonable, especially given the explanation that followed. "I arrange all your work, make partnerships with all the clubs and make sure you have somewhere to sleep. Without me, you'd be nowhere. Look at my life, Timea—I live to help you girls. I have no life of my own." It was true that he was with us all hours of the day and night. I felt a little sympathy for him when he pointed this out.

"Then you have your DJ fee of $40 per half day or $75 for a full day," he went on. "Plus you have your daily agency cut of $300 per day, which goes to Sasha." This was the number that worried me. It seemed pretty high. Elek must have seen the expression of concern on my face because he quickly tried to reassure me.

"But everything after that is yours to keep, don't worry. First you put it toward your debt to us, which is almost $3,000, then after that it's yours." Hearing the amount of my debt aloud was overwhelming. When I first left Budapest, I owed $3,500 there, plus I had to pay for my flight to Canada, which was about $1,000. On top of that was my flight back—half of which I owed to Bianka—plus my work permit fee of $150, plus the cost of my fake passport. The total I owed was now almost double what I'd started out with. I needed to start seeing the number go down instead of up.

Over the last several months, money had become the sole focus of my life. My mind was like a calculator, always adding and subtracting to see if and when I was going to end up in the black. *The girls last night earned $700 to $800 each. Take away their agency fees, debt repayment, DJ fees, motel charges and other expenses . . . they're keeping between $100 and $200 per day.* I felt a knot in the pit of my stomach grow until I converted it into forint. It was about a month's salary in my job at the TV station. Even though it was less than what I'd hoped, it was still a lot.

"You'd better get to work, Timea." Elek interrupted my thoughts. He was right.

10 | New Identity

AS LUNCHTIME CUSTOMERS ARRIVED at the club I began to walk around, trying to be sexy. I felt ridiculous. I tried to get the attention of some men by mimicking the other girls' coy looks and by running my hands over my breasts like they did, but I didn't have much luck. A couple of guys tried to talk to me, but since I couldn't speak any English, they got bored quickly. I didn't have the ability to ask them what they wanted, or get them to request songs.

Eventually the DJ called me to the stage. It was my chance to make some money, but the truth was, I just wasn't a very good dancer. Other girls were more experienced than me, or maybe just more naturally talented. After my songs ended, I stepped off the stage and began walking around again. I could see that Reka, Sylvia and Adina were very busy.

As the hours went on and more customers came in, I tried to get their attention so I could make money. At the same time, I was observing this new world, and the culture of the sex industry. The strange characters, the provocative costumes, the ugly scenery. I did my best to stay emotionally shut down and to keep it all contained; I continued to picture an electrical panel in my mind, each breaker labelled with a different feeling—fear, guilt, pain, shame—and I made sure they were all switched off. At one point I saw Tony come in, and I ducked into a shadowy corner so he wouldn't see me. I could smell his sweat as he walked right past. My empty stomach heaved.

The hours passed and I didn't make any money at all. At closing, the DJ wrote down my $75 daily fee as a debt since I didn't have any cash to pay him. In the car, Elek asked us to report our earnings before taking us to a couple of drive-through restaurants. Those who had earned the most got McDonald's, and the rest got Taco Bell. Again, I got nothing. I hadn't eaten for two days.

Back at the motel, we were allowed to get a cup of coffee from the machine in the lobby and bring it to our nightly family meeting. I once again filled mine with eight packets of sugar. We gathered in one room with Elek and János, and just like the night before, Elek sat us down on the bed like children and pulled out his notebook. A few girls lit smokes and someone offered me one, which I accepted. I had been an occasional smoker in Hungary—it was the norm—but this was my first Canadian cigarette. It was softer and smoother than what I was used to, but it did little to calm my nerves.

Elek ran through each girl's tally, asking what she'd earned and telling her what she owed while János collected and counted the money. Elek congratulated a blonde girl and announced in front of the group that she was the best worker so far, and that she had made the most money over the last four months. *Four months?* That seemed like a long time. Why hadn't she moved on to better work? János then went to the next girl and let her know in a matter-of-fact tone that it was her week to pay for the oil change and the car maintenance. The bill was a steep $360 on the top of her agency fee. I didn't know too much about cars, but it made sense that it cost that much in a rich country to maintain the big, fancy SUVs we were driven in. The girl handed over a stash of twenties without complaint. János counted and confirmed the correct amount; Elek made a note in his book and then handed $40 back to her.

"Keep this for food tomorrow. You worked really hard. I'll pay your motel fee tonight and we'll just carry it over to tomorrow." She nodded, grateful. "Look," he said, offering sympathy. "If you didn't have to pay for the car maintenance, you could have made an extra $360 today. Don't worry. You're doing great. Tomorrow you'll catch up." The girl smiled at him, doe-eyed.

Elek and János continued around to all the girls. Some owed money for special room charges like soaps and shampoos, plus phone cards, tampons, razors and toothpaste. They all had a lot of money that they'd earned, but it seemed like most of it ended up back with the agents. I could only figure that once girls had paid off all their debts and started to make money for real, they became free agents or got their own apartments or something. Those of us in the motel must either be pretty new or have huge debts to pay—maybe even bigger than mine. When it was less busy, and we weren't working all the time, I would talk to the other girls and get to know their stories.

Last, it was my turn, and again I had no money to hand over.

"I'm sorry," I offered. "I am not sure how to do this." I worried that Elek would be upset, but he was nice about it.

"I know you, Timike, and I know this is not what you're used to. Give it some time, but don't wait too long, because we have to send the money to Sasha ASAP. He asked Tony about it today." He looked around to make sure everyone was listening before going over my details yet again, breaking it down into concrete terms. "For the record, you owe $3,500. So, the minimum daily amount you need to make is $700 until you pay off your debt. Once that's paid, you need to start paying back everything that is adding up each day—Tony's fee of $140 per week, my fee of $140, your motel room, any extra charges, your share of the car maintenance and, of course, your daily agency fee. But don't worry, you can see how easy it is to make that money, right?"

He pointed at János, who waved a huge wad of bills at me. It added up to thousands of dollars, all of which the girls had earned in a single day. A sixteen-hour day, but still.

The next day I tried harder, but I still didn't make even $20. I wasn't given anything to eat, so I survived on soda water and orange juice from the bartender, cigarettes from the other girls (which eventually it would be my turn to pay for), and lots of coffee with sugar. We were always welcome to have coffee at the club since, after all, we had to stay awake and have energy to dance, plus it was free at the motel. Sleep deprivation made my mind foggy, but the pain in my legs and feet from wearing stilettos for sixteen hours was as sharp as knives. Worry consumed me. When would this change?

Elek was worried too.

"I'm trying to be understanding, Timea," he said in front of the other girls, sounding a little frustrated. "But you can't pretend to be a princess any longer. Everyone is working hard in this group. Everyone is earning their share. You need to pull yourself together and start making money."

I felt guilty and ashamed, like a child in trouble. I remembered a time when my teacher had scolded me in front of the class for a low mark on a math test. I'd felt terrible about myself, like I was letting everyone down. That's how Elek's words made me feel too.

I liked to be successful, to please people. While I didn't want anything to do with the world I now found myself in, I was unaccustomed to failure and I didn't know how to handle it. Elek was right— I had to pull myself together.

The problem, I realized, was in my head. I needed to switch gears. I'd shut away the good girl Timea, hoping I could spare her this whole scene and free her once I got to a better situation, but what I hadn't done yet was embrace a new identity. I needed to get into character and stay there. I tapped into my experience as a video director, and thought objectively about how a stripper must think and act. I'd been raised to believe that selling yourself was the worst thing you could do, and that there was only one type of girl who would do it: a bad girl. But I looked around the room at the other girls, especially Reka, and I didn't see them as bad girls. They were nice. They were hard-working. I didn't judge them. But I needed to judge myself, at least on a certain level, and that judgment had to be harsh. I had to become someone who could get this job done. I needed to forget about Timea and truly become Allison the badass stripper. I went to bed that night with new resolve. As soon as I shifted my identity, my luck would shift too.

The next day, I gave myself—Allison—a pep talk on the way to the club. Almost right away, a guy asked me to dance three songs. I made $60. The DJ was really pleased and said that I was the chosen one today, and that he would waive my $40 fee. *Awesome!* Now that I had a bit of money, I simply had to get something to eat. I found Reka and asked her to help me order something from the bar. She agreed but said we should make sure Elek didn't see. He was in a bad mood that day. In the car on the way to the club he'd complained that all us girls were so much work, giving him headaches, talking all at the same time. "Tonight," he'd said, "just get in the car and keep quiet until I tell you to talk. We're going to one place only for food. I'm not going to drive all over like I'm your slave."

Reka and I looked around the club and saw him at the far side of the bar, absorbed in watching sports on TV and drinking vodka.

Reka looked at the menu and explained that there was no Hungarian food. What did I want instead?

"Whatever is the cheapest," I said. That was all I cared about.

"Okay." She scrolled down the list of prices. "A grilled cheese sandwich."

"What's that?" I asked.

"It's where they melt cheese between two pieces of bread and fry it in a pan." It sounded strange, but it would do. All I was looking for was something to fill my stomach.

"How much is it?" I asked.

"Five dollars."

That was a lot, but I was desperate.

I devoured the sandwich in a few bites and wished I had ten more. It was the first meal I'd eaten in more than three days, since being on the airplane. I'd never experienced this kind of hunger—a deep gnawing in my gut—although at the same time I was so stressed that I'd lost most of my appetite. Back out on the stage, my luck seemed to run out as quickly as it came, and I didn't make any more money.

We stopped for food on the way home, this time at a coffee shop called Coffee Time. We all got just one small sandwich, but no one complained. Elek had ordered us to be silent and we were. At the motel we had our regular family meeting, but this time, I was able to say I'd made $60.

"Good, Timea," Elek said, his mood softening slightly. "You're finally getting it." He held out his hand for my money and counted it out. There were two twenties, a ten and a five. "There's only $55 here—where is the other $5?" he asked.

"Oh, I'm sorry," I began. "I was just so hungry that I bought a grilled cheese sandwich."

"You did what?" Elek asked in disbelief. There was an undertone of anger in his voice.

"I ate a sandwich, because I haven't eaten in three days. I didn't want to bother you." My voice was meek. I felt like a little girl again, like when my mom would get mad at something I'd done wrong, but I didn't know what.

"You just spent the money on yourself?" he asked, incredulous.

"I'm sorry," I said quietly. "I was just really, really hungry."

"And the sandwich was $5?" he asked.

"Yes," I said soberly, with my head down.

"That's an expensive sandwich," he said. All the girls listened and watched, except Reka, who looked away.

"I don't appreciate that, Timea," Elek said sternly. "It's almost like you stole from me." I shook my head. I'd never stolen anything from anyone. My mom was a cop. She would have killed me. Stealing was wrong.

"Listen, Timike, you owe me a lot of money. I've been patiently waiting for four days for you to get off your princessey little ass and start to make money. I understand that you need money, but you need to understand that we need money too. I've told you this a hundred times: I work for Sasha. He doesn't care about anything other than the business and getting paid. If you don't start making money, your brother is not going to be protected."

His anger was building, and all the girls watched to see how far he would go. "I need the money, and what do you do? The first chance you get, you spend my money. Do I go into your wallet and take your money?"

"No," I said, bewildered by this line of questioning. I hadn't meant to do anything wrong.

"And your family reputation," he went on. "When did you start stealing?" I shook my head and began to protest, but he cut me off.

"Listen, I've been very nice to you. And I would really appreciate it if you would start making money, for you and for me. So you need to get serious, start working for real, and stop spending."

I nodded, ready to move on from this discussion, but Elek wasn't finished.

"Now, you're a nice girl, Timea," he continued, "so I'm going to forget about this mistake, but I do need to teach you a lesson. Tomorrow, you'll give me $50 for this infraction."

"What?" The punishment didn't seem to fit the crime. It was like I was back in Communist Hungary.

"That's your penalty. I'm sure you'll never steal from me again. Are we clear?"

I felt like shit. I was trying to do my best, and now all I'd done was make more of a mess without even trying. *I'm an idiot.* I looked up at all the other girls; they seemed interested, but not sympathetic. Reka avoided eye contact and asked to go to the bathroom, and then the meeting ended. No one spoke about what had happened, and none of the girls offered me any comfort. It was becoming more and more clear that we were there to work, not to form friendships.

The next day, determined to make things right with Elek, I pulled out all the stops and did whatever I could to work harder, dance sexier and get those customers interested. I copied the moves of girls I could see were popular. I tried out a few English words on the customers. I acted coy and provocative. I wrapped myself around the poles on the stage and slid up and down. I did my three songs and got naked within the first hour, earned $60, put my bikini back on and marched up to Elek with three twenties.

"Here is my $50 penalty from yesterday, plus $10 because I feel really bad."

"Good, Timea, good." He nodded, but remained serious. "Now we can get back on track. You've still got another twelve or so hours here, so let's see what you can do. Good luck."

Over the rest of my shift, I managed to make another $150. On my way to the change room at the end of the night, I reported my earnings to Elek, who told me to give the $40 I owed to the DJ to keep in his good books, and the rest to him. He seemed pleased, overall.

"Much better, Timike—you see? You can do it! Now just add another zero to the end and we're good."

In the car, the other girls reported their earnings. They were all in the $600 to $1,000 range, three or four times what I'd made. On the drive back to the motel, Elek stopped at McDonald's, where he bought all the other girls burgers and fries. I didn't get anything. *Was I still being punished for the sandwich?* Relief came a few minutes later, along with another lesson about how everything worked. Elek pulled into Coffee Time, where he bought me an egg salad sandwich and a Nestea and delivered them to me in the car.

"Timea, the best girls get McDonald's. Not-so-good girls get Taco

Bell." Reka explained it to me in a whisper, but I'd already figured that out. "The lowest earners get Coffee Time." I took note, disappointed but grateful just to have anything to eat at all.

Back at the motel in our family meeting, Elek got out his notebook and on my page he took $110 off my debt, and then added on my daily fees. I did the mental math quickly and realized my debt had actually gone up, but I couldn't worry. I had to focus on the fact that I was starting to do better. Elek didn't make any note about the penalty, since I'd already paid it. We both knew I would never let it happen again.

11 | Rules of the Game

I'M A GLASS-HALF-FULL kind of person, and all my life I've been able to take something that started off bad and turn it around. I can always see the positive, and like in those American movies I loved to watch as a teenager, I believe that even though terrible things happen, somehow, eventually, good always wins out over evil. But every hour I spent in Canada tested my belief.

By day five, I was beginning to get used to my surroundings and could more easily and quickly slip into Allison mode. I made a little more money each day, and I was learning who was who in the agency and club, how things worked, and what the most important rules were: Never leave the club because we're in a dangerous part of the city and anything could happen. Never get into a cab because all cab drivers in Toronto are rapists. Never talk to anyone outside our group, because anyone could be an undercover cop or an immigration officer.

"You only trust me, János, Tony and our girls," Elek ordered. I took what he said to heart, because it instilled in me a bone-deep fear. I was a criminal, in Canada on a fake passport and I worked as a stripper. If I let that be known, or raised any suspicion at all, I could land myself in jail. If I went to jail, I could never pay off my debts and Sasha would kill my family. When I got out of this situation and into a babysitting job, I would easily learn English and make friends, and it would be great. But for now, I just needed to make money and remember the rules.

The hardest part of staying positive was dealing with Tony—harder than being hungry, tired and in pain from dancing for hours. He never missed an opportunity to violate me one way or another when we were alone, and seemed to come up with endless excuses to call me to his office. Our encounters continued to make me feel ashamed, guilty and dirty, but at least they weren't violent. He never hit me. Just as I got better at being Allison and switching off my emotions at the club, I got better at dissociating during those times when Tony took advantage of me—and, fortunately, they were always over quickly. Things were bad, but at least they were becoming a familiar bad. As long as nothing got worse, I would survive and eventually be fine.

When it came to money, my debt was going down a little bit at a time—at least as far as I could tell. It was hard to keep track with new expenses and figures popping up all the time. Elek let us know that our "family," as he referred to our small Hungarian group—Reka, Adina, Ilona, Ezster, Sylvia and me—needed to start saving for our own car. Once we had one, he could start driving us around and we could save on the cost of the drivers. I didn't plan on being around for long enough to invest in a car, but I nodded in general agreement. As Elek reminded us daily, things could only work if everyone got along. Besides, if owning a car was cheaper than hiring a driver, then so be it. I didn't dare ask about a bus or a subway, or cabs. As had already been made clear—they were much too dangerous.

For now, the agency had drivers—several, in fact. They drove us girls and our agents to and from different clubs on some sort of schedule that was never totally clear to us. The agents figured out the schedules, maintained relationships with the club owners and kept track of cash flow. So far, I'd only been to Temptations—Tony's club—but the other girls had been to other places. Drivers rarely entered the clubs, maybe just to have a drink while waiting for us to change at the end of the night. János was the one exception—he was an agent, but he also drove, did much of the accounting and was close with Sandra, the most experienced dancer who'd been with the agency for the longest. She was a little older than me, very blonde and very calm. She never caused any trouble—she just did her work, made a lot of money and handed it over every night. She seemed to have more privileges than the rest of us—a leadership role—and was allowed to escort a couple of girls at a time over to the twenty-four-hour convenience store across the street from the motel to buy cigarettes if we had a few minutes before leaving in the morning, or very late at night after we were back. János would give her the money and she would give him the change and a receipt so he could write it on our tabs. However, if someone wanted to buy a phone card and use the pay phone at the convenience store, Elek would supervise.

"Don't say anything about the work you're doing here, the name of the club or anything else," he reminded whoever was making a call. "You talk about the weather and shopping only. All the phones are tapped by the police who want to shut down the clubs or catch illegal immigrants." With all the surveillance and policing, Toronto almost seemed more communist than democratic. I hadn't expected that, but it was oddly comforting—not because it was good but because it was familiar.

I didn't have the money for a phone card, but it was okay, because I had mixed feelings about calling home. Part of me just wanted to hear my brother and my mother's voices and let them know where I was, but I also knew that their words would only be angry ones. I was sure that in their minds, I had simply run away from Hungary and our family, abandoning and embarrassing them, and leaving Zoli to deal with the apartment and the bills. Unless I was calling home to say that

I'd wired some money, there was no need for me to call at all. And what could I possibly say about what I was doing?

For now, I just had to try to keep the agency roles and rules straight, and stay focused on my goal of making as much money as I could as fast as I could, without upsetting anyone—the drivers, the agents, our "family," the rest of the girls or the big tough Ukrainian boss, Sasha, who I'd never met. I actually didn't know if he was in Toronto, Budapest, or somewhere in Russia. Sometimes I heard Elek talking to him on the phone in Russian, which I understood from all my years of taking Russian in grade school. The conversations were always very serious. I prayed my name would never come up.

At the end of another sixteen-hour shift, we girls—bone-weary, hungry, and with our legs and feet in agonizing pain—changed and divided up into cars by families. I was in a car with Elek, who as usual made the decisions about where we would go for food, and what we would buy. Although I'd succeeded in earning my highest amount so far—$340—it was still by far the least of the group. This meant I had the smallest budget for food, and I was again given an egg salad sandwich from Coffee Time. It was soggy and mushy but I gulped it down, followed by my Nestea ration, without one word of complaint.

During our family meeting, I was congratulated for earning slightly more, but then reprimanded because it wasn't nearly enough.

"We have an additional problem, Timike," Elek announced. "How many towels have you been using each day?"

"At the club?" I asked, confused. I hadn't used any yet. I hadn't set foot in the VIP room.

"No, here at the motel," he said.

"Well . . . I use a big one each day for my shower and a small one to wash my face at night. Why?" I couldn't imagine what the problem was.

"The towels cost extra," he said, "and you're ringing up quite a bill." He scribbled some numbers on my page in his book and then showed me the amount he was adding on. More than $100! He did the same on all the girls' pages and showed them. None of us had heard this rule before. Everyone began to complain, but Elek quickly shut us down.

"Enough! You girls are wasting, and we can't afford it. Your room already costs a fair bit, and now this. You need to be less selfish and keep focused on the bottom line."

Even though I hadn't meant to do what I'd done, I instantly felt very guilty. I could hear my mom's voice in my head, shaming me for wasting anything when I was little.

"How much are the towels?" I asked.

"The big ones are $20 and the small ones are $10."

Wow. This was the reality of being in a rich country. Everything was really expensive.

"I'm sorry," I said. "I'll be much more careful." None of the other girls said a word.

On Friday night, Elek walked Reka and me back to our room after the family meeting in Adina and Ilona's room. He said he needed to talk to us about something that had come up. It was after four in the morning and all I wanted to do was go to bed. It had been another long workday, seventeen hours.

"So girls," he began, "you might have a couple of visitors tonight—new guys who are coming to work for us. Just let them in and, you know, have a good time."

"What?" I had no idea what he meant. Visitors? We needed to sleep.

"Do they have drugs?" Reka asked. It was the first time I'd heard her mention drugs—did she want them for herself or was she trying to figure out what kind of guys these were? A lot of drug dealing went on in the club, but I'd never seen her use them.

"I don't know," Elek answered. "You can ask them."

"Reka, what's going on?" I asked, confused. What did she know about this? Was this normal? She'd been doing this longer than me—what wasn't she telling me, and why? Reka turned away and reached for a T-shirt from her suitcase.

"Look, just be good girls and let them in, and don't worry about anything," Elek coached us. "They are our contacts. They are here to make sure we are okay. Every group needs a protector. They are going to be our protectors." He said this like I should know exactly what he was talking about.

"Why do we need protectors?" I asked.

"This can be a dangerous business, Timike," Elek answered. "There are all kinds of agents at work who don't operate as well as we do, and they want to take our girls, our time at the clubs, our territory and even our cars. Plus, protectors can keep a watch out for police and immigration officers. Spies. Crooks. You have no idea what it's like. I protect you, and they protect us and all our hard work." I listened to his answer, noted the concerned look on his face and nodded. He was right—I didn't know what it was like—but it did sound dangerous.

Elek left and I turned back to Reka, who was now getting changed.

"Is that all true?" It wasn't that I didn't believe Elek, but it was a lot to process. I needed reassurance from Reka, or some kind of comfort. She offered none.

"Whatever," she said. "Who cares? Let's just go to sleep." She looked as tired as I felt, so I dropped it. But I couldn't get rid of the new worry.

I put on a clean T-shirt and underwear and crawled into bed. I wondered when we would get a chance to do laundry, because I was running out of clean clothes. I had brought enough for just a week, and I was still saving my pyjamas for later, when I was out of this situation.

We'd only just fallen asleep when there was a knock at the door. I crawled back out of bed and opened it, as Elek had instructed. Two guys were standing there. I recognized one—an older, over-weight man who I'd noticed talking to Elek in the club earlier that day. He introduced himself as Boris, a Serbian. Reka got up and sleepily came over to the door. She seemed to know the other man and they exchanged a few words in English. Then he left, but Boris came in.

"Reka," I whispered. "What's happening? What did you say?"

"Nothing much," she said. "I'm just going to go sleep in another room tonight." Now I was completely confused as well as terrified. Why was she leaving me here with Boris?

"What am I supposed to do with this guy?" I asked. "Weren't we supposed to talk to them? I don't speak any English, or Serbian!" I was getting frustrated, but Reka ignored it. She was evasive and nonchalant, shrugging her shoulders and turning her hands palm-up. Something had gotten into her.

"Just *chill* with him," she said, using an English word and waving her hand in his general direction as she headed for the door.

"What do you mean—*chill* with him?" I asked, repeating the strange word. I had no idea what *chill* meant. Reka ignored me and I watched her leave the room. I was so overwhelmed and sleepy that I just sat down on my bed and looked up at Boris. He sat down next to me and immediately began touching my face, my hair and my shoulders. Then he began to take off my clothes. And then I knew.

To be absolutely certain about what was coming, I looked him in the eyes. And I saw it. That look—a look I'd seen in Tony's eyes, in the eyes of the guy Bianka had set me up with in Budapest, and in the eyes of the guy in the TV studio long ago. It was the same look that's in an animal's eyes when it's just about to pounce on its prey— when it knows it's going to take what it has decided is theirs. I'd seen it on a few Discovery Channel programs when they came to Hungarian TV. The predator's pupils dilate; the irises go darker and become glassy. There is focus, yet absence at the same time. If you see this look, you know that you are done for. You are nothing but prey.

If there was a way out of what was going to happen, I didn't know what it was, I was too exhausted to protest, and too weak and scared to fight. Instead, I let him take off my underwear and I opened my legs. He climbed right on top and entered me. I turned my head to the side, closed my eyes and breathed to get through the pain. I slipped away into my safe place in the shadowy corner of the room and waited for him to finish.

A few minutes later, it was over. He got dressed, kissed me goodbye—which was almost the most disgusting part of the encounter because it made it seem as though there was affection or intimacy between us—and left. I lay there, my body numb but my mind racing. Who was he? Why did Elek send him? Was he one of our so-called protectors? The last thing I felt was protected. I felt violated, but like with Tony, it didn't seem like rape. I wondered if Tony knew about this. What about Elek? He had told me to have a good time with the guys. Was this what he meant? And was doing this part of my job? Everything that I'd understood about sex, crime, violence and relationships before coming to Canada was all mixed up. I didn't seem to know *anything* for certain anymore. One thing I could count on was the fact that in a few hours I had to be downstairs in the lobby with the other girls, ready to face another long day of dancing and make as much money as I could. The only other thing that was clear to me was that I desperately needed to shower. I felt very, very dirty.

I grabbed one of the thin, rough hand towels from the rack in the bathroom and took it into the shower with me. It would cost me another $10 but I didn't care. I scrubbed myself as hard and as thoroughly as I ever had in my life, but it did little to remove the filth of what had just happened. I thought of my godmother, who used to take care of me in the summers and who had bathed me in a big, metal tub in the middle of her farmhouse kitchen floor after I'd played outside all day. With her strong, Eastern European farmer's hands, she'd scrub me like I was a potato just pulled from the dirt. I would cringe and protest, emerging red-skinned and breathless, but clean. My godmother had nothing on me now. I was fierce and unstoppable, scrubbing myself until my skin was almost bleeding.

I cried tears of fear and anger, gasping to get my breath. *Get a hold of yourself, Timea! Stop being a drama queen. This is not that big a deal. Just wash everything and you'll be okay.* Tough love was all I had to offer myself.

I stepped out of the shower, patted myself dry with another hand towel and looked around for something I could use to soothe my skin. Reka had a bottle of body lotion on the counter so I grabbed it and squeezed a big dollop onto my hand. It smelled good, and I needed something to cover up the smell of *him*, which still lingered. I spread it all over my body, rubbing it in, trying to be gentle. Then I filled up the sink, unwrapped a little bar of hotel soap, washed out my jeans and T-shirt, and hung them to dry over the shower curtain rod. I went back into the room and laid out an outfit for the next day: another pair of jeans and a new T-shirt, still clean from home. Finally, I pulled the blanket off the bed and threw it on the floor. I crawled under the sheets on the side of the bed where Boris hadn't been, and tried to sleep. It was almost five in the morning.

The alarm went off at 10 a.m., as usual, although I wasn't sure I'd slept at all. I pulled myself out of bed, put on my clothes and went to the lobby, where I met Reka by the coffee maker. Reka who had abandoned me.

"So what happened last night?" she asked casually. "How long did you stay up?" I stared at her like she was a stranger, wondering if I even knew her at all. Had she known that guy was coming for sex, and just left me to figure it out on my own? Where had she really gone? Did she have sex with the other guy? I had no words, so I just shrugged off her question. "Not too long." Clearly, she wasn't the friend she'd once been.

In the car, Elek told me that Boris liked me.

"Timike, Boris likes good girls, and if you're nice to him, he can take you out shopping sometimes." I didn't respond. All I could think about was how dirty I still felt. I wished I could peel the skin off my entire body.

———

The scene at the club was the same as the day before. I managed to earn $240 dancing, and was able to avoid the VIP room again, which wasn't that hard. Since I wasn't a very good dancer, none of the clients asked me to do anything more. That was a relief, but I knew I needed to get better at dancing to make more money. I just couldn't get *so* good that the clients would demand more of me. I didn't know how I would manage that. Forgetting I'd ever been friends with Reka, I decided to look at her strictly as a colleague; I asked her and a couple of other girls to teach me a few more moves. I also got them to teach me all the numbers in English counting by twenties up to a thousand. I was literally starting from zero.

The club's no-touching rule never stopped the men from trying. In fact, it only encouraged them. We had to dance and do sexy moves while batting away the hands that grabbed us, like we were goods for sale in a market. There were a few security guards around, but not enough to manage the crowd completely, and they weren't really motivated to keep us safe. What they wanted, just like everyone else, was for the club to make money and not get busted.

One client took a particular liking to me and had me dance four songs in a row for him at his table. He sat in his chair watching me while drinking a beer and eating chicken wings, pants undone. He was middle-aged, overweight and generally unattractive. He was also strong. He pulled me toward him, forcing me down on his lap while he pulled out his penis.

"No touching!" I insisted, but he wasn't listening at all. Instead, within moments, he ejaculated all over me. It was disgusting—the wet feeling, and the smell. I jumped up and ran to the bathroom where I wiped myself off with water and toilet paper and willed myself not to be sick or to cry. I sat on the toilet for several minutes just trying to get my breath and figure out what to do next. The man owed me $80 for the four songs, and I needed to collect it. I hoped another girl would come in, and that I could ask her to get the money for me, or get a security guard. I didn't want to go back out there myself, but if

I didn't get the money and Elek had seen me doing all that dancing, he would accuse me of stealing when I didn't produce it at the family meeting. Then I would be fined, and would have to work twice as hard to make up for what I lost. And if I didn't get back on the stage soon, I'd be accused of slacking, which I'd learned carried just as serious a penalty as stealing. Ezster had been fined $100 a couple of days ago for taking a twenty-minute break.

I waited in the bathroom for close to twenty minutes, but no one else came in. Finally, I picked myself up and went back out on the floor. I looked around for the guy, but he had left; I looked around for Elek, but he was nowhere to be seen. I saw Reka, and she told me that Elek and János had gone to go pick up some other girls, so I didn't have to worry. I was off the hook, this time. They wouldn't know I'd danced for the guy.

As I danced the rest of the night, I tried to forget the whole thing. I told myself that it had happened to the badass Allison, not to me—not to Timea. Good Timea was strong and saw the glass as half full, and she would help me get through this. *Just keep on going*, she told me. *You're going to be okay.*

12 | A Day Off

ALTHOUGH I WASN'T RAISED with any form of religion, and under communism the government required volunteer work on the weekends, I did know the biblical verse about Sunday being a day of rest. By some kind of miracle, on Sunday morning—a week after I'd arrived back in Canada—Elek announced that we all had a day off. He gathered us in one of the other girls' rooms to talk about it.

The plan was for us to go shopping at Sherway Gardens, the mall across the highway from the motel, where we could buy makeup, hair products and whatever else we needed. Under normal circumstances, or back when I dreamed of sharing an apartment like the girls on *Friends*, I would have loved the idea of experiencing my first real Western mall, but not now. Now, I didn't want to go at all. I was too frightened, and I didn't have any money to spend. What if I got lost? What if a police officer asked me for ID? What if I was kidnapped? Elek and János talked about arrests, kidnapping and murder every chance they could.

"It happens here all the time, girls," they would say. "We're always reading about it in the papers. A lot of bodies get thrown in the lake." We were wide-eyed with horror. I'd seen the lake a couple of times from the highway. It was huge, more like an inland sea. I winced, picturing the bodies in it. "Once, that's how Sasha got rid of a girl like you—one who was always breaking the rules," they told me.

"So just remember," Elek said sternly as he prepared us for the shopping trip. "No talking to anyone outside our group, and don't leave my sight. You don't know who anyone is. There are a lot of spies in Canada, and remember, some of you are here on fake passports." He turned to look at me. "You'll be the first one to go to jail if you're caught."

"Can I just stay here at the motel and sleep?" I asked. My fatigue was extreme.

"Absolutely not," Elek said firmly. "We stick together as a group."

"But please," I begged. "I'm so tired."

"You can't stay alone." Elek reconsidered. "But Tony can keep an eye on you. He has to come anyway because he's going to look over the new girls arriving later on." I didn't like the thought of Tony "keeping an eye on me." I knew it would be much more than that.

"But Tony isn't coming until later," Elek went on. "So I'll get Boris to come by to take care of you before Tony gets here, so you can get some sleep." My stomach flipped over. Boris from the other night? *No.*

"It's okay," I said. "I'll go shopping."

"No, Timea, you stay here. You said you were too tired, and you are. It's done." He reached for the phone on the bedside table. "You can go back to your room," he said, motioning me toward the door. "I'll let Tony and Boris know." I had no choice, so I went back to my room, got into bed and pretended to sleep. Maybe Boris would leave me alone if I was sleeping. Maybe Tony would too.

A short time later, I heard the slide of a card unlock the door, followed by Boris's old, gravelly voice saying hello. I played dead, like I used to when I was hiding from Zoli as a little girl. I tried to make myself invisible, and it seemed to work. Boris lay down on the other bed and made some phone calls. Then, to my surprise, I heard him begin to snore just a few minutes later. I heaved a sigh of relief. *If he is sleeping, maybe I can actually sleep too.*

No sooner had I closed my eyes and relaxed than I heard the door open again. This time it was Tony. I felt my body tense with fear, but I kept my eyes shut, pretending to be asleep. He wasn't supposed to come until later. He called my name softly, and when I ignored him, he walked over to my bed and said my name again. I lifted my head a little, mumbled a hello and then put prayer hands under my cheek, tipping my head to show that I needed to sleep. He shook his head and held out a coffee and a box of doughnuts. I shook my head no, but he insisted, making me sit up and putting the coffee in my hand. I took a sip. He put the doughnuts down and then took my other hand and put it on the crotch of his pants, guiding me to rub him. He ran his hands over my hair and face, and then he took the coffee from my hand and put it on the bedside table. He undid his belt, unzipped his pants and put my hand inside.

Without missing a beat, he pushed me back to lying down, rolled me over onto my back and climbed on top of me. Rubbing up against me, he began to breathe heavily. He kissed me, and I could feel him getting aroused. His belt buckle jabbed into my hip, so I focused on that pain to distract me from what I knew was going to happen next. Then I tried to slip away in my mind, to my safe place in the shadows of the room. It was hard to breathe—his heavy frame pressed the air out of my lungs. He was more than double my size. I was utterly helpless.

Suddenly I felt something vibrate—the pager on his belt. He stopped what he was doing, wiped the sweat from his brow and reached down to his belt to look at the number.

"I'm sorry," he said, and kissed me on the forehead. I couldn't believe it. *Sorry?* It was an English word I'd learned. He clearly thought I was his girlfriend, and that I wanted this. What had I done to send that message? I thought back to the first time this happened, back in his office at the club only hours after I'd arrived in Canada. I should have made it clear then, but I was in shock—it had all happened so fast. This was all my fault. How was I going to get out of this? Did I have to break up with him? And what on earth was going on with Boris? Had he slept through all of this, had he watched, or did he just not care? Is this how relationships were in Canada—older men shared younger women? Was Boris going to take another turn with me? I had so many questions, and could make sense of nothing.

Tony did his pants and belt back up, kissed me again and left. I immediately got out of bed and headed for the bathroom. Boris sat up in the other bed; he looked at me and mumbled a greeting. I motioned that I was going to take a shower. I closed the bathroom door behind me, grabbed another $10 hand towel off the rack, placed it on the counter, undressed and stepped in.

Less than two minutes later, Boris was in the shower with me.

It was just like before, and just like Tony. Hands all over me, taking my hand and showing me what to do. He was gentle, but I didn't want any of it. I said no, but in my exhaustion it came out as a very weak protest. It wouldn't have mattered anyway; my body wasn't my own anymore. As Boris took me over to the bed, I could see that he was now fully aroused. I let my body become Allison's—the bad girl—then just a mannequin. I lay still and tried to relax my muscles as he entered me. I reminded myself not to feel anything. That's the only way I was going to be okay.

Soon, it was over. Boris kissed me, lit a cigarette and took a sip of his lukewarm coffee. He grabbed a doughnut from the box Tony had left on the bedside table and offered me one. Although I was certainly hungry, I had no appetite. I took a small bite and tried to let the sugar replace the taste of him, and of Tony, but it almost made me sick.

I got my T-shirt from the bathroom and put it on, along with a pair of underwear, and then went over to my bed and lay down, pulling the covers over me. Boris got dressed, made a few phone calls and turned the TV on to watch sports. He lay back down next to me on the bed like a king, remote control in hand and shirt unbuttoned to reveal his hairy chest and fat stomach. I felt flattened, used. I closed my eyes and tried to sleep, but I couldn't.

A couple of hours later, Elek returned from the shopping trip with the other girls and came to see me in my room. He and Boris exchanged a few words in their broken English and then Boris left. It was as though a parent had come home to their child, gotten a report from the babysitter, and then sent the babysitter home. Had I been a good girl? Elek asked. I had. I didn't cry; I didn't break any rules; I did what the babysitters wanted, except that they weren't really baby-sitters. It seemed more like they were my boyfriends, but I didn't want them to be. I thought about Ádám. For all our arguing, it was nothing like this. I missed him. I missed what we once had. If he knew about what I was doing in Canada, it would crush him like it was crushing me, even though we'd broken up. The only thing I could do, I knew, was keep my thinking focused and turn off my feelings. *Shut down. Be Allison. Make money. Get out of debt. Build a new life.*

When we were alone, Reka asked if I'd been able to get some sleep even though Tony and Boris were here. I didn't want to relive what happened, so I just nodded and said, "A bit." I didn't trust her anymore. For a second I felt a twinge of sadness, but I quickly switched it off. What power did she have to protect me, anyway? We were all in a fog. I'd never experienced such sleep deprivation, let alone starvation or physical labour. My body was sore from dancing all the time—especially my feet and knees—and my hands and inner thighs had blisters from pole dancing. Then there was my vagina, which hurt from all the unwanted invasions. Maybe Reka was going through the same thing.

The afternoon of our day off was fairly quiet, although it was still impossible to sleep. For whatever reason, our room had been chosen as the common room, and at least a dozen girls, plus Elek, János and a few drivers, hung out drinking coffee and watching TV. In the evening, Elek said there would be a party down the hall in his room, and invited us all to "go and do some stuff." By this I assumed he meant drugs.

"Come on, Timike," he coaxed. "Have some fun. You're always so serious."

"No, thanks," I said. "I'm good. I just want to sleep."

"Fine," he said. "It's up to you. Stay here, and don't go anywhere." His voice was stern. "There are cameras everywhere so we can see you, and you know how dangerous it is out there." He motioned toward the window, the outside world.

He didn't have to convince me. I knew I couldn't leave the hotel. Where would I go? I didn't speak any English, I didn't have any money, and I didn't have anyone to go to. Elek had our passports somewhere for safekeeping, but even if I'd had mine, it was a fake. Then there was the whole matter of leaving the agency and abandoning my debts, and what would happen to my family at home if I did. No, Elek didn't need to worry; I wasn't going anywhere.

"Are you going to the party?" I asked Reka. I couldn't imagine how she was getting by on as little sleep as me, but I also had the feeling she might be interested in the drugs. Maybe that's what had gotten into her lately and made her act so indifferent toward me. When I really thought about it, I didn't know her any better than I had when we were at school together. I didn't know what her life was like making porn movies in the United States, or how she'd gotten from there to here, to work for the agency. Although we spent hours a day together and shared a room at night, it seemed there was never any time to think straight, let alone have a real conversation. The club was no place to talk—it was too loud, and we had to work—and since our nightly family meetings never ended before four in the morning, sleep was always the main agenda afterward, unless we were sent *visitors*.

"Yeah," Reka said, shrugging. "Why not?"

As everyone got up to leave, I noticed Adina, the youngest in our group, hesitate. For a split second, I saw a look of fear on her face, as if she didn't want to go. Elek must have seen it too, for his demeanour became softer than it had just been with me.

"Come on, Adina," he said. "You're going to love it." I watched that fourteen-year-old girl go with Elek, saw her fall deeper into this dark world. I wanted to save her, but I couldn't even save myself.

I slept on and off that night, interrupted frequently by the girls, the drivers, Elek and some other guys coming in and out of our room. Sometimes they were checking on me, sometimes it seemed they were just changing hang-out zones. Everyone was high, and they partied until almost six in the morning. Around nine, I awoke to find two girls in my bed with me, three girls in Reka's bed and one driver asleep in a chair. In an hour we'd have to get up and start the work week. I got out of bed, went to my suitcase and pulled out the little Simba stuffed toy that Ádám had given me before I'd left Budapest the first time, just three weeks ago. I pulled a chair over to the window, sat down and looked out at the highway. I tried to remember the lyrics of the songs that used to lift my spirits, but I couldn't quite recall them anymore.

I focused on watching the traffic. First I noticed a big green highway road sign with place names and distances next to them: Hamilton 51, Niagara Falls 112, Fort Erie 138. The only place I recognized was Niagara Falls, and I couldn't believe I was so close to the world wonder I'd learned about in school. I closed my eyes and tried to imagine going there on a Sunday with the people I was going to babysit for one day. I imagined a nice family putting their arms around me with the waterfall in the background and the mist rising up behind us. We would all be smiling, and I would send the picture to my mother.

I watched as cars filled the parking lot of Sherway Gardens. They were mostly SUVs and minivans, and I still couldn't believe how big they were. A lot of them were pulling up to a big separate store adjacent to the mall, and I noticed for the first time that the sign had a backwards R in it, which was so strange to me. It existed in Russian, but I didn't think it did in English. Was it a mistake? I thought about my mom—that mistake would make her crazy. She was always one to point out things that were wrong and demand they be fixed right away, particularly when it came to city and community issues. If someone didn't have their snow shovelled ten minutes after it fell, she'd pull out her ticket pad and start writing. Same thing if a car was parked crooked on one of the streets in the district she policed.

I sat still in the window for a long time, watching parents and kids going into the store hand in hand and then coming out with big bags that looked as if they were filled with toys or games. There were parking spaces with pictures of strollers painted on them, indicating where people with babies could park. These were the families I'd thought I would be working for. This was the nice, free country I'd thought I'd be living in—a place where parking is saved for pregnant women or families with little ones. I watched the world outside my window and then turned to survey the room I was in—the world I was in—and a sinking feeling came over me. I was never going to be a babysitter. That was never part of the agency's plan. And now, even if a job somehow became available, I was too dirty and damaged to be around children. If I'd allowed myself to feel anything, I think it would have been heartbreak, but I kept everything shut down.

I grabbed a cigarette from a pack on the windowsill and lit it. Inhaling deeply, I tried to relax. Exhaling, I tried to think. *Come on, Timea. Be strong. You're going to get out of this.* After finishing the cigarette, I got up from the chair, went over to my suitcase, put my Simba toy back and got out a pen and the little journal I'd bought back in Budapest. I forced myself to remember the lyrics of one of my favourite songs, *Szállj Fel Magasra*—Fly Above the Clouds—by Piramis. I didn't want to sing them aloud and wake everyone up, so I wrote them down in my journal to soothe myself.

It was all I wanted to do—fly away—but the only way out was to keep working and keep earning more and more money. Today was Monday, a new day, a new week, and I would work harder than ever before.

13 | A Threatening Routine

AS A YOUNG GYMNAST back in Hungary, I warmed up for big routines by running around the gym, doing floor exercises, and focusing my mind on the most challenging component of my routine. Physical exertion got my adrenaline going, as did the fear of falling and failing. The one time I'd lost focus, I paid a huge price: I'd broken my back. I'd lost my dream. In my new routine of dancing and stripping, I wouldn't risk making the same mistake again. I drank a lot of coffee and smoked a lot of cigarettes, but what filled me with adrenaline most was fear—fear for my life and the lives of my family.

I had so much adrenaline that it often kept me awake through the few hours we were allowed to sleep each night—or rather, each morning. It made my body burn quickly through the calories in the one meal a day I was given, plus many more. I didn't have a scale to weigh myself, but I knew I was losing weight rapidly. The girls who weren't as skinny were the ones who got themselves into the VIP room frequently. They made more money, so they got a bit more food, and the clients they were with sometimes bought them snacks or meals. As hungry as I was, I didn't want that to be me. I kept focused on dancing and began earning a few hundred dollars per day.

Every day, while we danced, Elek sat at the bar, watching TV, having a few drinks, talking with other agents and keeping an eye on us. We checked in with him throughout the day, letting him know how things were going, if any clients were particularly disgusting or weird, and asking for permission to go to the bathroom or have a glass of water. For the most part, he acted like a coach or a big brother, but other times he was more militaristic. Together with János, he kept everything organized, keeping track of money, club contracts, drivers, schedules and the orientation of new girls. He made sure Tony was happy, and part of that was giving Tony and me time together. I didn't know how to tell Elek that I wasn't Tony's girlfriend, and I could no more break up with Tony directly using words than I could physically push him off of me, so I didn't try. I used my fighting energy and adrenaline to keep dancing.

As the days went on, I noticed a shift in the energy of the group. The girls who were doing well at the club and making good money were starting to get a little snappy with Elek and one other during our car rides to and from the club. They began complaining about their debts not going down and having to work so many hours. They began getting on Elek's nerves.

"Who do you girls think you're talking to?" he asked them sharply. "Don't forget who's the boss here. Don't forget about everything I've done for you."

A couple of the girls began showing up late to the motel lobby in the morning, and Elek blew up. He threatened to charge them $100 per minute if it happened again. Like berated puppies, they whimpered and obeyed.

Some aspects of the group dynamic reminded me of my camp experiences as a kid. Everyone behaved really well at the beginning, because we were a little homesick and everything was new. Then there was always a point mid-camp when we were comfortable and confident enough to question things, like why we had to wear bathing caps to swim, or why breakfast was the same every day. The novelty of all being in one cabin and sharing a bathroom would eventually wear thin and we'd start annoying each other. At that point, the counsellors would go over all the rules again and threaten us with loss of privileges—like movie night or candy—and then take us on a big hike or something to break up the tension. Elek and the other agents had a similar strategy with threats, but instead of finding ways to release the tension, they let it build. Except for the occasional supervised shopping trip, we weren't allowed to go anywhere; we could never leave the hotel or the club alone, never take a break. One morning, we learned about what happened to a girl who complained too much, a girl who tried to leave.

As we approached the car in the parking lot of the motel, waiting to take us to the club, we saw József—the Hungarian driver I'd met on my first night—smoking and pacing back and forth angrily. I'd seen him several times over the past month, and he was always calm. Not like this.

"What's wrong?" Elek asked.

"Stupid girl, fucking leaves the house! Tries to escape—and she thinks that she can make it to the police and report us!" József was incensed. "She thinks I'm the fucking criminal!"

"What?" Elek was shocked. I was too, my mind tripping momentarily on the word *escape*.

"She wants to report us, and put all the other girls at risk!"

We girls were listening intently, glancing at each other as we took this in. Was he talking about someone we knew? József swept his hand toward us, huddled together in our jeans and T-shirts. It was the end of May, but still chilly in the mornings.

"I don't know how you do this, Elek—how you handle them." He sounded exasperated.

"These are good girls," Elek assured him. "I don't have anything to worry about." He was right. There might have been a bit of complaining lately, but none of us would think of running off and leaving our debts behind, especially not me. Whoever this girl was, she must have been pretty screwed up, and irresponsible.

"So what did you do? Did she get away?" Elek asked.

"No, no, no," József said, shaking his head and half-smiling, triumphant. "János caught her at the end of the street. Imagine—she was totally naked! She just ran out and down the street like that. What a fucking idiot! Now the whole neighbourhood knows something's up."

I held my breath as I listened, trying to picture the scene. I didn't know that the agency had houses in neighbourhoods; I thought we were all at this motel. So who was this girl? She must have been on drugs. She must have broken the rules. József was right; she must be a real idiot. I glanced again at the other girls, whose expressions of judgment matched mine.

"Don't worry," József went on. "We got her back."

"Did you teach her a lesson?" Elek asked. We all listened intently in fearful anticipation.

"Oh, yeah," József said. "She gets it. It won't happen again."

"Which way did you choose? The baseball bat?" Elek asked. He was so calm and casual, I wasn't sure I'd heard him correctly. We stood motionless, waiting for the answer, picturing a horrible beating.

"No, the oil." József said. *The oil?* Adina's eyes met mine; they were wide with fear.

"Ah." Elek nodded slowly, approvingly.

"Yeah, me and János tied her up in the garage and showered her body with boiling oil for a few minutes." My stomach clenched in shock as József went on, proudly. "Man, the smell of burning hair—fuck!" He waved the air as though wafting away a terrible smell. "Have you ever had to do that?" We girls screwed up our faces as though in pain, picturing ourselves as the victims of this torture.

"No, no," said Elek, confidently. "I don't have to do that stuff with these girls. Right, girls?" We all nodded in unison, like puppets in a puppet show. Terrified puppets.

"What a bitch!" József went on.

"Seriously." Elek consoled him. "You're just trying to help her—help all these girls. You're up all day and all night, driving their asses around town like princesses, getting them work, helping them pay their debts, and this is what you get. Disgusting."

"Bitches, all of them," József said. "Are you sure about these ones?" He motioned toward us again.

"Yeah, yeah, yeah, they're all fine. You remember them, right?" He said each of our names. "All Hungarian, like us. We don't turn on each other." We all nodded in quick, scared agreement. "Now, let's go. They need to get to work."

We got in the car silently. I squeezed into the back, next to Reka, and Elek sat next to József, who drove.

"What the hell was that?" I whispered to her. She looked very pale. She put her index finger up to her lips. "Shhh," she whispered back.

I looked at another girl named Viktoria, who'd recently arrived from Hungary and joined our "family."

"Have you heard about this before?" I asked in hushed tones.

"Don't talk," she said. "Just don't talk." She turned to look out the window.

I gave up and tried to just watch the scenery too—the highway, the big cars—but all I could see was that girl in the garage, having boiling oil poured over her, screaming in agony. I could smell it. I shuddered and tried to push it out of my mind. At least I knew that would never happen to me, nothing even close. I would do whatever I was told and I would never break the rules. I wouldn't try to run away; I'd get out of this in the right way, by paying off my debts.

That day and night at the club were the same as all the rest, and we girls were pretty subdued on the way home. Elek and József took advantage of our silence to tell us more about what could happen if we ever decided to be as stupid as the other girl.

"There's a baseball bat in the back of the car, under the mat where the spare tire is. Does it still have the other girl's blood on it, Elek?"

József posed his question as innocently as if he'd asked to stop for coffee and a doughnut.

"Probably," Elek nodded. "That was a sad story, what happened to that girl. Such a waste." We all listened intently, riddled with anxiety. We didn't need to ask for the details; Elek willingly described what happened to her.

"Yeah, she really had us fooled! Seemed like such a good girl. Cute too. But if her body is ever pulled from the lake no one will recognize her after what we did to her face with the bat." He paused, and then turned to look at us in the backseat. "I think one of you has her passport." We all looked at each other. *Is it me?*

For the next few days, we were quiet. No one talked much, no one complained. We just worked, ate our McDonald's, Taco Bell or Coffee Time, handed our money over during the family meetings, and went to bed. But the peace couldn't last. We were too tired, too hungry and too stressed. Tension ramped up again. Something was about to give.

A couple of nights later, during the family meeting, Reka broke.

"You can't charge me for that," she protested over the cost of a car repair that had been added to her account. Apparently, the car had broken down during the day and József the driver had had to take it into the shop. We were collectively responsible for paying the bill. "I've given you over $2,000 in the last few days and my debt is only down by $350? That's bullshit." Her voice was strong. The rest of us froze, not knowing what was going to happen next. We'd never heard anyone talk back to the agents.

Elek's and János's faces immediately turned red with anger. "Do you know who you're talking to?" Elek yelled. "Do you have any fucking idea who you're talking to?" The brother Elek disappeared, and in his place was a furious dictator.

"I don't care," Reka said. "That's fucking bullshit. You don't charge that much for a small car repair. I've worked in the States; I've worked here. I'm not an idiot."

"Oh yeah?" Elek asked. "Come outside with me." He grabbed her by the elbow and led her out the door of our room. János stayed behind with us, shaking his head. The other girls and I remained frozen, looking at the floor.

Several minutes later, they returned. Reka was crying, but no one said or did anything to comfort her, not even me. Elek told us it was time for bed, so the other girls got up and left, and Elek and János followed. Alone with Reka, I asked her what had happened, although I was afraid to know. She just shook her head and said she didn't want to talk about it. Without even showering or changing her clothes, she got into bed, switched off the light and turned her back to me.

In the morning, seven new girls arrived from Hungary and Romania, and Elek announced we'd all be switching rooms and roommates. Reka and I would no longer be together, and I would instead be given one of the new girls, Hanna. I figured it was for the best—Reka's acting out could get me into trouble, and I didn't want that. Hanna was very quiet, very reserved—a Roma girl a few years older than me, although she looked very young. She carried her belongings in a plastic shopping bag, among them a photo of her son that she put on the night table. She didn't talk to me, other than a basic greeting and a few questions about what time we were leaving and where we were going. I explained the daily routine.

"Have you done this before—worked as a dancer?" I asked her.

"Yes, but not in Canada," she said.

"So then you know what to do, and if you have any questions you can ask me." I still wasn't an expert, but I knew my way around the club now and who all the players were. It almost made me feel good to have someone I could mentor a little bit. I was relieved not to be the new girl anymore.

The next two days and nights, I managed to make the most money I'd ever made: $500 each night. Elek was very pleased and rewarded me by taking $300 off my debt and letting me keep $200 for myself after I paid all my daily fees. He would hold onto my cash for safekeeping, since I didn't have anywhere to put it and he said all the housekeepers at the motel were thieves, but it was mine for the next shopping day or to send home. Hope surged. There was less than a week left for my brother and I to save our apartment, so as soon as I could, I'd have to send that money. I still hadn't been in touch with Zoli, but maybe after a few more shifts like this, I could call him and let him know how much I had. It might not be enough, but it would be something. Maybe the landlord would give him an extension.

I gingerly asked Elek what my debt was down to and he reported $3,000. I was surprised; by my mental calculations I'd earned almost $2,000, so it should have been far less, but it was true that there were a lot of expenses. I wished I'd written the numbers down in my journal, but so far all I'd done was write down some song lyrics to help myself feel better for a few moments when I couldn't sleep. Otherwise, there wasn't time. The next evening, I was hit with two more expenses: a $360 oil change for the car, and interest charges on my debt at 10 percent. Apparently, it was agency policy that new girls got to be interest-free for their first two weeks, but after that it was business as usual. I wasn't a new girl anymore. Elek moved my $200 savings over to the debt side of my page. I wouldn't be sending any money home.

Hanna, my new roommate, was suspicious. A few days later she approached me at the club and asked to talk. As she walked toward me I noticed how much thinner she'd become in just a week, and that she had the same big, dark circles under her eyes that we all had.

"Timea, can I trust you?" she asked, sounding nervous.

"Yeah, for sure," I said. She was looking out at the dance floor and all the tables with the clients and the girls—at the whole scene—as though assessing it all from a distance.

"I worked in Germany and other countries as a professional prostitute, and this is not right. This is not how it works. These guys are robbing us blind. This is illegal!" She spoke quietly, but emphatically. I listened without looking at her, acting normal so as not to call any attention to us.

I didn't want to believe what she was saying. If I believed her, it would mean accepting that my situation was far worse than I thought—that I'd signed up with a corrupt agency. I glanced around nervously to make sure no one could hear us talking, especially Elek. He had made it very clear: no rebelling, no talking behind his back and no backstabbing.

"It's different here," I offered. "I know Elek from home. He wouldn't do anything illegal—he used to be a police officer. This is how it works in Canada."

"How do you know?" she asked. "Have you worked anywhere else?" I admitted I hadn't, and immediately got a sinking feeling in my stomach. *What if she's right? What if Elek is the criminal, not me?* It was too much to think about, that someone would intentionally take such advantage of me—someone I knew from home.

"We can't talk about this," I said, and turned to walk away. I was riddled with fear. *What if she's a mole, and Elek is testing my loyalty?* I couldn't take a chance. I headed over to the other side of the club, hoping Elek had seen me from wherever he was. I needed him to trust me, to see that I trusted him. I tried to put Hanna's idea out of my mind, but I couldn't. If she was right and we were all being exploited, then I'd never get my debts paid. I felt the panic rising inside me, and did my best to push it back down. *You're okay. Just keep breathing. She's wrong. Keep dancing.*

But it was hard to keep breathing, let alone dance. My feet and legs were in agony. My mind was filled with worry. Tension was building more and more each day among the girls. Despite Elek's threats, there was arguing over everything, and everyone was on edge. We were all hungry, exhausted and frustrated that our debts weren't getting paid off. I tried to stay out of it, but it was difficult. I pulled into my own internal world and repeated song lyrics in my mind over and over so that I couldn't hear the bickering.

Elek did his best to control the growing tension by constantly—but indirectly—letting us know what could happen if we rebelled.

One day, in the car on the way to the club, he began venting to that day's driver, Karoly.

"Oh man, am I tired!" he complained. "There is so much shit going on. Not these girls"—he motioned toward us in the back-seats—"but the other groups I take care of." He turned his head to look at us over his shoulder. "You guys don't know how hard I work. There's all kinds of stuff I have to do when I'm not taking care of you." We all listened intently. "It's all just a big headache. Probably not even worth it anymore."

Karoly piped up with a suggestion. "There's always the baseball bat. You know the best way to use it, right?" Elek was all ears, and Karoly continued.

"Just hit them in the back of the head first, then on the back, then the back of the knees, and they will collapse. Then you just beat them a couple of times, and then, well, your problems are over." The girls and I listened, our breaths held. I could almost feel the blows.

"Come on, man," Elek protested. "Really?"

"Trust me," Karoly said. "You'll appreciate this advice."

The girls quieted down for a couple of days, but then the fighting and bickering returned. Our family dynamic got worse by the day. Reka had begun smoking weed—I think in the VIP room or some-where else in the club—and Elek was pissed about it.

"Where are you getting it from?" he demanded. "And why are you spending your money on it? You still owe us!" She laughed it off and said clients gave it to her. This only angered Elek more.

"Don't make me get the baseball bat," he warned. "Don't make me become that guy. It won't be fun, feeling the bat on your head, in your back, on your knees. And it won't be fun for me if you make me do it. Do you know how many girls' blood is already on that baseball bat? You don't want to add to it." Reka didn't look fazed. I couldn't tell if it was because she was stoned, or if she had just truly stopped caring, but it was scary. In such a short time, she had become com-pletely unrecognizable to me as my girlhood friend.

"Do you know how easily I could just put your black-and-blue body in a garbage bag and throw you in the lake?" Elek asked, his voice raised. "No one will ever find you." He looked at all of us in turn. He could never hurt me, could he?

"Why do you guys make me do this?" he asked, exasperated. My whole body was tense with fear. I pictured myself sinking down to the bottom of the lake, pictured myself dying here. I couldn't let that happen. There had to be a way out of this.

On the way home from the club that night, Reka lost it—and this time, she didn't hold anything back. "You know what, Elek?" she asked, her voice pitched. "Fuck you! I'm not giving you my money anymore." Elek turned around in his seat to look at her.

"What the fuck did you say?" he asked angrily.

"This is bullshit. You're cheating all of us," Reka snapped. "I'm going to call the police." At the drop of the word *police*, Elek told the driver to pull over and stop the car.

"Get out," he ordered Reka. It was almost 3 a.m., and there were only a few other cars on the road.

He got out and walked around to Reka's side of the car. He opened the door and pulled her out.

"What the fuck did you say?" he hissed.

"I said, I'm going to call the police." Reka was defiant. Elek grabbed her by the hair and pushed her up against the car, pinning her body with his.

"You say that again and I promise you, you will not breathe anymore." I wanted to jump out of the car and stop Elek, but I knew that could only end badly, with me not breathing either. I stayed in the car with the other girls, all of us still and silent except young Adina, who was shaking.

"Get your hands off me!" Reka screamed. Elek pulled her hair tighter.

"Your mother, and your little sister—no one will be breathing anymore. So get your ass back in the car and shut the hell up."

Reka continued screaming and struggling. Still pinning her with his body, Elek stuck his head inside the open car door so he could look at us.

"Tell her to get in the car!" he yelled. "If the police come, you're all going to jail and it will all be her fault!"

We all started yelling and pleading. "Reka, please, get in the car!"

"Fuck you all!" she shouted angrily. Elek put his hand over her mouth, overpowered her and forced her into the backseat, where she continued to swear at us. I wanted to throw up. What was going to happen now?

Adina, who I'd seen do lines of coke every day at the club since the motel party, bent over and starting rocking and crying.

"Why is this happening?" she cried, pulling out handfuls of her own hair. I didn't know if she was acting this way because she was high or having a nervous breakdown. She was sitting next to me, so I put my arm around her and rubbed her back gently. She calmed a little bit.

Hanna was sitting on the other side of me, silent.

By the time we reached the motel, Reka had calmed down a bit and so had Adina. Elek warned us not to make a scene, and we quietly went to one of the rooms for our family meeting. The accounting was done quickly, and Elek told Hanna, Adina, me and the other girls—now more than twenty in all—to go to our rooms. He needed to deal with Reka.

"What do you think is going to happen?" I whispered to Hanna as we left the room. Although she was new to our agency, she had more experience than me. Maybe she'd seen something like this before.

"Don't talk," she said.

"But what's going on?" I needed to know.

"I don't know, but this isn't how it's supposed to be. This is not good." Every muscle in my body tightened. All I could picture was Reka being stripped, tied to a chair and having boiling oil poured over her like that other girl—the one who'd tried to run away.

"I'm leaving. I need to get out of here," Hanna suddenly said.

"Where are you going to go?" I asked, fearful. "How are you going to leave?" She didn't answer. I told her the hot oil story but she shrugged it off.

"I'm not planning on getting caught," she said firmly, before opening the door and walking out of our room and out of the motel, leaving everything behind.

The next morning, Reka and Hanna were nowhere to be seen. We all pretended that everything was fine, that nothing had happened, even though I had a terrible feeling that something awful had happened to Reka. Images of the baseball bat, the hot oil and the lake took over my mind. Elek asked me where Hanna was and I said I had no idea, which was true. At the club, I tried to act normal. I danced, stripped and worked some tables with guys who invited me over, but all I could think about were the two missing girls. I wanted to talk to Adina, but I could hardly look at her—it was too painful. She'd lost so much weight, and her eyes were vacant, with big black circles under them. I didn't dare look in the change room mirror at my own face. I kept my head down. I didn't want to anger Elek. After last night's scene, and whatever he'd done to Reka, my sisterly feelings toward him had changed. I'd seen something different, something sinister.

When we got back to the motel at the end of the night, Elek told the girls I'd been in the car with—Sylvia, Adina, Ilona and Viktoria—to go into Sylvia and Adina's room and wait, and then he pushed me toward my room. The other girls weren't back yet. He opened the door with the keycard, stepped in, looked at Hanna's side of the room and ordered me to pack her stuff.

I hesitated.

"Where is she?" I asked, not really wanting to know. The answer wouldn't be good.

"Don't worry about it," he said. "She's not breathing anymore and neither is Reka. Now pack up her shit." I could hardly breathe myself, picturing Reka as I'd known her in trade school, laughing and chatting with me between classes. Then I pictured her dead, beaten with a baseball bat or burned with hot oil and lying at the bottom of Toronto's lake. Then I pictured Hanna, who had tried to run away but had been caught and was at the bottom of the lake too. I reached for a plastic bag in the corner of the room and began filling it with Hanna's clothes and few personal items. I paused when I saw the photo of her son, still leaning up against the lamp on the bedside table.

"Yeah, go ahead. Pack that shit up too," Elek said, emotionless. I put the photo in the bag, and then gave the bag to Elek.

"Hopefully her little son isn't in the house in Hungary as it's burning," he said. "Now let's go." I followed him back down the hall to the family meeting like a robot.

Everyone behaved normally at the meeting, as though nothing had happened. As though two of us had not just been murdered. I passed over my $500 in earnings to János and watched as Elek scribbled in the notebook. I was more scared than ever, but I didn't want them to sense my fear. I needed to be strong, and for them to know I was part of the team, that I was working harder than ever. This was the only way I could protect my life.

That night, my debt went down, and then back up again as usual. Elek had snapped back into his encouraging coach-like demeanour.

"Don't worry, Timike," he offered, in his brotherly tone. "Look how much you've improved in a short time. I think she's ready for a new opportunity, don't you, János?" János nodded enthusiastically. "Tomorrow we're going to take you to a new location, where you can make really, really good money, okay?"

I nodded yes, having no idea what I was agreeing to.

14 | The Massage Parlour

IT WAS A WARMER, brighter morning and the sun hurt my eyes as I walked from the motel to the car with Sandra—the most senior dancer and János's favourite girl. There were only a few minutes a day like this where I was out in sunlight, and I'd made it a habit to take in a big breath of fresh air, but after yesterday's events, I could hardly breathe at all. I also didn't know where I was being taken, so I steeled myself. Wherever it was, I just hoped I would be safe and able to make some better money, and maybe—just maybe—I could call my brother and tell him how much. I couldn't be exactly sure of the date, but I believed it was May 31—the last day on our lease. There was still a shred of hope, and I held onto it.

Sandra and I got into the car, where Elek was waiting with a driver.

"Good morning, Timike," they said, almost cheerfully. Their good moods were a complete mismatch to all that had gone on the night before, and over the last several days. I pretended too.

"Hey, guys," I said with a smile. "So where are we going?"

"It's a surprise!"

The route was different from the one to the club, so I forced myself to enjoy the change of scenery. Since I'd first landed here five weeks ago, and then returned three weeks ago, spring had fully arrived and now everything was green. For a few moments, I put everything out of my mind and remembered that I was in Canada, one of the most democratic, rich and beautiful countries in the world. Maybe this was the day I'd been waiting for—the day when things got better.

We pulled up in front of an office building that had a few retail stores on the ground floor. My hope swelled. *Are we going to be cleaning offices?* I would gladly scrub a hundred toilets instead of dancing. If I could make money doing anything other than selling my body, I would be happier. Besides, I was a way better cleaner than I was a dancer. That much I knew for sure.

Sandra and I got out of the car, but Elek and János didn't.

"Don't worry, Timike, Sandra will take care of you. We'll be back to pick you up at the end of the day, and we'll go to the club for the night shift." My heart sank a little, knowing the dancing wasn't yet over, but I let it go. Whatever this was, it seemed like a step in the right direction; there were no neon signs with naked women here.

"Have you been here before?" I asked Sandra.

"Yeah, I come here sometimes," she replied. "You can make a lot of money here, like a thousand dollars."

I was impressed. "What do you do?"

"You'll see," she said.

Sandra led me through the main glass doors, then through a maze of hallways and up three flights of stairs. After a couple of minutes, we came to a frosted-glass door. She opened it and we walked into the reception area of what seemed like a spa. The floor was white tile and the walls were white with a couple of posters of tropical flowers on them. There were a few folding chairs along one wall, a desk in the middle and several doors lining each side of a corridor behind the desk. It smelled like a pool—like chlorine—and also like scented candles. *Okay*, I thought. *This is good!*

"It's a massage parlour," Sandra said, gesturing around the room with one arm, as though revealing a prize on a game show. Then she pointed to the ceiling, where a security camera hung in each corner. "It's a really safe place," she said. "The managers are in another room and they can see everything, so you don't have to worry about the clients getting out of line." *Okay, so I'm going to be giving massages? I guess I can do that.* I'd never had a massage in my life, but maybe I could pretend to be Phoebe on *Friends*; she was a massage therapist. I didn't have to be the badass Allison here.

Next, Sandra pointed to a sign above the desk area. "Do you understand any of it?" she asked. I shook my head; I knew the few English words the girls had taught me at the club, but only to hear them. I couldn't read anything in English. She began translating the sign, which was a list of services and prices.

"Clients can choose whatever item they want, or a package," she explained. She went down the list. "Back massage—that means hand job; head massage—that means blow job; and full service—that means, well, you know."

I didn't know for sure. But I could imagine. The price next to it said $200. All my hope and positive thinking began to sink like a ship. This wasn't a massage parlour. It was a sex parlour. I wasn't safe here at all.

"Sex," Sandra said simply. "You have sex with them."

"I can't . . ." I began to protest.

"It's not a big deal. You just lie down, open your legs and let them do their thing. It's usually over in five minutes." Just like every other time I'd had my job explained to me in this country, the words and their meanings didn't match the nonchalant way they were said. It was like I was being shown how to scoop ice cream in an ice cream parlour, not how to be a prostitute in a "massage" parlour.

"All customers want a 'happy ending,'" Sandra went on casually, as though describing the most popular flavour of ice cream available. "You know—an orgasm." I was in shock.

Moments later, while I was still standing there dumbfounded, the first customer walked in. He was a very average-looking, middle-aged man with a receding hairline and pot belly. For a split second, I thought maybe he was lost. I hoped he was lost.

"Do you want to take him?" Sandra asked.

"No, no, you can definitely take him," I said, instinctively stepping back. Sandra smiled at the customer, grabbed a towel from a stack on a nearby shelf, opened one of the doors and motioned him into a room. I watched her as she efficiently handled all of this. She looked so normal. She was wearing a miniskirt and T-shirt, and low heels. She looked like she should be going shopping or out for lunch with a friend, not about to perform a sex act on a stranger.

I sat down in one of the folding chairs and didn't move. I didn't hear anything other than the sound of a shower starting, and then stopping after a minute, and then some moaning. I watched a clock on the wall. Exactly six minutes later, the guy walked out and left. Sandra came out shortly after with $200 in her hand.

"You see?" she said with a smile. "Easiest money you'll ever make."

"What did you do?" I asked, incredulous and yet morbidly curious.

She laughed. "He was such a loser. I just took my top off and he came."

"That's it?" That wasn't so bad.

"Yup. And you know the rule of the business, right? It's one cup of tea." I didn't, so she explained the industry standard. If the guy wanted a second cup of tea—another orgasm—he had to pay for it.

"It doesn't always happen like that," Sandra went on. "But you'd be surprised how often it does. These guys are so hard up for it they'll come at the drop of your pants. Such losers." I hoped for a day full of losers.

A few minutes later, three young Russian guys, probably sixteen or seventeen years old, walked in.

"You wanna take them?" Sandra asked.

"Not really, no," I said.

"Security is watching in the back," she said quietly, motioning toward one of the cameras. "You better. They report to Elek and János."

I hesitated.

"You have to take them," she insisted. "It's your turn."

"All of them?"

"Kids like this pool their money. It's a group rate."

"What do I do with them?" I asked, feeling pressured. The guys were already looking at their watches.

"Just take it easy, make them take showers, take your top off. Dance a little like at the club. You'll be fine. They probably only have enough money for hand jobs anyway. Make them show you the money first. Three hand jobs would be $60."

I listened to the instructions and then tried to snap into being Allison, but I couldn't do it. My surroundings were new, I was wearing my own T-shirt and jeans, and everything was happening so fast. I was Timea, and I was frightened, but I let Sandra lead me and the boys to the door of one of the rooms. I went in first. There was a massage table in the middle and a shower stall in one corner. Some towels were stacked on a wall rack next to it. There was no other decor whatsoever, save for a wall calendar featuring a picture of a topless girl. We all crowded into the room and one of the guys locked the door behind us.

"Okay guys, here's the shower," I said with nervous cheer in my grade-school Russian. I opened the door to the shower stall and waited for one of them to get in.

Instead, one of the boys pushed me in and all three of them began tearing off my clothes, like I was a new toy on Christmas morning.

I didn't even have time to try and stop them. Then they turned the water on and told me to take a "sexy shower." I ran my hands over my breasts and butt, hoping it would be enough for them. They watched and laughed as they undid their belts. I glanced up to the ceiling corners to see if there were any video cameras. There weren't. No one was watching me; no one was protecting me. These guys could do whatever they wanted.

After a couple of minutes, they turned off the water, pulled me out of the shower and pushed me onto the massage table. They each took their pants off and rolled on a condom, and I was momentarily relieved. I already feared getting pregnant from Tony or Boris, and the more men I was exposed to, the more I knew I was at risk for all kinds of nasty stuff.

They took turns touching me, squeezing my nipples, fingering me. Getting turned on. I froze and didn't fight, but I couldn't seem to slip away to my safe place like I could with Tony or Boris. As I lay on the cold massage table and stared up at the ceiling, I willed myself not to cry, not to scream. Just do what Sandra said: lie down, open my legs, let them do their thing and hope it would be over quickly.

One of the boys climbed on top and roughly entered me, while another grabbed my hair and the third forcefully rubbed my breasts. I felt cold and exposed; there was absolutely no way I could even attempt to protect or cover myself. I was utterly vulnerable and help-less. The first boy finished, and the second jumped on. He was rougher than his friend, and it hurt. I was dry, and my muscles were tense.

Okay, Timea, it's okay. I began to console myself. *It's just your body. It's not what's inside you. No one is here. No one can see what's happening. It's okay. It will be over soon.*

After the third boy took his turn, it was finally over. I looked at the clock; it had all taken close to forty-five minutes. The boys, happy and laughing, thanked me for a good time, placed a stack of bills on the massage table, near my feet, and left. I wondered if it was their first time with a girl.

As soon as they left, I numbly reached for a towel and sat up on the table. Then I carefully stood and stepped back into the shower, where I scrubbed myself under hot water. Afterwards, I used the towel to scrub down the table. Then I sat down for a moment. Closing my eyes, I was finally able to forget the last hour and slip into a new safe place for a moment. It wasn't just into a shadowy corner of a room, like before; that wasn't enough. This time I pictured myself in a beautiful field of flowers. I was wearing a long white dress that flowed out behind me. I walked around and picked the flowers. There was soft music playing. *No one can touch me. Nothing can hurt me. I am safe and free.* I breathed.

I opened my eyes and picked up the money. They'd left $200— payment for one "full service" package, not three. I left the room, saw that one of the other doors was closed, and sat down by the reception desk for a few minutes until I saw a customer leave. Then Sandra came out.

"How did it go?" she asked casually.

"Not too well," I said. I told her what happened.

"All three? Timea, you're not supposed to do that! You got ripped off." She sounded disappointed in me.

"You should have told me!" Suddenly, I was angry. "I didn't know what was happening. I've never done this before. I thought we were going to be cleaning an office today."

Sandra looked at me with pity.

"Sorry, Timea, I thought you understood."

"How many times a day do you do this when you work here?" I didn't want to know, but I had to know. What was expected of me? Would I have to do that again?

"Eight or ten," she said. "It depends on how long I stay and what the customers want. Full service is expensive, so most of them just order something cheaper."

"I can't do that again today," I said earnestly. "I'm in too much pain. Please, don't make me."

"Elek is going to be pissed if you don't make money today."

"I just can't. I don't care. I'll make it up dancing tonight. Just please, don't make me take any more customers." I was desperate, wanting only to protect myself from more pain and humiliation. I didn't want to be a prostitute. I wanted to cry but I swallowed my tears. If I started crying I would never stop.

"Okay," she said sympathetically. "I'll cover for you." Relieved, I thanked her and promised to pull my weight by doing all the cleaning, folding towels, and anything else that needed to be done—anything but servicing customers.

Sandra was right. When Elek arrived to pick us up in the late afternoon, he was none too happy about what had happened with the three high-school boys. I begged forgiveness, and promised to make up for my lost income that night and in the days to come. I tried to appeal to any sense of compassion he might have for little Timike, from back home.

"Please, Elek—I can't do this. I can't have sex for money. Dancing, no problem. I can do that. But I can't have sex."

He agreed.

"I get it, Timike. I should have known. I forgot you are just a beginner. You weren't ready." I was relieved, but not completely off the hook.

"But you do need to shape up and start making some real money. Consider yourself on trial. I need to see you bring in more money or there are going to be consequences."

15 | Fantasia

ONE STEP FORWARD AND TWO STEPS BACK. That's how things always seemed to go with the agency and with my account. Days and weeks passed and I danced as much as I could. I earned more and more, and should have been closer to clearing my debt, but new obstacles presented themselves daily, most of which I never saw coming.

First it was about the car we were saving up to buy so that we could get rid of the drivers. It was $7,500, which we apparently had, but then it needed a new engine and that was $5,000. Next, we needed a light bulb for the headlamp, which was $500, plus, of course, the weekly oil changes at $360 each. These were necessary because the car was driven all day, every day. Then it was our accommodation. The motel had become too expensive at $55 per night per girl, plus all the towels, soaps and shampoos, so we were starting to save for an apartment. It would be more economical in the long run, Elek and János explained, but first we needed to have enough to pay first and last month's rent, plus a damage deposit, and then buy all the furniture. We all had to do our part to contribute, so equal amounts were added to our tabs: $1,400 each.

The good news was that I was finally becoming one of the biggest earners, even without going to the VIP room. I'd remembered how I'd earned top praise in gymnastics, chorus and so many of my other activities growing up—not necessarily by being the best in technical ability, but by being the most spirited and enthusiastic. On stage, I forced myself to smile and look like I was having fun, and it drew customers to me. I went as far as lap dancing but then handed guys off to other girls for the VIP room.

"Look at you, Timike!" Elek exclaimed at a family meeting, after I'd reported a good night's earnings. "What a little superstar! You're really starting to bring it in."

"You know, we have a lot of new girls coming soon," János chimed in. "You could move up in the agency. You could help us out with them—teach them what to do and keep them organized and on time—and we could pay you." A promotion could be good, and maybe it would bring an end to the extra work I was already doing. Most nights, "visitors" like Boris came to our rooms at the motel. Then there was always Tony. He was calling me to his office during my shifts at the club more than ever. Sometimes it was for full-blown sex; other times it was for touching, kissing and one-sided satisfaction. We never spoke. Well, sometimes he whispered a few words to me, but I didn't understand any of them and I didn't want to. The only word I did understand was *baby*, and I cringed every time he called me that. I wanted these visits with him to end, and one day I thought of a way to make that happen.

I'd noticed in the seven or eight weeks that I'd been in Canada that while my business was going up, the other girls' business was going down. They complained about it at the nightly meetings, especially Adina. We had the same clients over and over again, but they were always looking for something new. They got used to us, but rather than change clubs, they preferred that the club changed girls. With

János's announcement that new girls were coming from Hungary soon, I saw an opportunity to request a move, get away from Tony and maybe make more money. I figured Elek was more likely to go for my idea if it came from a group of us, so I talked it over with Adina and Viktoria and got them on board.

"The guys here are getting too used to us, and we think we could make more money by going to another club," we told Elek one night.

"It's not a bad idea," Elek said, considering our suggestion. "Change is good, and I heard they need more girls at a really big club north of the city. It's a longer drive, which is more expensive, but if you can really earn more, it could be worth it."

Two days later, the three of us were driven to Fantasia, a huge club in an industrial area of someplace called York Region, which seemed to still be part of Toronto. From the outside, it looked like a big warehouse, except that it was painted a light pink. Like at Temptations, there were no windows, but there were no signs either. There was nothing to indicate that it was a strip club. I guessed that it was a word-of-mouth kind of place.

As we pulled up around 11 a.m., Elek let us know that a couple of things would be different here at Fantasia. For one, he and János wouldn't be coming in. "We have a Hungarian guy on the inside, and he'll be watching you to make sure you're working and not slacking off." I didn't like that we would be watched by someone we didn't know, but as long as the inside guy wasn't like Tony, it was already better than Temptations.

"Also, this club is open until 6 a.m., so we'll be back then," Elek continued. "It's a long shift, sure, but just think of how much money you'll make." Nineteen hours of dancing? Would the food rules be different here, too? I wondered, but I didn't ask. I'd learned that there was never any point in asking ahead, because I'd never get answers. We only found out the rules when someone broke one.

"Don't talk to anyone, don't talk to any girls, don't look anybody in the eye, and just mind your own damn business," Elek ordered. "It's a very strict club, and it's a rough club too. It's not like Tony's little club, understand?" We nodded. "So just go in there and do whatever you have to do to make money," he went on. "And in this club, there are many more ways to make money."

I thought back to the massage parlour and instantly felt a wave of nausea, but I pushed it down. I could do this. I'd be able to get by, just as I'd done until now. I looked over at Adina. She was another story, and I was worried about her. She was completely addicted to cocaine now and spent her time exclusively in the VIP room, and never on the stage. I didn't know what she would do—or, rather, what she wouldn't do in this new club. She was never just dancing.

Before we got out of the car, Elek surprised us each with a gift—a small, plush-animal backpack for holding our money, body spray, tampons and lipstick. Mine was a pink bunny. "Good luck, girls," he said as we stepped out. "Make me proud!"

We walked to the side door of the club, where a security guard stood. He was big, bald and built, with a thin moustache and beautiful green eyes that softened his otherwise intimidating look. He addressed us in Hungarian, but with an accent I couldn't place, then led us down a hallway toward the change rooms, explaining operational procedures as he went.

"Over there is the main dance stage and the DJ booth," he pointed out the obvious. The space was enormous, with dozens of black tables and chairs. The walls and ceilings were all painted black and the floor was dark grey industrial carpet. Strings of flashing lights and coloured spotlights set the club mood and made it feel like the middle of the night.

"You tell the DJ your songs and you pay him at the end of the night," he continued. "Your daytime manager sits over there, and then there will be a nighttime manager later. Over there are the VIP rooms." He pointed at a long row of doors, each manned by a security guard. "It's $10 per fifteen minutes for the first few. Further down the hall they are $15 and $20, because those rooms are a little nicer. You pay the guard." He paused. "Now, who wants to know what's upstairs?" I said nothing, but Adina and Viktoria expressed interest, so they left me to wait while they ran up the stairs with the security guard. They came back a few minutes later, but didn't offer a report, and I didn't ask for one. I was sure it was something like the massage parlour—a place for full sex. Exactly what it looked like, and how things worked up there, I planned never to find out.

"Have you girls ever been to a club this big before?" the guard asked. We all shook our heads. "It's a little different here, a little more dangerous. Don't look in the other girls' eyes, because they might think you want to fight them. If you see a gun or a knife, just run." My heart began to pound. At Temptations, the clientele was older and fairly subdued. Most girls were Eastern European, like us, and tame. I'd never seen any kind of fight.

"Don't leave anything around, don't drink from a glass unless the bartender hands it to you directly, and never let your guard down," he went on without missing a beat. "This place is owned by bikers and there have been shootings and stabbings before." The three of us absorbed everything, our feet rooted to the floor in fear. The guard paused for a moment, as though he was noticing us for the first time. "You don't look like you belong. You sure you wanna work here?" I didn't want any of this at all, but here I was.

"Okay then," he said, taking our silence as a yes. "Just be safe, girls, be safe." He pointed us toward the change room, and he left. We looked at each other and then around the room. Just like at the other club, there were racks of dancer and stripper clothing and piles of shoes. About a dozen girls were getting dressed, doing their makeup, styling their hair and spraying perfume, and more were arriving every minute. The girls looked different from the ones I danced with at Temptations—not all Eastern Europeans. They were all different shapes, sizes and races. Some were tattooed; some had fake boobs, fake hair and long, fake baby-doll eyelashes. Some of the girls seemed so young—thirteen or fourteen—that they could've been baby dolls themselves. Seeing them made my heart hurt, but I quickly shut off my feelings. There was nothing I could do for them. I had to stay focused on my own goals, and, in this new club, my own survival.

Adina, Viktoria and I picked out outfits from the rack like we had at Temptations, and stowed our jeans, T-shirts and backpacks in lockers without locks. We left the bright lights of the change room and headed into the dim light of the club. It was at least ten times the size of Tony's club, with three bars, a huge main room and stage, countless tables, security guards at every turn, a row of cashiers, pole-dancing booths, a coat check, a big DJ booth, plus all the VIP rooms. Music blared from the speakers, and strobe lights flashed. As customers sat down at tables, girls began to fill the floor. The men were as different as the girls in the change room. Many of them wore business suits; others were more casual. While Tony's club felt like a mini Eastern Europe, Fantasia was international.

To say I was intimidated is an understatement. I was truly terrified. This was a whole different ballgame from Temptations, and I was in the big leagues now. The confidence I'd felt two days earlier when I suggested we try out another club was gone, and I wished I could go back to Tempations where I was many guys' favourite dancer, even if it meant having to be with Tony. I put my hand up to feel my little bob haircut and my tiny hoop earrings. Despite everything I'd been through, I still looked like a babysitter—albeit a skinny, very tired babysitter. I was going to have to make my way here somehow, and get through even longer shifts than I was already used to.

Adina, Viktoria and I went over to the DJ, who introduced himself in English as Chris. He was wearing a huge cowboy hat and had a big, friendly smile and twinkly blue eyes. We gave him our dancer names and our lists of three songs. While Adina and Viktoria made their way around the floor, I hung back by the coat check where a stunning woman stood behind the counter. She was biracial, with light brown eyes, curly lashes and a very warm smile. She began talking to me, and called me *honey* repeatedly. I didn't understand what the word meant, but from the way she was talking I knew it was a term of endearment. Her tone put me at ease in this daunting new place.

"Towel, honey?" she asked. No, I didn't need a towel. "Gum?"

What was *gum*?

"Gum? Gum?" she said loudly and slowly, followed by a chewing motion. Oh, *gumi!* Gum.

"Yes, please," I said in English. I hadn't had a piece of gum since I was in Hungary. She passed me a piece and I unwrapped it and put it in my mouth. It was fresh and minty and tasted clean. Immediately, though, the flavour of it ignited my appetite. I was ravenous. Without Elek here watching my every move, maybe there was a way I could actually eat something. I would have to figure out what the rules were around eating, but only after I had earned at least a little money to spend, and once I found out who his "inside contact" was. Maybe it was the Hungarian security guard who had shown us around, or one of the managers? I'd have to be careful, and make sure I didn't get caught breaking any rules.

As I watched the main room get busier, my nervousness made way for a bit of excitement. Yes, it was more dangerous here, but there was also more possibility. Elek had said that this place was one of the hottest clubs in the city, and I could see he was right. Temptations was slow and old, but Fantasia was fast and cool, and I could make a lot of money. Then I'd get out of this dancing and sex work thing altogether.

"Allison!" Chris the DJ was calling me. "You're up next!" He pointed toward the stage as a new song began, one I hadn't put on my list. I looked at him in confusion. This must be a mistake. But he just nodded and motioned for me to go up. As I walked toward the stage in my high heels and bikini, I heard the first few beats of the song. *I know this one!* "It's Raining Men"! I had made a video for this song about a year ago, back in Hungary, when a remix by RuPaul had become really popular worldwide. The record label began hiring small, independent companies to make videos with subtitles for various Eastern

European countries, and I did the Hungarian version with Ádám and Endre. Just hearing something familiar from my old life felt good. I let the music start to fill me up. I didn't remember what the English words meant but it didn't matter. I walked past the tables that were now filled with the lunchtime crowd. It might as well have been midnight on a Saturday, it was so busy. *Just dance,* I told myself. *Just forget about everything and get up there and dance.* I stepped onto the stage, turned around to face the audience, closed my eyes and began dancing like my life depended on it. I got so deeply into the beat of the song and so focused on my goal of success that I lost my fears, my inhibitions and all track of time. I felt free.

When the song ended, to my surprise, the whole club rose to its feet in a standing ovation. Everyone was clapping and cheering, even the waitresses and the coat check lady. A long line of men who wanted to request private dancing immediately began to form near the stage. I couldn't believe it. Even though I was excited, I was also worried. What would they want from me and how would I manage them? I didn't know how things in this club worked. As I stepped down from the stage, one of the managers came over, spoke to the guys at the front of the line, and then pointed to the first of the VIP rooms, taking me by the elbow and turning me toward it with a little push. I didn't know if it would be like the VIP room in Tony's club, which wasn't good. For all I knew, the VIP rooms here could be like the massage parlour. I just wanted to get back onstage and dance, but I was already being shuffled through the door.

The VIP room wasn't any darker on the inside than the main club was. In fact, it was pretty much the same, only a little quieter—and it was huge, almost like its own club. Dancers were walking around and a few were pole dancing or at tables, but nothing *bad* was happening. There was a security guard in the room reminding everyone in a stern voice, every few minutes, that there was "no touching." Here, it seemed that rule actually meant something.

With the risk of being touched gone, I could dance, laugh and make the time fun. And just as it had worked at Tony's club and on the dance floor moments ago, it worked in this VIP room. The guys were content to watch me, tease me and flirt with me—they didn't need anything more. No one jerked off, asked for a towel or tried to touch me. A cashier near the doorway wrote down every guy who sat at or near my table, and what they had to pay for fifteen minutes in the room. When their time was up, they were ushered out—either back to the main room or down the hall to another VIP room and another girl, or even upstairs, depending on what they wanted— and more guys were brought in.

After a few hours in the VIP room, the security guard gave me a short break. I had some soda water from the bar, and then got back onstage. The DJ gave me another song with a great rhythm and I danced my heart out. At the end, I had another lineup for the big VIP room, and I found myself back there for a couple more hours, just dancing for easy money.

Around 4 a.m. the night manager told me I could take a break, go to the cashier to get some money, and buy myself something to eat. I was shocked—another moment of freedom, and a welcome chance to refuel. I definitely needed more than soda water to get through the next two hours. I went to the change room to grab my pink bunny backpack, and then to the cashier. As she punched numbers into a cash register, she told me she'd loved my performances, and congratulated me on a successful first shift. I'd earned $1,500—more than double the most I'd earned in a single day at Temptations! I couldn't believe it. I felt as proud as when I'd earned my first Trailblazer badge, and my first high score in gymnastics. There was some shame mixed in with the pride, but I did my best to brush it off. Of course, there would be the usual charges taken off of my earnings, like the DJ's fee, the coat check fee, and the club's cut, but it was still a big wad of cash. I stuffed it into my backpack and imagined the look on Elek's face when I gave it to him. At this rate, I'd be out of debt in a few days.

I went to the bar and ordered a big plate of French fries, which I took out to the hallway near the change room and wolfed down in a few minutes. For the first time during this whole ordeal, I almost felt happy. Things were finally starting to go my way. I returned my empty plate to the bar, inhaled a big breath, summoned up some more energy and headed back out to the dance floor. I could hear the DJ calling my name. I walked with confidence to my place on the stage, putting my bunny backpack down on the floor close to me. My song started and I did my thing just like before, dancing with abandon. As soon as I was done, I started down the steps toward the lineup of men that was forming, grabbed my backpack, and noticed immediately that it was lighter than it had been when I'd put it down. My stomach dropped and a hot wave of nausea passed over me. I unzipped the pocket. It was empty. I'd been robbed.

There was nothing I could do and no one I could go to for help. All I could hear in my mind was the security guard saying, "Don't talk to anyone, ever." *You're an idiot, Timea!* I was furious with myself for being so stupid. I was being punished, again, for my naivité. All I could do was go back into the VIP room for my last shift of the night, try to make some money back from the guys who'd lined up after my song, and prepare myself for whatever Elek's reaction would be. The only thing I could count on was that he wouldn't know how successful I'd been, so he wouldn't know that I'd both made and lost a fortune on my first night. If I came out with even a couple hundred dollars, I'd be okay. I could make as much money tomorrow as I did today.

For the next two hours I did my best to dance and pretend as though nothing had happened, but I was crushed. Who had robbed me? I got my answer in the change room, as the club was closing. Two tough-looking girls were standing by my locker, counting a big wad of bills. They were covered with piercings and tattoos, which I'd never really seen on women before. Without thinking, I did what I'd been told not to: I looked them in the eyes. Instantly, like wild dogs, they took this as a call to fight, and began yelling at me in English. One of them pulled a knife and held it up to my throat. I didn't need to understand their words to get the meaning. I put my hands up as though to surrender, and said, "I'm sorry" in Hungarian over and over until they backed down, knowing they'd made their point. They slammed each locker door they walked by on their way out of the room, just to make noise. When they left, I broke out in a sweat, defeated.

My heart racing, I tried to play it cool when Adina and Viktoria walked in a few minutes later. I told them to just get dressed quietly so we could leave. Outside, as we waited for Elek and János in the early light of a June morning, they told me about their night. Both of them had gone to a couple of the VIP rooms, given a few blow jobs and hand jobs, done a few lines of coke, and gotten lots of invitations to go upstairs. They had seen a few fights break out and drunk guys tossed out. The other girls scared them too—especially the two they'd just seen walk out of the change room. I filled them in on what had happened to me so that it wouldn't happen to them.

"What are you going to tell Elek and János?" Adina asked. "Viktoria and I made over $800 each. How are you going to explain that you only have $240?"

"I don't know," I hesitated, uncertain now about my plan to simply lie. If Elek suspected I had kept money for myself, I might be punished. "I think I'll just tell them the truth and promise that I will make it all back later today." We'd be back in five hours to start a new shift.

"Well, you better decide," she said. "Here they are." I watched as the new black SUV pulled up, our car. János was at the wheel and Elek was in the passenger seat. Nervously, I got in and waited for the inevitable.

"So, how did our rising star Timike do?" Elek asked cheerfully.

"Well, I did extremely well. You were right, Elek, this club is awesome!" I responded with cheer and confidence, hoping it would cushion the blow of the bad news I was about to deliver. "Unfortunately, all my money was stolen from me. I'm sorry. I'll make it back today."

Elek turned around to look at me, his eyes bulging.

"What? Are you fucking kidding me?"

"No, I'm sorry, I'm not."

János piped in. "You better be telling the truth, Timea. If you're stashing money for yourself and we find out about it, you know exactly what's going to happen to you and your family." He pulled his index finger across his throat as though it were a knife.

"I swear I'm telling the truth. Have I ever lied to you before?" I asked sincerely.

"This is your last chance, Timea," Elek warned. "No more fucking up, or you'll be fucked up. Remember what happened to Hanna and Reka?" I nodded and turned my head to look out the window at the highway and all the morning commuters on their way to normal jobs. I understood.

Back at the motel, I took out my journal and pen. I wrote my fake name—Andrea Hernuss—and the names and phone numbers of a few of my family and friends. If anyone ever found my journal, it would mean something had happened to me, and I hoped that person would have the decency to notify my next of kin. If the police found it, they would know to trace me as Andrea. Then I wrote a note to Elek, in case he ever found my journal—if ever things did get so bad that I had to run away. I wrote something that would throw him off.

Dear Elek, I wrote. *I lost it completely. I spoke with my family and I have to go home asap. I am not trying to take off, cut you short or steal from you. I will come back.* These were all the terms that he, János and the other drivers used when they accused us of being traitors. They were the worst infractions a girl could make, and they carried the harshest penalties. I needed to protect myself, and start to think ahead, just a little.

16 | Unravelling

I WASN'T THE ONLY ONE starting to think ahead. After my first nineteen-hour shift at Fantasia, Elek drove me and the other girls home to a new motel. He and János worried that the police had been tipped off to our living arrangements, and that they were coming to raid Motel 27. While we'd been out working, they'd gathered up our suitcases and made plans for us to stay somewhere else until we had the money to get an apartment.

I couldn't make out the name of the new motel but it was very similar to Motel 27. Across the street there was a McDonald's with a children's play area and a big, red, plastic slide—something I'd never seen before. For a moment I wondered if we were now in a better part of the city, somewhere less dangerous, but the quality of the new motel assured us we weren't. Adina and I were given a room that smelled of stale cigarettes and had only a small window and one double bed. There was just a blanket and some worn, wrinkled sheets on it. I could no longer see the toy store or the Niagara Falls sign, just several one-storey plazas that looked run-down. Before arriving in Toronto, I'd heard about a really big tower—the tallest structure in the world—but so far I hadn't seen it. Maybe that had been a lie too.

It was 7:30 in the morning when we checked into our new home, and we fell into bed without even showering. I felt like I had only blinked when the alarm went off two hours later. In the lobby, Elek offered us a coffee and a doughnut since he hadn't bought us any food after our shifts a few hours earlier. We ate the doughnuts and drank the coffee in the car and arrived back at the club just before it opened at 11 a.m. The bald, green-eyed Hungarian security guard with the strange accent was there again to let us in. He still didn't say much, but he did translate a sign I asked about: "Early Bird Special." It was a two-for-one deal offered until noon for the first customers to arrive: a striptease with blow job for $30. I shuddered. I was going to have to go straight to Chris the DJ, request the same songs that had brought me so much money yesterday, and try for a repeat of my dancing-only success.

That day and night passed in much the same way as the previous day. I was a dancing sensation! I turned down all invitations to go to the dirty VIP rooms, pretended not to understand the word *upstairs* when guys suggested it, ate another plate of French fries, earned $1,240 and kept it all safe. Elek and János were pleased. Another day went by, then a week, then another. I thought about calling my brother, but I feared his anger. I still didn't have any money to send him, since all of it went toward my agency debt and expenses. Although I was bringing in more than $1,000 per day, unfortunately, our new motel was almost double the price of the first one (due to the summer tourist season, Elek explained), and even though we now owned our own car, we spent a lot more on gas and oil changes because of how far Fantasia was. At our family meetings, Elek and János assured me my debt was going down, but only by $50 to $100 most days. At least it was headed in the right direction.

As much as I'd been able to keep myself safe so far by being the most popular, fun dancer on the stage, there were still moments when some of the clients would get rough and try to touch or grab me. Fortunately, a security guard—usually the Hungarian—was always nearby, ready to throw the client out. One day, after he had pulled me away from a dangerous situation, I thanked him and then asked him a question that had been on my mind.

"Do you work for Elek?" I wanted to know if he was the one who was watching me and the girls in our group, and if he reported back to Elek.

"Who's Elek?" he asked in his strange accent.

"Oh, never mind," I said. His question was my answer. I changed the subject. "Where are you from?" I asked. "I don't recognize your accent."

"I'm from here," he said.

"Here?" I hadn't considered that he could be Canadian-born, and that his accent was Canadian.

"Yeah, my parents are from Hungary so I grew up speaking it at home, but I was born in Toronto." I wondered what his life growing up had been like, compared to mine. I wanted to ask more, but I needed to get back to work. I didn't want whoever Elek and János had watching me to see me slacking off.

But before I went back onto the floor, I asked one more question. "What's your name?"

"Julius," he said. "You?"

"Allison," I said.

He smiled, knowing it was just a stage name. There was no way that any girl my age who was born in Hungary would have the name Allison.

"Nice to meet you, Allison." He winked.

Over the next few days, I noticed when Julius was working and when he wasn't. I also took closer note of the DJ, manager and bartender schedules, to see if I could determine who Elek's inside guy was. If I knew who was watching me and when, I could protect myself from being reported for talking to anyone, taking breaks or buying food. I could also talk to Julius safely if the inside guy wasn't around.

Julius explained that all the guards, managers and bartenders worked either day or night shifts, though I couldn't tell which was which because everything ran together in the loud, dark club. I noticed the waitresses and the coat check ladies swung shifts too, and that none of the dancers who were there when we arrived at 11 a.m. were still there when we left at 6 a.m. It became clear that no one worked the entire nineteen-hour day except the girls in our group. I wondered if that meant Elek had more than one person watching us, since I couldn't seem to find someone who was there all the time.

"Do you know who the guy is who's watching me here?" I asked Julius a few days later when I took a short break from dancing to sip some soda water. I'd taken my glass over to where he was standing by the side door to the club.

"What do you mean, 'watching you'?" he asked.

"Well, the guys who drop me off have other girls to take care of, so they have someone here on the inside to keep an eye on me and the other girls in my group."

"Who drops you off?" he asked, furrowing his brow slightly. He glanced down at me while keeping his bald head facing straight ahead and his arms crossed in security guard stance. He was a giant compared to me.

"Our agents. You know, the Hungarian guys Elek and János."

"Why don't they come in?" he asked.

"They're too busy," I explained. "They have other girls to take to other clubs."

"So they have someone here watching you?" He seemed genuinely curious and a little concerned, and his reaction took me aback a little. Wasn't this a standard practice? Maybe he hadn't been working in this industry very long. "Why?" he asked me, before I could ask him anything else. "Why do you have to be watched?"

"So that we don't leave," I explained. "You know, because it's so dangerous out there."

He lowered his gaze so that he was looking straight at me. There was a confused look on his face, but he didn't say another word. I began to feel awkward, as though I needed to explain myself.

"Also, I guess in case the police come." I filled in the silence with what else I knew.

"Why would it be a problem for you if the police come?" he asked, still looking directly at me. My stomach knotted. I had said too much. What if he was an undercover cop?

"Oh, never mind," I said with a small laugh. "Sorry, I don't know what I'm talking about. I better get back to work." I turned and started walking away.

"Hey, Allison!" he called after me. "Come back." Now I was really nervous. Could he tell I was an illegal? I took a few steps back toward him.

"What?" I asked, trying to be casual.

"You see that girl over there?" He pointed at a woman standing at the far end of the floor. I couldn't tell if she was a dancer or not. She looked classy in her red dress and black heels. I figured maybe she was a head waitress or coat check manager or something.

"Her name is Maria," he said. "She's Hungarian. Go ask her your questions."

"Is she a dancer?" I asked. "She doesn't really look like a dancer."

"Yeah, she is. High-end. There's a girl here for every kind of guy that walks in. Just go talk to her," he insisted.

"That's okay," I said. "I'm not supposed to talk to anyone outside our group. Forget about it."

"Says who?"

"Our agents, the guys who drop us off."

He took a breath in and exhaled slowly. "Okay, look," he said, facing me directly. "I don't know who you are other than Allison, and you don't have to trust me, but you don't belong here. Go and talk to Maria. Tell her what you just told me." He looked and sounded genuinely concerned.

I thought about what Elek had drilled into me: *Never talk to anyone outside our group.* Yet there was something in my gut that told me to believe Julius over Elek. Julius was kind, and seemed to be actually interested in my well-being, not his own. He'd given me no reason to be afraid of him. I decided to take his advice and approach Maria.

"Hi," I said to her casually, in Hungarian. "Um, that guy over there said I should come and talk to you?"

"Sure," she said. "What's up?" She spoke Hungarian the same way that Julius did, so I knew she'd been raised in Canada too. I didn't know how to start our conversation, or where I even wanted to go with it. Luckily, she spoke first.

"I've noticed you've been here for a while now, and you're great on the dance floor, but why don't you ever go upstairs?"

"I don't even know what *upstairs* means exactly," I said, sidetracked.

"They're rooms for sex," she said simply. "You can make $300, $400, $500 dollars per client up there."

"Oh, I don't do that," I said, shaking my head. "I'm just a dancer."

"So then why are you here? Most girls want to make money the fastest way possible. Who brought you here?"

"The Hungarian guys, Elek Pécsi and János something. I don't know his last name."

"Who are they?" she asked.

"They're my agents."

"Your agents?" she asked, eyebrows raised.

I nodded. The knot in my gut was getting tighter as I watched Maria's reaction to my answers. She exhaled slowly, as though she was putting a puzzle together in her head.

"How much of your money do you give them?"

"Well, it's a little complicated because of all the expenses," I began.

"And what I owe them for getting me here from Budapest." Maria listened intently. The look of concern on her face drew my worry. "Why, do you know them?"

"I don't know them," she said, "but I know their kind." What was that supposed to mean?

"What about you," I asked, suddenly feeling as though I needed to stop talking about myself and my situation. I'd already said way too much, and I didn't know Maria or Julius, or where this was going. "Who do you work for?"

"I work for myself," she said. "I come here for a few hours, I make a few hundred dollars, and then I leave."

"What do you mean 'you leave'?" I asked.

"I finish my shift and then I go home. I have another part-time job, and a son."

"How do you get here?" I asked, piecing together what she was telling me and trying to picture her life.

"I drive myself. I have a car."

"You drive?" I asked, surprised. I didn't know of girls who drove themselves to clubs.

"Of course. Why wouldn't I?"

"Well, because of all the police, spies and rapists," I explained.

"What are you talking about?" She was bewildered.

"Well," I began, "I guess if you were born here you might not know this, but Toronto is full of spies and undercover cops looking for people who are here illegally, and if you're caught you go to jail. And all the taxi drivers are rapists."

"Are you here illegally?" she asked.

"No, I have an exotic dancer work permit," I said, leaving out the part about my passport being a fake. I had to change the subject, quick, before I said any more. "I actually just wanted to know if you know who is watching me and the other girls in my group. My agents told me they have someone here on the inside."

Maria looked at me directly, now very concerned. "There is no one here watching you, Allison. Why are they saying there is?" I didn't know how to answer.

Seeing the expression on my face, she said, "Listen, we should talk more, but not now. I need to get back to work. Find me tomorrow." I nodded, but wasn't sure if I actually would talk to her again. Was she a friend, or someone else who was going to take advantage of me?

The next morning on the way to the club, Elek told Viktoria, Adina and me that we needed to call him three times per day to report on our earnings. He had bought a cellular phone so that he was always within reach, and he gave us the number and some quarters for the pay phone inside the club.

"My guy on the inside is going to be calling me too," he said, "so make sure you're telling me the truth." I decided I should try to keep an eye on who made phone calls to see if I could pinpoint our watchman, although it would be almost impossible since I was on stage or in the VIP room for all but a few minutes per day.

Just before we got to Fantasia, we stopped at a gas station with a pay phone so Elek could show us how to use it. I made my first call to him from the club a few hours later, and reported my earnings of $330.

"Oh, I know," Elek said. "I got a call from my guy. Good girl, Timike." It was creepy, being watched, but all I could do was follow every rule and somehow try to figure out who Elek's "guy" was.

Sometime in the afternoon, I saw Maria near the stage, and when she spotted me, she beckoned me over. I glanced around as I walked toward her to see if anyone was tracking me. In the crowded club, I didn't see anyone who seemed focused on me.

"How's it going?" she asked.

"Good, fine," I said. "But can I ask you something?"

"Go ahead."

"Do you think Julius is my agents' guy on the inside?"

"What do you mean?" she asked.

"I mean, is he the one watching me and the other girls in my group, and reporting back to our agents?"

"Julius? No, no, no. He's not involved in anything like that. He's a straight-up security guard."

"Then do you have any idea who it might be?"

"Honestly, Allison, like I said before, no one is watching you. I think there's something fucked up with your whole situation," she said.

My whole situation? She didn't know my whole situation. She had no idea how the agency had helped me get here, what I faced back in Hungary with my debts, and how I had no other way to make the kind of money that I needed. Elek and János wanted to help me. Yes, there was the other stuff—the Sunday night drug parties, the "visitors" they sent, the stories of what they did to other girls, and what they'd done to Reka and Hanna, but they were protecting me. I worked for them. I had signed a contract.

But—what if Maria was right? What if there was something messed up going on? I couldn't really imagine what it was, nor was I ready to find out, so I left Maria standing there and went back to dancing. I called Elek a few hours later to report another $410 earned, and then one last time around 2 a.m. about another $590. I'd spent $10 on fries and a soft drink at the bar, but I didn't mention it and neither did he. It made me wonder if his guy had seen me and it was allowed, or if he hadn't seen me at all. How many girls was he watching anyway? Just our group of three, or were there more? Even keeping track of the three of us in the huge club would be hard, especially with all the VIP rooms and, of course, upstairs. I had to figure out who the guy was.

The next day, Maria found me and invited me to step outside for a smoke.

"Outside?" I asked in disbelief. This would be an incredibly dangerous move. What if someone saw me leave, or some taxi driver was waiting to attack us? Besides, weren't all the doors locked? I'd assumed so.

"Don't worry," she said. "We'll just go to the back and Julius will keep an eye out to make sure no one sees us. We can talk a bit more."

As scared as I was, I couldn't resist her invitation. The idea of standing outside in the July sunlight for a few minutes was very appealing, but beyond that, I really did want to talk to her. I was afraid of what I might find out, but even more afraid not to. Deep down, I knew she was right—that something didn't quite add up in my situation—and it wasn't just my never-ending debt repayment.

"Come on," she said, beckoning me to follow her. We walked away from the stage, down the hall past the VIP rooms and over to the door Julius was guarding. Maria asked him to take us through the hall to the exit door at the back, and to keep an eye out. He nodded, and we slipped behind him and into the hallway. It was cooler than in the club, and for a moment I enjoyed the feeling of the air on my skin. I was so used to feeling dirty and sweaty that I'd almost forgotten what it felt like to be otherwise. Maria led the way toward the door and pushed it open. I couldn't believe it wasn't locked. Bright, warm sunlight beamed down as we stepped out onto a small metal landing with a handrail and a few steps leading down to the parking lot. I squinted and looked at the industrial area around us; I realized we were at the back of the building, not the side, where Elek and János dropped us off each morning. Maria took off one of her heels and wedged it in the door to keep it open. Then she took off the other one so she was barefoot, and invited me to do the same. I almost didn't want to take my shoes off, knowing how hard it would be to put them back on, but I did and the relief was instantaneous.

Maria pulled a pack of cigarettes and a lighter from the little black purse she wore over her shoulder and lit two of them.

"Here," she said, passing me one. "Nice day, isn't it?" I nodded, feeling the sun on my skin. Usually I got quite tanned in the summer, out all the time in Budapest, running around for work and all my projects. Now my skin was just a pasty white. I avoided the mirrors in the change room because it hurt to look at the dark circles under my eyes, my skinny body and gaunt cheeks. Somehow, I looked both older and younger. I had turned twenty-one back in June, but I'd ignored my birthday. There was nothing to celebrate.

"Those guys—the ones that dropped you off," Maria began, "are pimps." She took a drag from her cigarette.

"What are you talking about?" I asked, stunned. "They're not pimps! I'm not ... pimped." Pimps managed prostitutes. I knew this from the movies and a few times my mom had cases in the red light district. Elek and János were agents managing exotic dancers on a work program approved by the Canadian government. I knew that "exotic dancer" meant "stripper," and that there were a lot of opportunities to do much more than just strip, but Elek and János didn't force any of us to have sex with customers. It was our choice.

But then there were all those motel "visitors"—our protectors, and others, who came for sex. And there was Tony. I didn't want to go there.

"Yes, they are, and yes you are," she said, exhaling a big puff of smoke.

"No way," I said. "No way."

"Okay," she said. "How much money do you have?"

"Well, I give it all to them and they write it down, and they take off all the expenses. So, I have money, I just don't *have* it." As I explained aloud, the story started to sound a little weak.

"How long have you been here? How much have you made?" Maria asked.

"I came April 27 but had to go back to Hungary for a while. I returned on May 18, so I've been here about two months, and I've made a lot—"

"How much?" Maria interrupted.

"I have the $150 I made so far today, but the rest is in my agency account."

"What's the balance in your account?"

"I'm not too sure," I stammered, thinking back to the last few nights of family meetings. They'd been rushed, and I hadn't paid close attention. Now that our workdays were longer than ever, all I could think about at 7:30 a.m. was sleeping until 9:30 a.m. "Not too much because I'm still paying off my debt and there are a lot of expenses, like the oil changes . . ." I let my words trail off, feeling foggy. All these weeks I'd been thinking of nothing but numbers, but now I realized that I'd somehow lost track. I felt like an idiot.

"Oil changes? For his car?" Maria asked.

"It's our car."

"Have you seen the ownership card in your name?" She looked at me straight in the eyes, and I knew I couldn't lie.

"No . . ."

"How much do you pay for oil changes?"

"Usually around $360."

"What?" Maria's eyebrows shot up and her mouth fell open.

"It's a big SUV and they drive around all day." I explained what I'd been told.

"Where else have you gone? Have you seen much of the city in your time here?"

"Nowhere, actually. I'm just here to work, and I can be a tourist later when all my debts are paid off and I have a different job. I wanted to be a babysitter, but when I got here, well, it just worked out differently."

"And you said you're not allowed to leave the club?"

"No. I can't leave the motel either. It's too dangerous." The way Maria was asking questions reminded me of being interrogated at the airport, like I was stupid and everything I was saying was being picked apart. I wanted to be taken seriously, to be believed.

Maria considered my words, and then asked another question. "Were you always this skinny? I've been watching you, and you only eat once a day, and hardly anything. Why is that? You must be starving." She put her hand on my waist then and gave it a gentle pinch, feeling my bones.

"I am, but the food is too expensive to eat more than once a day. That's the agency rule—one meal per day." As I repeated the words Elek had drilled into me and all the other girls in my own voice, I realized it was ridiculous—and cruel, inhumane. Maria looked appalled. I suddenly felt very light-headed, and reached for the hand-rail behind me.

"Look at me, Allison," Maria said. I followed her order and looked into her eyes. They were deep brown, and in that moment, filled with sympathy. They were the eyes of someone who cared about my well-being, not only my debt. "When you're ready to leave them, you let me know and I'll help you."

"Leave the agency?" I thought about Reka and Hanna. I thought about the girl burned by hot oil. I thought about the police. I thought about jail. I thought about my mom and my brother back in Hungary. "I can't leave." *No one can leave.*

"And why not?"

"Because I have a fake passport," I confessed. Then I felt defensive. "I got myself into debt, so I signed up with the agency. I wanted to come here, and they tried to help me. That's how it is. I owe them, and I can't leave until I'm paid up." She looked at me, listening and waiting, as if she knew there was more. I thought about the newest rule that had been laid out for us by Elek during a recent family meeting, when some new girls had arrived. If any girl ran away, she would be charged $500 for each day that she was gone, and she would be found. That much was certain—she would be found. And if she wasn't found quickly enough, her family would be found. I told Maria about the rule.

"So they're threatening you?" she asked.

"I wouldn't call it threatening," I said. "They're trying to run a business and they have a lot of clubs and a lot of girls, plus they have a big boss they have to report to and he is really strict. He's Ukrainian, and you know how Ukrainian guys are." I sounded just like Elek.

"Okay," Maria said slowly and clearly. "I'm going to give you my number and you can call me when you're ready to get out of this, or just talk to me here."

"Don't write anything down," I said. "I can't have anything on me or they will find it. We're not supposed to talk to anyone else. I'm already putting myself in jeopardy right now." I put my shoes back on, crushed out my cigarette and reached for the door handle. She put her hand over mine.

"When you're ready to leave, I'll help you," she repeated firmly.

"I can't leave!" Why couldn't she understand? I pulled my hand back from under hers and let go of the door handle. "If I leave, they will call the police. The police will find me and put me in jail because of my passport. Or, they'll find me themselves and it will be worse than jail. Don't you get it?" Maria listened intently but didn't say a word. "And Sasha will find my brother in Budapest—they already told me they can't protect him from Sasha." It almost felt good to get it out, to tell someone. But as I said the words I realized more deeply than ever just how trapped I really was. There was no way out. I dropped my hands to my sides. It was hopeless.

"Who's Sasha?" Maria asked.

"The big boss, the Ukrainian."

She shook her head. "There's no big boss, Allison. There's no Sasha."

"Yes, there is," I said. "I've heard them talking on the phone." She let this argument go.

"So who is watching you here?" she asked.

"I don't know; I can't figure it out."

"You're here almost twenty hours every day. Have you ever seen anyone who is here as much as you and the other girls in your group?"

"Well, no, but I'm always busy dancing, so I can't pay attention."

"Allison, there is no one here watching you. No manager would let someone hang around here twenty hours a day for free or just to have a few drinks and some food. And this club doesn't work with pimps—they're the lowest of the low. Sure, a lot of the girls have them, but they're not allowed inside."

"They're not allowed?"

"No, they aren't."

That was when it hit me. Maybe Elek and János really were pimps. Did Natasa, back in Hungary, know that she was recruiting for pimps? That her boyfriend was a pimp? Did the drivers know that they weren't working for an agency? All of this information made my head spin. No, Maria was wrong. Maybe Elek and János weren't the nicest guys, but they weren't pimps.

"They have no idea what you're doing in here all day," Maria assured me. "They have no idea how much you make, how you make it, what you wear, what you eat, how many pieces of gum you chew, what the fees are, nothing. They know nothing." I stared at her in disbelief. "You could walk out of here right now and they wouldn't know until they come to pick you up and you're not here."

"But they'll find and kill my brother . . ."

"Bullshit," she said. "It's all bullshit."

Feeling dizzy, I sat down on the metal step and put my head between my knees. I had no idea what to think, who to believe or who to trust.

"Wait here," Maria said. "I'll be right back." She slipped inside the door and left me sitting out on the step, the door still wedged open with her shoe. I looked around at the parking lot and the other warehouses. There wasn't much going on, just a few people getting in and out of cars. I couldn't read any of the signs. I could see a highway off in the distance, and cars on it. I looked up above the door for a security camera—there wasn't one. I scanned the tops of the other buildings for guards or cameras, but everything looked normal and quiet. I began to panic. What if a taxi drove by and the driver saw me and came for me? Or a police car? Maria was crazy if she thought I could simply walk away from the agency. In all the time I'd been in Canada, I'd never been anywhere but the motel, the massage parlour and the clubs. I knew no one in this city. I wished I'd kept the phone number the lady on the plane had given me, even though I knew I would be too embarrassed to call someone so much like my mother. I had nowhere to go and no way of surviving on my own. I had to stick to the plan. I only had a few weeks left on my visa and then I could leave Canada and go back home. I would pay my debt and make sure I had something left to bring back to Budapest with me, to Zoli. Then, once I cleaned up that mess, I could start over and get a real job. Maybe I could move somewhere else and put all this in the past.

"This is Petra," Maria announced suddenly, interrupting my thoughts as she came back outside with a woman in tow. "She's also from Hungary. Tell her who you're working for." Petra was different from Maria—edgier, with tattoos and piercings, but she smiled at me. I'd seen her in the club once or twice but had never spoken to her because she intimidated me, and because I wasn't allowed. I was surprised that she was Hungarian.

"Elek and János," I said, hesitating slightly. I didn't know her, and didn't know if I could trust her.

"Those fucking guys are losers," she said fiercely. "They've tried this before with other girls. You have to get rid of them." Her words and tone startled me. What exactly did she mean by "they've tried this before with other girls"? All this new information clanged around in my mind, crashing into everything I'd believed about the agency.

"When does your work permit expire?" Maria asked me.

"In three weeks."

"Then forget about them. I'm going to help you make your money and keep it, and take it all home with you."

"Are you crazy?" I asked, incredulous. "I mean, thank you, but I don't think you understand. They know everything about me and my family. They're going to show up at my house in Budapest. I already went back there once and they sent someone to follow me, and the

recruiter came to my house with a big, mean guy and threatened me."
My words were rushed and fearful.

"What are you, twelve years old?" Petra asked. I couldn't quite tell
if she was being sarcastic.

"You don't understand," I said.

"Fine, we'll leave it at that," Maria said. "But my offer still stands.
You let me know when you're ready to leave and I'll help you. You
can stay with me."

"You'll be putting your life at risk, because they will find me at
your house."

"We'll make a plan. I've seen enough of these asshole guys take
advantage of girls like you."

I was nowhere near ready or willing to make a plan. I was too afraid,
too tired, too hungry and too confused. I was completely alone in
Canada, which so far had proven to be the most dangerous place I'd
ever been, despite being known as one of the best countries in the
world. My life, and the lives of my family, were at stake. I knew nothing about how Mom and Zoli were, if they still loved me, or if I would
ever see them again. My fear was as big as my shame, and I didn't
know who to trust. All I knew was that things always seemed to get
worse, and I was running out of time to make them better.

17 | Upstairs and Outside

BACK INSIDE THE CLUB, I headed straight for the bathroom. My head was spinning, and I was hot all over, like I had a fever. I felt nauseated, but my stomach was so empty there was nothing I could throw up. I splashed some cold water on my face but it didn't really help. I went into a stall to pee and that's when I smelled a terrible odour. Something was wrong.

I went to the coat check lady to ask for some painkillers, and then to the bar for some water. For the rest of the day and night, I danced my songs, downed painkillers and took small breaks when I could. When Elek came to pick us up at 6 a.m., I told him I wasn't feeling well and asked if I could possibly sleep in and go to the club later, to give myself some time to recover.

"No way, Timea," he said firmly. "We're not going to waste time and gas making two trips to the club just for some little princess who thinks she deserves a break."

The moment I got to our room, I crashed. When I awoke two hours later, my fever was higher than before.

"I think I should go and see a doctor," I said to Elek. I hoped he was in a good mood, and would see the beads of sweat on my forehead, and that I really wasn't well.

"You? Go to a doctor?" He laughed. "You have to have a health card to go to the doctor in Canada, and all you have is your fake passport." That was the end of the conversation.

In the car on the way to Fantasia, he ramped up the pressure to make more money, intimidating me, Adina and Viktoria with threats of violence. He focused mostly on me, since my work visa expired in a few weeks. I was going to have to go back to Hungary, but if I went without my debts paid off, there would be serious consequences, he warned.

"If you want to keep your family safe, you have to return to Canada, and we'll add the cost of another work permit and another flight to your account."

Even after my conversation with Maria and Petra, I knew I couldn't go back to Budapest. What did I have to go back to? I'd disappeared on my family and Ádám. There was no way I could show my face without an explanation as to where I'd been, but telling the truth was not an option. Besides, Elek had already let me know that if I stepped out of line, he would make sure to tell my mom, brother, Ádám, and everyone at the TV station that I'd gone to Canada to be a prostitute. So I couldn't go home, but I also couldn't stay at Fantasia after my visa expired. The managers there were careful—they didn't want to be shut down. And if I couldn't work at Fantasia, where I made the most money, I would be sent back to Temptations, where I'd have to deal with Tony, back to the massage parlour, or somewhere even worse. I had no options.

At the club, I felt sicker than ever. No amount of painkillers would bring down my fever, and I had a lot of abdominal pain now too—terrible cramping and a shooting pain through my pelvis, and the smell from my vagina was rancid. I tried to dance and forget about how I felt by losing myself in the music, but for the first time since I'd arrived at Fantasia, it was impossible.

The pretty coat check lady pulled me into a quiet hallway and pulled a Thermos out of a bag. "Soup, honey? You want soup?" I nodded yes.

It was early afternoon on a Tuesday and the club wasn't too crowded yet, so she asked Julius to let us into one of the empty VIP rooms so I could eat and then lie down. I was burning up, but also shaking with chills. Julius laid some clean towels over me to try to warm me up.

"Do you want me to take you to a doctor?" he asked gently.

"I can't go to a doctor," I said weakly.

"Why not?" he asked.

"I just can't," I explained. "Don't worry, I'll be fine." I didn't have a health card, and I also couldn't leave the club. Even though Maria had insisted that Elek and János didn't have anyone on the inside watching me, I wasn't convinced.

Julius and the coat check lady left me in the VIP room to rest, locking the door behind them, and checking on me every so often. I slept on and off for hours, but I didn't feel any better, which only made me worry more. What was wrong with me? Had I contracted some sexually transmitted disease? Was I going to die? Then another thought crept in. If I didn't die from this disease today, I would be killed. I had been so sick all day that I hadn't been able to dance. If I didn't have any earnings by the time Elek picked me up, after a nineteen-hour shift, it would be game over.

I had to do something to make some money, and quick. There was only one thing I could do: go upstairs. I'd take three or four pain-killers at once, get through it, and make $500. Maybe Elek would believe that it had been a slow day. If I could do whatever I had to do up there twice, then I could make $1,000 and he wouldn't question me at all. I thought about this plan as I slipped in and out of sleep and feverish dreams. Finally, I decided I could do it, but I'd have to wait until Julius's shift ended. He was so kind to me, and I didn't want him to know I was going to prostitute myself. I wanted to have just one person in my life who thought I was a good person.

Sometime around 11 p.m., Julius came to the VIP room. His shift was over, but he would stay if I needed him. His kindness made my heart hurt. No one had been this nice to me in so long, but I said no. I knew what I needed to do, and I couldn't do it if he stayed. I thanked him, and he let me know that the coat check lady had his number and she could call him for me if I needed anything.

"Please, Allison," he said softly, "call me if you need help."

I rested a little longer and then sometime after midnight, I asked one of the girls in the change room if she could get me some more painkillers from the coat check lady. On an empty stomach, and in such a high dose, it didn't take long for the pills to take effect. I stood up, put on some heels and wobbled back into the club, heading straight for Chris the DJ in his big cowboy hat. I danced to one of my songs, and as soon as it was over, a balding man in his late forties came over to me.

"Upstairs?" he said in English, pointing up with his index finger. I nodded, avoiding his eyes. We walked over to the security guards at the bottom of the stairs. Both looked surprised. I was known in the club as innocent Allison, a good girl among bad girls. I wasn't an upstairs girl.

One of the guards said something to me in English. Though I didn't understand the words, I understood his tone, and it was one of concern. He was asking me if I was sure. I nodded. He looked up to the security guard at the top of the stairs and gave a nod. We proceeded up, where the guard entered a code into the lock on the door and it clicked open.

The customer and I walked in. Just like the VIP room downstairs, this room was like a whole other club. Individual rooms lined the far end, and my customer walked over to the bartender, handed over some money and got a key to one of them. He came back over to me, grabbed my hand and walked me toward the door. It was dark inside, but I could see the bed in the middle. It was covered with a white sheet but no blanket. The man began taking off his clothes, and motioned for me to do the same. That was fine with me; I needed to get this over with. As I stripped off my bikini bottom, the terrible smell I'd hoped I could hide behind body spray wafted out. The customer, with his jeans down around his ankles, stopped suddenly, sniffed and made a face. He said something in English and I smiled and waved toward the corner of the room, as if to indicate that the smell was coming from somewhere else. He stepped out of his jeans, took me by the shoulders and began kissing me. He moved down my body, kissing my breasts, my waist, and was on his way south when he stopped and made a sound of disgust. He pushed me down on the bed and quickly began to put his clothes back on. Then he left the room, leaving the money behind.

It was "buyer beware" in the sex work industry, and I knew the customer wouldn't complain to management because Fantasia's security guards were notorious for beating up men who asked for their money back, no matter the reason. It was one of the only protections we girls had, although it wasn't really us the guards were looking out for; it was our money—and the club's cut of it—that was being protected.

I put my clothes back on, grabbed the cash and made my way downstairs to the change room, where I took a shower and put on my own T-shirt and jeans. Then I grabbed some towels that were lying around and lay down on the floor in a corner, closing my eyes. Except for the noise of girls coming and going every so often, and the muffled club music in the background, it was quiet. Finally, I slept.

I woke up to Julius tapping my shoulder.

"Come with me," he whispered in my ear.

"I can't," I said. I could hardly move.

"You need to come with me."

I tried to stand up but I was too weak to walk, so he picked me up and carried me out the back door of the club and to his car. He put me in the front passenger seat and pushed it back as far as it could go so that I was almost lying down. Then he buckled me in, got in the driver's seat, and drove out of the parking lot and away from the club. I didn't know where we were going, and I almost didn't care. I was in such excruciating pain, I felt like I was going to pass out. The clock on the dash said it was 2:10 a.m.

Soon we arrived at a hospital where Julius walked me slowly to a nurse at a desk in Emergency. I didn't have any ID, but whatever he said to her—plus how I looked—made her take me to an examination bed right away and pull the curtain around for privacy. She gave me a hospital gown to change into and put me on a scale. I weighed 120 pounds when I'd first left Budapest two and a half months ago; now I weighed 89 pounds. Then she checked my vitals and learned I had a fever of 104 degrees. She called a doctor over and together they asked me lots of questions, using Julius as a translator. I was in too much pain to be self-conscious, but I did want them—and Julius—to think I was a good girl. They asked if he was my boyfriend or if I worked for him, and I said no, that he was a friend and that we worked in the same nightclub. They asked me about my sexual activity, and I answered their questions as though I had a boyfriend at home I was faithful to, not as though I was working in the sex industry and couldn't count all the men who'd had their way with me.

They asked me what painkillers or other drugs I'd taken, and if I had any alcohol in my system. They asked about my period and if I could be pregnant, or if I'd tried to give myself an abortion. Had I put anything unusual up inside me? I told them about a sponge I'd used instead of a tampon. Sandra, the dancer who'd taken me to the massage parlour, had given it to me over a week ago, telling me it was better than a tampon because there was no little string to hide while stripping. The medical team looked at each other, asked Julius to step outside, and then began a painful internal exam. They found a piece of the sponge still inside me from several days ago; it had become infected. They told me the infection could spread all through my blood and become fatal if I didn't take antibiotics right away.

Once the sponge was removed, and I was cleaned inside and out, the doctor gave me a large dose of antibiotics and told me I could go. No one asked for my ID or demanded payment for anything. I had the chills now, so Julius went out to his car and brought back his sweatshirt for me to wear. Then he took me by the elbow and guided me back to his car. It was almost 4 a.m. I still had time to make it back to the club before Elek came at 6 a.m. As soon as Julius began driving, I fell asleep.

About twenty minutes later, I woke up when the car came to a stop. We weren't at the club. We were at a townhouse in an unfamiliar neighbourhood. I hadn't been alone with anyone for months who hadn't tried to take advantage of me, and I hoped Julius was truly as nice as he seemed. If he did try something, I figured he'd at least steer clear of intercourse, since he had just seen everything and knew I was unwell.

He came over to my side of the car, opened the door and held his hand out to me. I stepped out, and he put his arm around my shoulders and helped me walk from the driveway, through a gate to the backyard and then down a set of stairs to a basement entrance. Inside there was a couch, a coffee table, an end table with a lamp, and a TV.

"Where are we?" I asked.

"This is my apartment," Julius said softly. "You can sleep here for an hour and I can still get you back to the club on time." He reached for a blanket and told me to lie down on the couch. I did, and he tucked the blanket around me. It smelled clean and fresh. I'd never been in a real home in Canada, and it was comforting to know they actually existed.

"Go to sleep, Allison," he said. "You're safe."

"It's Timea," I told him as I drifted off. "My real name is Timea."

———

An hour later Julius woke me up and gave me some toast and jam he had prepared.

"How are you feeling?" he asked.

"Like I could sleep for days," I said, "but the pain is much less. Thank you so much." I didn't know what to make of his kindness. He hadn't tried anything with me; instead, he'd looked after me. No one had been this nice to me in months. We left a few minutes later and got back to the club just before 6 a.m. Julius let me in through a back door, and I headed straight down the hall to the change room where I found Adina and Viktoria changing back into their clothes. They hadn't noticed I was gone, and minutes later, when I got into Elek's car, it was clear that he hadn't been informed either. I handed over my cash with an apology about it being a slow day for me because I hadn't been feeling well. He didn't make a big deal about it.

I sat back in my seat quietly while the other girls talked. *No one had noticed I was gone.* Just like Maria had said, there was no one watching me. Elek and János had lied about that. For the first time, I really began to wonder what else they'd lied about, and what the real truth was about how the agency worked.

I needed to talk to Maria again.

18 | Busted

THE ONLY THING PREDICTABLE in my life as a dancer was that it was unpredictable. The next morning, my plans to talk to Maria quickly went awry. We arrived at the club at 11 a.m., but it was filling up much more quickly than usual for lunchtime. There were a lot of men at the tables, the bar and on their way upstairs. There were more dancers too, it seemed—many I had never seen before. Something was going on.

"What's happening?" I asked Petra. She didn't know but agreed that something was up. The atmosphere felt different, but neither of us could pinpoint exactly how. There seemed to be tension in the air.

Our instincts were right. No sooner had we finished our first couple of dances then suddenly the music went off, all the lights in the club came on and we heard a loud male voice shouting, "Police! Police! This is a raid! Everyone put your hands up!" I didn't understand the words but I could see what was happening. More than two dozen undercover cops had risen from the tables and bar where they'd been pretending to be customers. They flashed their badges and motioned for all the men to line up on one side of the room. A dozen more cops in uniform burst through the main door. They moved to block every door and hallway. Some female officers dressed as dancers pulled out their badges from little purses just like ours and flashed them while yelling at us to put our hands up. They got all the staff on the other side of the room, and all the girls on the stage. Terror flooded my heart and immediately put me into a state of panic. I didn't notice how any of the other girls were reacting; all I could see in my mind were images of my mother strangling me. My nightmare was coming true: I was being arrested. Me, the daughter of a police officer. *I am going to jail.*

The female cops organized me and the other dancers into a line across the stage. There were so many of us, easily more than fifty. Next to me in the line was a young Hungarian girl, blonde and sweet, in a string bikini, who also spoke English. She translated what the police were saying so I could understand. They were going down the line and asking everyone their name, age and citizenship. I could hardly think straight, I was so scared. When I went to jail, everyone at home was going to find out what I was doing here and who I'd become. Elek would let Sasha know, and Sasha would no doubt find my brother and my mother. First they would tell Zoli and Mom about me, then they'd try to get money from them, and then, if they couldn't come up with it, they'd harm or kill them. And what would happen to me? I racked my brain, trying to remember the birthdate that was on my passport, and said my name and age over and over in my mind as the police came down the line toward me. *Andrea Hernuss. September 21, 1973. Almost twenty-five years old.* I had to get out of this. *Don't screw up.*

The girl who was translating for me whispered,

"You are one of Elek's girls, right?"

I didn't say anything. She could be a cop.

"Don't worry, I won't get you in trouble and you're going to be okay. I used to work for him. That's how I came to Canada. My name is Zsófia."

I looked at her with surprise but still didn't say anything. In the background, I watched as men were put in handcuffs and led out of the club. There was a lot of commotion. It was a crazy and hectic scene.

"I don't work for them anymore, and neither should you," she said.

"I can't talk to you," I said, watching the police come closer. After they spoke to each girl they told her to go to one side of the stage or the other. Which side would they make me go to?

"Name and age?" an undercover officer asked me loudly.

"Andrea Hernuss, twenty-four," I said in Hungarian. Zsófia translated. Both she and the officer seemed surprised by my age, and rightly so. I was actually twenty-one but I looked sixteen. They didn't buy that I was twenty-four.

"Over there," the officer said, pointing to one side of the stage. He asked the name and age of my translator, and sent her with me. I shuffled over to where I was told to stand, barely able to walk thanks to my infection, which was still painful. I saw Maria on the opposite side of the room, but she didn't see me. Then two police officers in uniform appeared with the day manager in handcuffs, and a box of papers and files. One of them announced that we'd be going down to the station in police cars, two girls in each car. We were handcuffed and then led outside where the parking lot was full of squad cars. The sound of the handcuffs closing around my wrists almost made me faint. All I could see in my mind's eye was my mother, in her police uniform. I could hear her saying she disowned me. I didn't feel like Andrea, and I couldn't escape into being Allison, even though I was dressed like her. I was Timea Nagy, a young, stupid girl from Budapest who had shamed her family.

I'd been driven in more cop cars in my lifetime than I could count, but always as the daughter of an officer—never as a criminal until now. I willed myself not to cry. I needed to keep it together for whatever was coming next—an interrogation, a jail cell, a phone call to Elek or home. A short time later we arrived at a big, modern building. The stations on Csepel Island where I'd spent my childhood were completely bare bones, and I remembered my mother bringing her own light bulb to work, so unreliable were even the basic facilities. With its huge glass walls, shiny and clean tiled floors, and big potted plants, the police station in Toronto looked like a palace.

The police officers sat us girls down in a waiting room, and I looked around, immediately seeing Adina. I looked closer at the other girls and noticed they were all young like her. Maybe this was what the police were looking for—underage girls, not illegal immigrants. That could be good for me, since I wasn't underage—not in my real identity, nor in my assumed one. None of the men from the club, staff or clients, were anywhere to be seen. Maybe they'd been taken to another station. I wondered if Julius was okay. The officer who'd carried the box of papers out of the club came in and called out our names one by one, pulling out photocopies of our passports and work permits. I was one of the first to be called into another room for questioning, where a translator was waiting with two serious-looking male officers. *Don't say anything*, I told myself. *Just stay quiet*. They looked over my paperwork and then at me. They asked who I worked for, how long I'd been in Canada, if I had sex for money, and if I bought or sold drugs. I didn't answer any of their questions. I just shook my head and shrugged my shoulders. One of the officers leaned in a little closer.

"Are you doing this work because you want to be doing this work?" he asked. The translator put it into Hungarian for me. I nodded.

"Who's Tony?" Tony's name was on my work permit.

"He's my agency's manager."

"Are you sure?"

"Yes."

"Is he nice to you?"

"Yes," I said, remembering how Elek had asked me that after the first time I went to Tony's office. I would never use the word *nice*, but

I also wouldn't use the word *mean*. He just seemed to think I was his girlfriend, and that he could have sex with me whenever he wanted. Since I didn't see him anymore, I could only guess he'd moved on to another girl.

"Can you let me go please?" I asked the officer. I wanted this to be over and to get back to work.

"We have a concern," the other officer said. "You look very young." *Oh, God.* They knew my passport was fake; they could tell just by the photocopy. "How old are you?"

"Twenty-four."

"What's your name?"

"Andrea Hernuss."

"When were you born?"

"September 21, 1973."

"Are you sure?"

"Yes."

The officers exchanged a few words between them, and then they left with the translator, locking the door behind them. I waited for over half an hour with every scenario possible running through my mind, none of them good. When they returned, they took me to a large cell where more girls were. I sat down on the floor, put my head in my hands and prayed, begging God to let me go free without my mother finding out what had happened. A few girls shouted at the police to let us out, while others lay down on the floor and tried to sleep. None of us knew what was going on, although a couple of the girls had been through a bust before and they said we didn't have to worry. The police did this all the time and they weren't really interested in us, unless they were sure we were in our early teens. They busted clubs more for drugs, weapons and money laundering, one girl said.

A couple more hours went by and then some officers came in and said that we were free to go and that they would be taking us back to the club. I wasn't going to jail. I was so relieved. Back at the club, we changed out of our dancer clothes, and I called Elek to come and pick us up. The club would re-open to clients the next day, but Elek and János thought we should lay low for a while in case there were still cops around. They took me and the other girls straight to a new club that had just been opened by a Russian guy he knew named Sergei, and dropped us off at the side door.

Lucky's was a small, quiet club, and the bartender was Sergei's grandmother. She had baked cookies that morning and left them on the bar. It made for a strange scene: girls walking around a stage in bikinis and home-baked cookies on the bar. Lucky's was nothing like Tony's dirty, smelly, disgusting club, and it was definitely nothing like Fantasia, where you were more likely to see someone get stabbed than someone eating a cookie. Sergei looked like a 1930s Italian-American mafia guy from the movies, complete with a pinstriped suit and fedora, but he was very friendly and so was his grandmother. I was able to make conversation with both of them using my grade-school Russian. I took a cookie when offered, and no one made me pay for it. I danced, made a few hundred dollars, and then went back to the motel with Elek and the others at 3 a.m.

The next morning at Lucky's, a friendly Hungarian waitress named Beatrix arrived at the same time we did, and once Elek and János had driven away and were out of sight, she pulled me aside.

"You know they're scum, right?" she said. "Sergei hates them, but he needs girls so they're allowed to drop you off as long as they don't come inside." This is pretty much what I'd been told at Fantasia—that Elek and János were the lowest of the low, not even allowed through the door.

I wanted to ask what more she knew about them, and was about to ask her if they were pimps, but then something happened that shocked me to my core: Reka walked into the club, like she'd risen from the dead.

I couldn't believe my eyes. For a split second I wondered if I'd died, and if this was heaven, hell or somewhere in between. I excused myself from the conversation with Beatrix and walked toward Reka.

"Timea?" she asked when she saw me, and came closer.

"Reka?" I blinked and my head started to spin. It was her! I threw my arms around her, overjoyed yet completely confused.

"What are you doing here?" she asked calmly, seeming a little taken aback by my zealous hug.

"What are *you* doing here?" I asked, almost shrieking. "You're alive!"

"Of course I'm alive. What did you think happened to me?" she laughed.

"Elek and János said you weren't breathing anymore. I thought they'd killed you." Tears pricked at my eyes. She understood and hugged me back.

"No, I left," she said. "I'd had enough. Elek was yelling at me, threatening me with a baseball bat, and I just ran away and got into a cab. I went to another club I'd heard about, worked there, met someone who works here, and now I'm here too. You don't need a work permit here, no one checks. I've made $5,000 since I left, and it's all mine." I was stunned. Everything I'd been made to believe about the agency was quickly dissolving. Reka was alive. She'd been able to leave Elek and János. She was safe. She was working, making money and keeping it all. She even seemed more like the girl I'd once known, back in trade school. I wondered if Hanna was alive too, and if she'd managed to escape and get back home to her son.

"Where do you live?" I asked.

"With a friend of Beatrix," she said. "Beatrix is awesome. Be sure to get her number in case you ever need anything." I nodded.

"And Timea," Reka said in a low voice. "You need to get out of the agency too."

I knew she was right. I knew they all were right—Reka, Maria, Julius, Petra and Zsófia. I needed to start making a plan.

Part III | ESCAPE

19 | Allies

I NEEDED TO GET BACK TO FANTASIA so I could talk to my new friends—my real friends—Julius and Maria. I didn't know if I could 100 percent trust them, but I had to try. For two and a half months, I'd been doing nothing but what the agency told me to do, but I still hadn't paid off my debt, nor did I have any money to send home. I had just over two weeks left on my work permit and then I would have to return to Hungary. What would I have to show for my time in Canada—for all this pain and suffering, hunger and exhaustion? And even if I could somehow pay off my debt to the agency in the next two weeks, what would I do back in Hungary? I had huge debts there. These questions consumed me, and during what little time I had to sleep, they kept me awake. I had to make an escape plan, or I risked being trapped in sex work forever.

The next morning, Natasa the recruiter arrived from Budapest.

"Nice to see you, Timea!" she said cheerfully, as she rolled her suitcase into the motel lobby as we were heading to the car.

"What are you doing here?" I asked, surprised to see her. Elek hadn't mentioned she was coming.

"I'm on a little business trip for the agency," she said. "We're bringing over fifteen new girls in a couple of weeks, and we have to figure out what we're going to do with you and the other girls whose work permits are ending. You know, you still haven't paid off what you owe us. What have you been doing?"

"I've been working twenty-hour days," I said, defensively. "I should be close."

"Yes," she said, nodding with approval. "Elek tells me you've become quite good. You know, we could use you. You can go back to Hungary with him and János—they have to renew their work permits too—and we'll get you a new work permit. Then you can come back here with the new girls and get them organized and trained. Consider it a promotion." She said it so firmly that it seemed the decision was already made.

"I'm not sure," I said, stalling for time so I could pull my thoughts together. I hadn't expected to see her, or to be having this conversation. And I didn't like the idea of being responsible for bringing more girls into this line of work, or of continuing in it myself. I wanted out.

"Well, what else are you going to do?" Natasa asked. "You should know that everyone is talking about you back at home. You have a bad reputation. I don't know who started the rumours, but everyone is saying that you left your family to become a prostitute in Canada." I felt as if my stomach had fallen to the floor. Her words confirmed one of my worst fears. The disgusted and distraught faces of my mother, my brother, my colleagues and friends flashed in front of my eyes, each one stabbing my heart.

On the way to the club, Elek repeated Natasa's idea. "Timea, tonight at our family meeting, you can start your training by collecting all the money from these girls, okay?" he said, motioning to the others in the car. I knew it wasn't really a question. "And you need to get on them to make more money when they're at the club. No one is making as much as they're supposed to, and we need to get the apartment before all the new girls arrive." His voice turned serious. "Today, everyone needs to bring in at least $200 more. Got it?" Everyone began to protest.

"Shut up! All of you just shut up!" Elek yelled, silencing everyone. "Don't forget who's in charge here. You do whatever you have to do to make the money." I decided to take a different approach to complaining, something more measured. "Elek," I said, trying to keep my voice steady. "I should be keeping my money for myself now. I should have paid everything off. I need my money to take home with me."

"What the fuck are you talking about, Timea? And what is this attitude? We give you a promotion, so now you think you're the big boss?" He was angry.

"I didn't mean that," I said, backing down. "I just mean that I've been working hard and I should be finished soon. I was making at least $1,000 a day at Fantasia, but I still don't have my own money."

"You're way off," he said. "You've got $1,200 left on your debt. You're forgetting that you still have to pay for your return ticket home before you leave, plus you're on for the next oil change, and everyone has to pay for the apartment. It's not my fault everything is so expensive." I couldn't believe what I was hearing. *I'm not even close to paying off my debt?* It was ludicrous. I didn't know what to say, but even if I had, Elek wasn't going to give me a chance to speak. Instead, his tone softened slightly, back to his brotherly way, which I hadn't heard for a while. "Don't worry, Timike, you'll like the apartment. And when you come back here, maybe you can have your own room." *He has no plans to ever let me out of the agency.*

"Can I go back to Fantasia then?"

Elek considered my request. "That's not a bad idea. I'll take you, but it will cost an extra $100 for gas."

"No problem," I said, relieved I'd be back with my new friends.

———

At the club, I told Maria and Julius that I had to make more money than ever, and why.

"When are you going to truly understand that these guys are pimps, Allison?" Maria asked. "They are the bottom-feeders, the scum of everything. You need to get away from them."

"But they will hurt my family," I said desperately. It wasn't that I didn't understand; I was scared. More scared than ever. I felt like I was being pulled under water.

"Is there any way you can tell your family and they can hide somewhere for a while?"

"No, absolutely not. My mom is a cop. Her life will be over, and so will my brother's. I can never tell them. This is my problem to fix."

Maria had an idea. "Okay, so why don't you 'go missing' for the next several days? You can stay with me or with Julius, you can earn all the money you need at Fantasia, and then you can give me whatever you still owe your pimps. I'll give it to them after you go back to Hungary and they'll be off your case."

"What about my family?" I asked. Maria thought for a moment.

"Your pimps probably won't let their big boss know right away, if he even exists. They'll try to find you on their own first. Didn't you say they told you that they get fined if they lose a girl? You probably have time." That made sense.

"How will I buy a plane ticket?" I asked.

"I'll help you. You give me the cash and I'll get you the ticket. There's a travel agent near my other job." I thought about it and punched numbers into my mental calculator. I had thirteen days left, so I could earn $13,000. I could spend $1,000 on a plane ticket, leave behind a few more thousand to pay my remaining debt, and I could take home the rest. I was beginning to feel better. This could work! Except for one thing: I would need my passport, and I didn't know where Elek kept it or how I could ever get it from him.

"You can do it, Timea," Julius said confidently. "I'll help you. You can stay with me, with Maria or even with Chris. You're his favourite, and he's a good guy. I'll get you to and from the club, don't worry, and I'll never let those pimps in here to look for you." With Maria and Julius's support and protection, I could do it.

The next day, I brought an extra T-shirt with me to the club, and tucked a pair of underwear into my little pink bunny purse. I couldn't take all my personal belongings at once because I couldn't risk some-one noticing and becoming suspicious, so I would take what I could. The biggest obstacle to overcome was how to get my passport.

Elek dropped me off at Fantasia but told the other girls in the car that they were going to yet another new club. No one asked any questions; they were just happy to get a few more minutes of sleep on the drive. At the club, I asked Maria if she could find out how much a one-way ticket to Budapest would cost, as well as if I could leave on the last day of my work permit. I told Julius about my decision too. He was happy for me, and promised to help in any way he could. I got the feeling he had a crush on me, and it was sweet. If I'd had any ability to feel anything other than fear, shame and anxiety, I probably would have had a crush on him too.

I danced all day, trying to make as much money as I could. At around 5 a.m., one of the waitresses came to the VIP room where I was dancing and told me that I had a phone call. I followed her through the club and to the bar, where the bartender handed me the phone.

"Hello?"

"The car broke down and we can't come and get you." I recog-nized Elek's voice immediately, and he was furious. "It's your fault! You were supposed to pay for the oil change this week but you didn't make enough money, and now we have car problems." *My fault?* There was no point in trying to defend myself. "So you're going to have to get a cab, and you're going to pay for it, and whatever you have to pay for the cab you're going to pay us too, as a fine!" he railed on.

"What?" I acted as if I'd misheard, hoping he'd hear for himself how senseless his accusation was.

"Yeah, so if the cab is $70—and you will show me a receipt—then you're going to pay me $70 too!" He was livid. I had no choice but to agree, get back into the VIP room, and dance my butt off for the next hour. When the club closed, I made my way outside to the parking lot and sat down on the curb in the early morning light. I put my head in my hands but didn't let myself cry. I hadn't let myself cry too much since I'd arrived in Canada, and I wasn't going to start now. I was terrified of cab drivers—they were rapists, Elek had always said, but clearly he cared less about my safety now than about money. Maybe he didn't really care about me at all anymore. Although it was warm outside, I shivered. Maybe I should find Julius. He could tell me what to do.

Then, as if I'd summoned him telepathically, he appeared next to me.

"What's going on, Timea? Where's your ride?" he asked. I told him what happened and about the cab.

"I'll drive you home, no problem. Where do you live?"

"At a motel," I said, ashamed to admit that I lived there. But if he was shocked or upset by this information, he hid it. There was no judgment.

"Where is it?" he asked.

"I don't really know," I said, feeling stupid. I didn't even know where I was right now—I just knew it was somewhere in Toronto, which was in Canada. I described the McDonald's with the playland, hoping it was a one-of-a-kind and that it would help us find the motel, but Julius said they were all over the city.

"Do you think you could direct me?" he asked. "Like, could we try to find it? Or if I showed you a map, could you show me?"

I'd been driving the same route every day now for several weeks, so it was possible I would be able to. I began to describe the highway with big ramps and a few landmarks.

"Let's go, then," he said, pulling his keys out of his pocket and taking my arm. We walked to his car and got in. "Which way?" I pointed

My only baby picture (5 months old), with my brother, Zoli (1977).

Me at age 9, the good little communist, proudly wearing my Little Drummers Uniform in front of a map of the Eastern Bloc (c. 1988).

Proudly holding my Student of the Year award in 1989 (age 12).

Me as lead drummer in the daily school flag parade (c. 1988).

Mom and Dad on their wedding day, standing in front of the most expensive car Mom could find (1970).

Enjoying the summer, age 12 (1989).

The TV Teddy Bear, instructing all of us how to brush our teeth, put on our pyjamas, and go to bed (1970s–1980s).

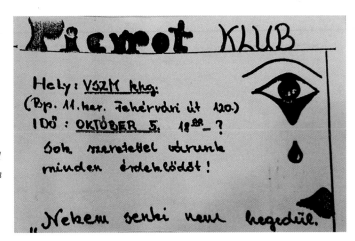

The Pierrot Club poster I hand-drew and distributed in downtown Budapest with my friend Aniko (1990).

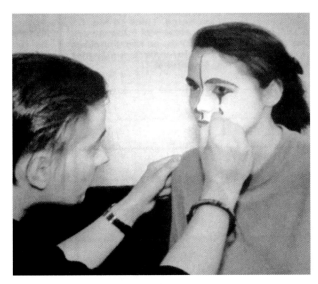

Pierrot doing my make-up like his, before we interviewed for a newspaper article (1992).

In my role as live-to-air TV announcer at age 16 (1993).

The view from my room at Motel 27: the highway sign showing my proximity to Niagara Falls, and the store with the backwards "R." (This photo was taken years later by my co-author, Shannon.)

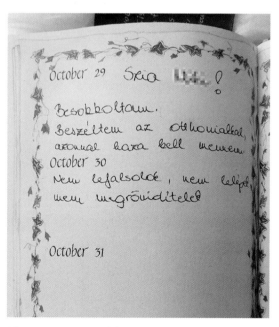

The note I wrote to Elek in my journal, in case he ever found it (see page 172).

Budapest, August 25, 1998, right after my escape.
I'm wearing clothes from when I was 12.

Medieval Times, 2001. Andre (beside me) was very scared, so I helped him through the experience; years later, his mother found me and sent me this picture.

My mom, Eva Ilona Both, when she came to Toronto in 2006.

March 2015 reunion with my father, Gyula Zoltan Nagy. This picture was taken following my mother's funeral.

Me and my brother, Zoli, on his trip to Canada in March 2015. We're having fun in front of the camera for Mom as we spend time with her before she dies.

*Receiving the 2012
Prime Minister's Volunteer
Award from Prime Minister
Stephen Harper.*

*The Walk With Me fundraiser
gala with Sergeant Mike Josifovic
(left) and lawyer and patron
Rob Hooper (right), two of
my heroes (January 2014).*

*This 2014 photo was taken at
one of my police trainings as
this officer told me he'd seen
me when he was undercover
and I was a trafficked dancer.
It was an emotional moment
for both of us.*

One of the best days of my life—being presented with my Canadian citizenship at a special ceremony on July 1, 2012 (Canada Day)—with one of my RCMP heroes from Project OPAPA, Lepa Janovic, by my side.

Addressing the new Global Taskforce on Human Trafficking at the United Nations in New York (September 2018).

Dan and me on our wedding day (September 2018).

toward the road we always came in on, and we began our journey.

"Okay, so do you see a big, big tower when you're driving?" Julius asked. Yes, I had finally seen it once we started coming to Fantasia. The tower hadn't been a lie: it stuck straight up into the city skyline, like a sewing needle coming through fabric. I nodded. "Where is it when you see it on the way home? To your right or your left?"

"Mostly in front of me, but a bit to my right."

"Okay, now what about the lake?"

"It's behind the tower, straight in front of me when we're driving down the long road the club is on. Then we get on the highway, and the lake is to my left."

"The road the club is on is Yonge Street—the longest street in the world," Julius said. "It goes north for almost 2,000 kilometres. It also divides the city into east and west." He was treating me like a tourist, and it was nice. I thought about the Danube, and how it divides Budapest.

"Can we just head up north then?" I asked, only half-joking. It would be nice to just run away. I smiled at Julius, and he smiled back.

We continued making our way toward the general direction of the motel until I started recognizing more and more landmarks. We made a few wrong turns, but not many. On the way, Julius pointed out more interesting things about Toronto, and I asked him about the kids' store with the backwards R in the sign that I could see from my first motel. He chuckled, and then explained that it was called Toys R Us, and how the R and the fact that it was backwards was simply a play on the word are.

The hour it took us to get to the motel in morning traffic was the most pleasant I'd spent in my whole time in Canada, despite being stressed and so tired. For sixty minutes, I wasn't a sex worker; I was a real person with another real person who genuinely wanted to get to know me.

When we finally saw the motel across from the McDonald's, Julius parked a couple of streets away so I could get out and walk there, just in case Elek or János were watching for me. We probably had half an hour before they would start to worry over my whereabouts and call another agency driver to hunt me down.

"Timea, please tell me more about how you got here and what these guys are like." Julius's green eyes looked right into mine with what I knew was sincerity.

I took a breath and began to tell him what had happened back in Hungary, how I'd signed up with the agency to be a babysitter, but how when I got here it was nothing like what I expected. Once I started talking, I couldn't stop. Though it was hard to tell the truth, it felt good to get it out, and Julius listened intently and patiently. I explained the debt I had with the agency, all the expenses there were, the fines and penalties, the threats, how I was never allowed to leave the motel, and how I was only fed once a day. I told him how they told us that everyone in Toronto was dangerous, that it was a city of spies and police who were always on the lookout for illegal immigrants. We had to stay with our agents or we were at risk of death or jail, yet staying with them was also dangerous. I told him about the girl who'd been washed in boiling oil. I told him about Hanna and Reka. I told him that the only way I could keep myself safe was to follow the rules—no matter what they were—and make back the money I owed. The only part I didn't tell him about was Tony and what he did to me, or about the massage parlour and nighttime "visitors." I couldn't utter those words.

When I was finished, Julius looked at me. "Timea, this is all wrong. None of this should be happening to you. You're being taken advantage of." He reached out his hand and put it gently on my shoulder. "But we can't talk now because you have to get inside before they wonder where you are." He was right.

"Thank you," I said. "For everything."

"See you in few hours, Timea."

I walked toward the motel feeling more hopeful than I had in a long time. It was as though I'd been given one little candle in the dark cave I was trying to find my way out of. At the same time, I was nervous about what would happen next.

Elek was waiting for me in the lobby.

"Where's the taxi?" he asked.

"I just got him to drop me off at the McDonald's because we were on the other side of the street."

"Did you go in and spend any of my money?"

"No, I came right here."

"Where's the receipt for the fare?"

"He didn't have receipts."

"Well, then how much was it?"

I pulled a number from the sky. "It was $96."

"I'm assuming you tipped him, so it was an even $100?"

I nodded. He put his hand out.

"Give me $200 for your penalty—$100 for me and $100 for János." The rules had changed again.

I got the bills out of my purse. What did it really matter? In my mind I now knew that I was going to escape. I handed him the money and then went upstairs to sleep for two hours until the next workday started, when I would test the first part of my plan. I had to make 100 percent sure that what Maria and Julius were telling me was all true: that my agents were really pimps, that they didn't have anyone watching me in the club, and that I was going to be able to leave when I was ready.

The next morning, right after Elek and János dropped me off, instead of walking into the change room and getting dressed in my stripper clothes, I walked right out the back door of the club. I looked around; there was no sign of them, or anyone else. No one called out for me and there was no one waiting with a baseball bat. I crossed over to the other side of the parking lot, trying to play it cool, but I was a bundle of nerves. I glanced up to the roofs of the other warehouses in the area almost expecting to see assassins, or the Russian soldiers I'd grown up with, but there was no one. A couple of cars drove by, but they didn't stop. Then one pulled over to the side of the road and braked suddenly, skidding loudly. My heart stopped, but I forced myself to keep walking. If someone *was* coming for me there was nothing I could do other than try to hide in plain view. Out of the corner of my eye, I saw two girls get out of the car and walk into the club. Then the car drove off. I was safe. I walked for another couple of minutes, crossing the road and heading into an adjacent parking lot. A few cars pulled in, parked, and people got out and went into the warehouses. Some were carrying coffee cups in those paper trays. They seemed to be normal people going to normal jobs. I was beginning to relax a little.

Then I saw a police car in the distance, driving toward me. *Oh my God, Elek knows I escaped and he called the police! They are coming to arrest me. I'm going to jail.* But the car drove right past me, as though I was invisible, as though they hadn't seen the 89-pound girl with the big, dark circles under her eyes, carrying nothing but a small pink bunny backpack. I was safe, but rattled. Heart pounding, I sat down on the curb for a moment. When I'd calmed down, I got up and walked a little farther. I'd never been left unaccompanied or unsupervised for this long in Canada, and I'd never been outside on my own.

Suddenly, realizing how vulnerable I was, I panicked. I turned and started running back to the club at full speed. I couldn't get back fast enough. I reached the main door, stopped to catch my breath and then walked inside. Julius wasn't on shift yet, but there was another daytime security guard, one I didn't know. He checked for my name on the list of dancers and let me in. I went straight to the change room, and as I took off my jeans and T-shirt, I tried to slow my breathing back to normal. *I didn't get caught. No one is after me.* I could leave, and I had people who could help me.

20 | Making a Plan

THE NEXT DAY, I brought a few extra clothes with me from the motel to Fantasia. I was putting them in my locker when the day manager came in with three women, one older and two middle-aged. They were well-dressed, all in black, but looked distraught and were speaking Hungarian in hushed tones. Their accents were like my mother's, not Canadian like Julius's. I immediately began to eavesdrop, my shoulders instinctively tensing. These women were here for a reason, and it probably wasn't good. The manager called for Julius to come and translate, and then showed them to Zsófia's locker. The older woman opened it, took out a T-shirt, held it to her face and cried into it. Another woman asked Julius if Zsófia had any friends who would want to come to her funeral. Her *funeral*. I went cold all over. Zsófia was dead? It couldn't be.

Moments later, the manager left with the women and Julius came over to me, his face drawn. "Timea, you have to get out of this work. This is not the place for you."

"What happened?" I asked.

"Zsófia was found in the subway. She was hit by a train. Nobody knows exactly how it happened, but she's dead. That was her grandmother, mother and aunt. They came from Hungary."

I felt sick. Had she jumped or been pushed? I didn't want to know the answer.

"Did she know your guys?" Julius asked.

"Actually, she did know them," I said slowly. "She said she used to work for them."

"You need to get out of here, now." Julius was insistent. "Unless you want it to be your mom coming here to get your body."

The thought of that was too much for me. "Let's go talk to Maria," I said.

We found Maria over by the DJ booth with Chris. They were both upset by the news of Zsófia's death.

"We need to get you away from your pimps soon," Maria said fearfully. She translated for Chris, who nodded, and we all began to piece together my escape plan. Julius had told Chris a little bit of my story, and Chris offered to let me stay at his house. It was the furthest one away from the club, and he had two dogs, so it would be the safest. I was touched that he wanted to help me—he barely knew me. The language barrier made it hard to connect, but he was warm toward me, smiling, tapping his foot and moving to the music in his booth—always with his cowboy hat on. If we had spoken the same language, and if our situation had been different, I'm sure we would have become friends over our love of music. Julius said he could easily arrange transportation or take me to Chris's himself, depending on when I was actually ready to leave. That would have to be a last-minute decision, because I still needed my passport.

Maria suggested I spend a few days simply resting and lying low after I left, so that it would seem like I'd just disappeared. While I was safe with her and Julius, and most of the staff at the club knew and liked me, we couldn't be sure about everyone. The last thing we needed was for Elek and János to hang around outside the club or for them to send someone in to look for me, and for one of the other dancers or guards to tell them where I was. When a few days had passed and I was ready, I would come back to work and make as much money as I could before flying back to Hungary. I hadn't slept in months, so having a few days to rest sounded like heaven.

Maria had found out that a one-way plane ticket would cost only about $800—less than I'd been charged by the agency for my other tickets—and that she could book one for August 16, eleven days from now, and a couple of days before Natasa had decided that Elek, János and I would all go back to Budapest together, at the end of my work visa. I knew I needed to get to Hungary before them, to have some time to figure out what to do. I had to see for myself what was going on back home—what my family knew and what rumours were going around. Depending on that, and if I'd been able to leave enough money behind in Toronto to pay the agency off, I'd plan my next steps.

But I couldn't put my plan into action until I had my passport in my hands. While I waited for an opportunity to look for it, I made sure that Elek, János and Natasa didn't suspect a thing. I went along with their request that I take on more responsibility by collecting the money from the other girls at family meetings. I was the only one still going to Fantasia after the bust—testing it out to see if it got as busy as it had been—and in the meantime, Elek and János were getting the other girls settled at the new clubs they'd found. They were under pressure to get ready for all the new arrivals that would be coming, and there was a lot for them to do. Elek's temper was short, and he made more and more threats to us. Natasa's presence only made things worse, as she agitated everyone and interfered with Elek's management.

A day or so later, Natasa announced she was going back to Hungary to get the next shipment of girls organized. Elek had an announcement too. "We did it, girls—we've finally got our new apartment!" he said like a proud papa. "We're moving today, and there's enough room for everyone, plus all the new girls coming."

"That's awesome," I exclaimed. "Thanks, Elek!" I acted as if I were excited and on-board; the more I pretended to embrace my new role in the agency, the more Elek and János trusted me, and the less they'd suspect I was planning on escaping.

Elek and János drove me and three other girls directly to the apartment after our shifts at the clubs—it seemed to be in the real downtown of Toronto, as there were a lot of tall buildings and the traffic was busy, even in the early hour of the morning when we got there. We pulled into an underground parking lot, got out and into an elevator, went up to the tenth floor and down a nondescript hallway. The apartment must be huge, if it was going to fit more than twenty dancers, plus Elek and János. Elek opened the door to our apartment and we followed him inside—Adina, Sylvia, Ilona, Viktoria, Sandra, a few others and me. János closed the door behind him.

"Ta-da!" Elek exclaimed, spreading his arms wide and presenting the apartment to us like a magician who'd just pulled a rabbit out of his hat. "Our new place!" None of us responded with nearly his enthusiasm.

There were three bedrooms, two with stacks of thin foam mattresses for us to sleep on and our suitcases and plastic bags with personal items tossed in a corner, and one with two real beds, for him and János. There was a small kitchen and a living area with a few more foam mattresses and no other furniture to speak of. In the bathroom was a shopping bag of basic items like tampons, razors and body spray. There was no safe like there had been in our hotel rooms, and no sign of our passports. I couldn't think of how I might get into Elek's room to look for them, but I would have to find a way. Where else could the passports be? What if Tony had them?

"Isn't it great," Elek asked, smiling. "There's a swimming pool, and a little store downstairs where you can buy sandwiches." Who was he kidding? No one would be going for a swim or running down to buy a sandwich. He must be practising his welcome speech for all the new girls, the ones who thought they were going to be baby-sitters too.

I pulled one of the foam mattresses from the stack onto the floor, as did the other girls. We were all exhausted, and after another twenty-hour workday, all we wanted to do was sleep for our allotted few hours. In spite of how tired I was, I made sure to wake up before everyone else to give myself some extra time to get ready. I wore two T-shirts, two pairs of underwear, and I tucked one more T-shirt into my little backpack. I would have to leave all my nice pyjamas behind, the ones I'd never worn. An extra T-shirt I could explain if I had to, but pyjamas, no. On the way to Fantasia, we dropped off the other girls and János at the new club, and then Elek and I stopped for gas. I moved to the passenger seat, and while Elek pumped the gas, I discreetly popped open the glove compartment.

I couldn't believe my eyes. The passports were there! Right at my fingertips were more than twenty Hungarian and other Eastern European passports.

My heart racing, I glanced behind me to look at Elek. His back was to me as he stared at the pump. Quickly, I began rifling through the pile, looking for mine. I saw one with a photo of Adina but someone else's name, a bunch with other girls' photos and real or fake names, and then I saw Reka's. I looked back over my shoulder and saw that Elek had finished pumping. I heard the sound of the pump handle being placed back on its cradle, and Elek closing the gas tank door. I quickly but quietly closed the glove compartment door, but then reopened it when I saw him walk into the store to pay and buy cigarettes. I checked two more passports, finally finding mine. I swiftly tucked it into my backpack and then made sure everything looked as it had when Elek left the car. Had I been able to test my blood pressure in that moment, it would have been through the sunroof.

Elek came back and, to my surprise, tossed me a chocolate bar and then asked if I wanted a smoke.

"Things are good, now, aren't they Timike?" he asked. "Just like I told you. Now we have a nice place to live, a nice car, and when we all come back after our trip to Hungary, it's going to be better than ever." I nodded, took a drag off my cigarette, and exhaled slowly, praying he would not open that glove compartment for a few days. Adrenaline coursed through my veins but I had to play it cool.

"Why are you so quiet this morning?" he asked. He could tell something was up with me. I had to come up with an explanation, and quick.

"Yesterday, I saw a girl's family come to get her things from the club. She was killed by a train."

"Yeah," Elek said, glancing at me. "I heard about that too."

"It's sad," I said.

"Well, let's just say she was a drug addict and she wasn't a good listener. She pissed someone off that she shouldn't have," he said flippantly. "You see what happens to bad girls?" I began to sweat. Did he know what I was planning?

"Yeah, she didn't appreciate everything she had," I said, trying to change the subject. "But I do. And today is going to be good. Hopefully it's going to start to pick up. The manager is making some plans to get more customers again, making some new special offers."

"I'm glad to hear that," he said, nodding approvingly. "Because you still have a long way to go."

That day and night at Fantasia, I danced like mad and earned almost $2,000. I gave my passport to Maria so she could book my plane ticket, and I gave half of the money to Julius to keep for me until tomorrow.

"Great news!" I told Elek excitedly as I handed him the other half of my earnings at our family meeting that night. "Tomorrow a professional hockey team is coming for a special VIP event. Maybe you can pick me up a few hours later so I can earn more money." Although this wasn't true, it was completely plausible. Fantasia was popular and some girls claimed they had seen Canadian celebrities, athletes or big businessmen in the club before.

"Great, Timike!" Elek said. "I always knew you were a good girl. How about you just call me when you're ready to be picked up?" I agreed, knowing it was a call I would never make. Before lying down on my foam mattress to go to sleep, I stuffed my journal and stuffed Simba toy into my pink bunny backpack and said a silent goodbye to all of my other possessions, and to the other girls. It was my last night with the agency. Tomorrow, I would escape.

21 | Disappearing

IT WAS A BEAUTIFUL summer morning in early August when Elek and János dropped me off at the club for the last time.

"Be good to those hockey players," Elek said with a smile as they drove away. I prayed I would never see them again, then turned and walked into the club where Julius, Maria and Chris were all waiting.

"Ready?" Julius asked.

"Ready." I tried to sound more confident than I felt.

Chris handed me the key to his house, and described—with Julius translating—how to get in. He gave me some treats to give to his dogs, told me their names, and said not to be afraid. They were friendly and would be easily won over by food. He told me which room I could sleep in, and to help myself to anything I needed.

Maria gave me a duffle bag for my things, so I went into the change room and gathered all of my stuff from my locker, taking care not to let any other dancers see. Julius gave me the $1,000 I'd asked him to hold for me from yesterday, and I tucked it into my backpack. Then they all walked me to the back door where a black limo was waiting. I was escaping in style!

"The club has a relationship with this limo company," Chris explained. "So this is our gift to you." I was stunned. It was all so surreal—to experience such luxury after such deprivation, such kindness after such cruelty. I would have been happy to make my escape in the back of a pickup truck.

"Just call the club for anything," Julius said, giving me Fantasia's number on a piece of paper. "And we'll make sure those pimps know you're long gone when they come around looking for you. You can just rest for a couple of days."

Maria nodded. "And when you're ready to come back, just call the limo, give them this address, and someone will come and pick you up."

"But I can't speak English," I said.

"Right, okay, so call the club and just ask for one of us and then say, 'ready.' We'll take it from there," Maria reassured me.

"And I'll see you at some point," Chris said. "But if you're sleeping I won't wake you." I couldn't even imagine how it was going to feel to sleep and not be woken up after a couple of hours.

"Thank you guys, so much. I don't even know what to say." If I'd had the energy, I would have cried. I hugged each of them, and got in the limo.

The driver was an Indian man with a turban who greeted me with a warm smile. I felt nervous being alone with him, but trusted my friends would not have put me in danger. As we pulled away, I waved at my new friends, my allies. Then I put my head back on the cushy seats, closed my eyes and exhaled slowly—all the breath it felt like I'd been holding for months. A small smile drew across my face as I pictured Elek and János coming to pick me up hours from now only to find out that I wasn't there. I imagined them going to the door of the club and having it slammed in their faces by Julius. I thought about them driving all over the city trying to find me, like a needle in a haystack. But a dark, heavy feeling grew in my heart when I thought about them contacting Sasha and sending guys to find my mother and my brother. All I could do was hope that they would spend at least a week trying to find me before they let the big boss know. It was very bad for them if they lost someone, as they'd always told us girls. They would have to pay off the girl's whole debt, plus a $5,000 fine to the agency.

"That's why we never lose anyone," they'd said. And I believed them. It was better for them if they found me and killed me, and told Sasha I'd been killed in a stabbing at the club, then to tell him they'd lost me. I had to believe that I had time to pay off the agency, get back to Hungary and save my family. Maybe I would even go to the police and tell them about the agency. Leaving the other girls behind at the apartment, and knowing there were so many more coming, bothered me greatly.

The driver turned on some music in a language I'd never heard before and began singing along. It was beautiful—soft and melodic— and I almost fell asleep as we drove out of the city and into the country. I watched out the window as we passed by rolling green hills, farmhouses and garden nurseries. I hoped somehow I could come back to Canada and see all of its beauty I had missed. After about forty-five minutes, we turned into a community of what looked like newly built brick houses with attached garages and the same type of tree planted outside each one in the middle of the front lawn. A few minutes later, we pulled into the driveway of Chris's house. I started to get very nervous again. This was unfamiliar, and I was alone. What if Elek and János had somehow followed me? What if they were waiting for me? I had to be brave. I got out of the car and walked up to the front door, key in hand. I heard barking. There were windows down each side of the door and the white faces and bright, icy-blue eyes of two huskies appeared, one on each side. I reached into my duffle bag and found the dog treats Chris had given me. I opened the door and held out the treats to the dogs, who instantly stopped barking and started wagging their tails. Inside, I locked the deadbolt behind me, as Chris had instructed. I took off my shoes but kept them in my hand so the dogs wouldn't chew them. I stepped into the foyer and looked around at my new surroundings.

There was a small living room to my left with a couch, chair, coffee table and TV, open to a dining room next to it. In front of me was a hallway, so I followed it down past a small bathroom to where it opened into a sunny kitchen that was bigger than any I'd ever seen in Hungary. The house was cleaner than any place I'd been in Canada by far, except maybe the airport. I went upstairs, followed by the dogs, who were now my friends. There were three bedrooms and another bathroom. One bedroom was Chris's, one had a desk and computer in it, and the third was the guest room Chris had described, with a double bed made up for me. The carpet was soft under my feet and felt heavenly. It didn't stink of beer, cigarettes, sweat and semen. There was a glass of water on the bedside table next to a clock radio that told me it was noon. I put my duffle bag down on the floor, drank the whole glass of water at once, took off my jeans and got into bed.

The next time I opened my eyes and looked at the clock it said 4:13 a.m. I'd slept for over sixteen hours! I got up, went to the bathroom to pee and then got back into bed. I woke up at 1 p.m. the next afternoon to find a sandwich on the bedside table, along with another glass of water and a note from Chris, the only words of which I could understand were "Hi Allison." I wondered if we'd all forgotten to tell him my real name in our planning and execution of my escape. He'd drawn a little smiley face as well. I was so unaccustomed to these simple acts of kindness that I was almost suspicious of them. It had been so long since I'd been treated well. Was I in a dream? What if the water was poisoned? *No. You've been in a nightmare, and you're waking up from it.* I rubbed my eyes, feeling groggy. I wolfed down the sandwich, and then ventured into the bathroom to have a shower. Chris had put out a clean towel for me. It was soft, not like the rough motel towels that cost $10 and $20, and not one of the little white towels at the clubs for lap dancing. It was just a nice, normal bath towel for a nice, normal person.

Was I normal again? I felt so different after sleeping for almost twenty-four hours. But I was still tired, so after my shower, I put on a clean T-shirt from my duffle bag and went back to bed. This time, though, my sleep was interrupted by all kinds of nightmares—about men, clubs and being chased, and travelling on an airplane. I also had a beautiful dream in which I was back at communist summer camp, and a weird one where I was in the McDonald's play area eating *guylas*, a Hungarian soup.

When I woke up, it was morning again and there was another sandwich waiting for me. I ate it and got dressed. I was ready to get back to work. I had eight days left before my flight to Hungary, and I needed to make some cash. I found the slip of paper with the number for Fantasia on it, and then dialled the number on the phone in the kitchen.

"Chris?" I asked when someone answered. "Chris DJ?" I didn't even know the words to ask for him, only to say his name.

"Hang on," the person said. A couple of minutes later, I heard Chris's voice say hello.

"Allison," I said, then repeated it. I felt so dumb, not being able to communicate with more than one word.

"Allison!" he said, and then asked me something that was probably *How are you?* Silence. I didn't know how to answer.

"Ready?" he asked. This word I knew.

"Ready," I said.

"Hang on," he said. He called for Julius. After a couple of minutes, Julius came on the line. He asked how I was and I told him I'd done nothing but sleep, and that I felt better. I was ready to come back to work, if it was safe.

"Those guys came for you yesterday and today, but I told them I hadn't seen you. They were really mad, but I told them not to come around again. I think it's okay now. If they come again, don't worry. Even if you're here they won't know." I shuddered, knowing that they were looking for me, but I felt protected by Julius.

I decided to bring all my stuff with me since I didn't know where I would be sleeping that night. Chris's place was far from the club, and I couldn't expect my friends to pay for the limo every day. Maybe I could stay with Maria, or even with Beatrix from Lucky's—I still had her number. Julius had offered to let me stay with him, but I declined, worried that our friendship could turn into something more than I was ready for.

Back at Fantasia, things were different, even after being away for only two days. I was a free agent now, which meant I could keep every dollar I earned, and because I was so rested, I would dance my heart out. But since the bust, everyone at the club was still on edge, paranoid that there were undercover cops everywhere. There had been a lot of turnover in both the staff and the clientele. Some of the more reliable dancers had moved on to other clubs, and there were more "bad girls"—rough girls who got into fights and did drugs. The same roughness was reflected in the clients, since the more "proper" businessmen weren't coming around as much, to avoid police. There was more violence and more fear, and fewer staff to manage it all. That first day and night back I made more money than ever, but it was hard to maintain my role as the crazy dancer girl who didn't do much else. There were new customers who didn't know me, and they wanted more than my dancing.

At the end of the night, Adina came into the club looking for me, and my heart stopped.

"Timea!" She raised her voice and grabbed my arm, holding me close to her. "Elek told me to tell you that every day you spend away from us he is adding $500 to your debt," she warned. "Don't make it any worse. Just walk with me out to the car and apologize. Say you made a mistake."

"I can't do that," I said as calmly and firmly as I could, shaking off her grip. "I'm not going back." I tried to channel the defiance I'd seen that time in Reka. "Don't tell them you saw me," I ordered. "Say nothing."

She looked at me, and I could tell she understood that I was serious. She nodded in agreement and hugged me. She left, and I ran to Julius to ask him to look outside for Elek's car and make sure it was gone. It was. Julius hadn't seen Elek or János, but I was still scared.

I called Beatrix at Lucky's and asked if I could work there part-time and stay with her instead of continuing at Fantasia, since I knew that Elek and János weren't allowed inside there either, and it was the only other club I knew apart from Tony's. I had to be very careful. With only a week left in Canada, I couldn't afford to let anything go wrong. Maybe after a few days I could swing another shift or two at Fantasia, but not right away, not while Elek and János were still angry and looking for me. I would make less money at Lucky's, but at least I would be safe. I asked Beatrix if she'd seen Elek and János lately.

"They don't come around here these days," she said. "Sergei hates them and they're in some sort of trouble with the Russian mafia, so they're staying away from all Russians." I was confused. Did that mean they were in trouble with Sasha? Sasha was Ukranian, but was he also in the mafia? I wondered if the trouble was about me—the girl they'd lost.

Julius offered to drive me to Beatrix's place that night, after his shift ended. He was only on until 10 p.m., and now that I was working for myself I could come and go when I wanted. The freedom felt amazing. By 10 p.m., I had earned another $1,000 and was happy to leave early—hours earlier than I'd ever left a dancing shift my whole time in Canada. I gave him the address of Lucky's—it was somewhere just west of downtown he said, near the intersection of two major streets, Bloor and Dufferin. Bloor Street ran east–west and the subway line was under it, he told me. I liked how he took the time to explain things to me, and to make Toronto seem less sinister. On the way there, he asked if he could take me somewhere nice first. Even though I was tired, I said yes.

"You should see the lake before you go," he said. I shook my head as horrifying images of the water flashed in my mind. The only thing

I knew about it was that it was where all the bodies of dancers and prostitutes were thrown after they'd been beaten to death. I shared my fear with him.

"Timea," he said softly, "it's a beautiful lake, called Lake Ontario, for the province. I'll show you." I liked the way he said my real name, in his Hungarian-Canadian accent.

We drove to a parking lot by the edge of the water, got out of the car and began walking along a path. Although it was late, there were still lots of people on it, and we could see the beautiful skyline of the city. It was breathtaking, especially with the tall tower pointing to the sky and stars.

We sat down on a big log by the waterfront and talked—a normal conversation, about music and what Budapest was like (he'd been there only once), and a lot about what I'd been through. He looked at me with care and concern, reaching for my hand at one point and holding it. In that moment, I fell in love with him. He was my saviour—the one who told me I deserved more than the nightmare I'd been led into—and I loved him for it.

He leaned in to kiss me tenderly and I let him.

22 | Running for It

WORKING AT LUCKY'S for the next few days was the closest I was going to come to being with a nice family in Canada, the experience I'd been promised by Natasa when I signed up with the agency. At Lucky's, the presence of Sergei's grandmother and her cookies lightened the whole atmosphere and made it seem not as much like a strip club as it was. It was in a busy area of the city, not in an industrial area like Fantasia, but the club was pretty quiet. The clients were older, all Eastern European men. I danced, but I also helped out cleaning the bathroom and wiping tables in my own jeans and T-shirts.

When I wasn't working, Beatrix made me feel at home in her apartment, giving me clean sheets to put on the couch where I slept, and welcoming me to help myself to food. The first thing I made was scrambled eggs on toast, and it felt wonderful to not have the gnawing hunger pains anymore. I tried not to gorge myself because I didn't want to seem like I was taking advantage of Beatrix's generosity, although it was tempting with lots of food available. Also, I still had a lot of anxiety from everything that had happened and didn't have my full appetite back yet. What helped ease my anxiety was doing normal activities again, like preparing food and having a shower when I wanted. I even did a load of laundry, something I hadn't been able to do for months.

One morning, Beatrix needed to run some errands before our shifts at the club. "Will you be okay here by yourself?" I'd never been alone at her place, but didn't see why I couldn't be. She said she'd only be gone an hour and a half or so.

"For sure," I said. "I'll be fine." I could just watch TV, not that I could understand anything in English.

"Help yourself to anything you want," she said. "There's lots of food in the fridge, and my boyfriend might stop by—he does his laundry here." The idea of a stranger—a man—stopping by triggered my anxiety, but I had no reason to think Beatrix was setting me up for something awful, like Elek had done so many times. She'd been nothing but kind and caring. As if sensing my anxiety, she described her boyfriend as really nice and relaxed.

"It's because he smokes a lot of weed," she said with a laugh. As she was about to leave, she remembered something else. "My dentist's office is going to call. The secretary is Hungarian. Do you think you can answer the phone and take a message?"

"No problem," I said. I was beginning to realize there were lots of good Hungarians in Canada, just like I'd been told in the beginning: Maria, Julius, Beatrix, and now a dentist's secretary.

"Thanks, Timea," she said. "See you in a bit." She quietly closed the door behind her, leaving me alone in her apartment for the first time. I lay down on the couch and closed my eyes. My mind was full of images of the terrible things that had happened to me in the past few months, but I tried to push them away and think of happy things now that I was in a safe place. I remembered the Danube, the smell of fresh pine needles at camp, and the bright Saturday morning market. I sang a few lines of Pierrot's "Step into the Light" and remembered going to his concerts. Everything would work out in the end, I told myself. I could recover from all of this and start over. I didn't know how, but I had to believe.

I had just finished making toast when Beatrix's boyfriend arrived. I offered him some breakfast but he declined and just asked me to tell Beatrix he'd see her later in the day. Then he left. After eating, I stepped out onto the balcony and looked at the view. It wasn't particularly pretty—lots of tall apartment buildings and a big parking lot below, not unlike my complex on Csepel Island—but it was Canada, a place that I now knew had beauty and some good people. I sang a few lines of another one of my favourite songs—one that reminded me of freedom—and then decided to have a shower. I knew I could use as many towels as I wanted, and that I could take as long as I wanted, but it was hard to get Elek's voice out of my head. "Towels cost $20, Timea. Water is expensive—you need to be in and out in three minutes." My taste of freedom at Beatrix's was delicious, but I realized it was going to be a long time before I could recover from all of this, and that my ordeal wasn't over yet. I still had to get back to Budapest and face the consequences there.

I dressed, made myself a cup of tea and then turned the TV on in the living room to distract me from my thoughts. I found a sitcom I'd never seen before and paid close attention to the words to see if I could understand any of it. A short while later, the phone rang. I remembered that Beatrix said her dentist's office would call, so I picked up the receiver and nervously cleared my throat, hoping to sound like the professional I'd once been back in Hungary. "*Szia?*"

"Timea?" It wasn't the secretary, but it was a voice I knew. My stomach dropped and my heart immediately began racing. It was Elek. "Is that you?" he growled. I didn't say another word.

"What the fuck are you doing there, you little bitch?" I couldn't breathe, and I couldn't say a word. How had he found me? How did he get Beatrix's number?

"I know exactly where you are," he said. "We're coming to get you. Now."

Panic took over my body. I kept silent, but my breath was quickening. Could he hear it? I angled the phone away from my mouth.

"We're on our way, Timea. You're gonna pay us for every day you've been gone, on top of the massive debt you already owe us. And you'll pay in more ways than one," he hissed.

I dropped the phone. Only one thought raced through my mind: I had to escape. I knew what Elek and János were capable of. If they were as close as he said they were, I only had a few minutes to get out of here. Beatrix's apartment was on the eighth floor. If I took the elevator down, I might run into them. If I took the stairs, they could trap me there. There wasn't time to phone Julius, Maria or Sergei at Lucky's. Even if I'd known how to call the police, I couldn't—I was a criminal. There was no one who could save me.

My thoughts were scrambling. I ran to the balcony door. As I opened it, there was a loud banging on the front door. I remembered fastening the chain lock after Beatrix's boyfriend left, but I couldn't remember if I'd turned the deadbolt. There was no time to check.

"Timea! We know you're in there. Open this door!"

Elek. I looked around desperately for a place to hide.

"If I have to break this door down, not only will you be sorry, your family will be too! I will chase them down in Hungary. I'll cut your mother's throat, cut your brother's throat, and we're going to fucking kill you too!" I had never heard him so angry.

I saw the balcony. It was my only way out. I ran to the sliding doors and opened them quietly. I stepped out, closed the door behind me, tightly clutched the railing and looked down. An eight-storey drop. No, I would die for sure if I jumped. To my right, the next balcony was about four feet away. It was half full of camping equipment— tents, sleeping bags and backpacks. If I could leap onto it, I might be able to hide under that stuff, or maybe the door to the apartment was unlocked and I could hide inside. If I didn't make it, I'd fall to my death.

Jumping was my only hope. I could hear my heart in my ears even above the sound of Elek banging on the door and yelling. I had no other choice—jump and take my chances, or stay and be tortured and killed.

I swung one leg up and over the railing, then the other, so that I was standing on the edge of the concrete balcony floor, holding only the railing for dear life. *Don't look down.* I summoned the little gymnast that was still somewhere inside me and prepared for the most important vault of my life. Like I'd been trained to do all those years ago at school, I took a big breath, focused my eyes on where I wanted to land—on a pile of sleeping bags—and jumped. I made it! For a moment, it felt like time stopped, and then started up again in a panic. I quickly tried to open the sliding door. It was locked. I knocked on the door, knowing I'd terrify the neighbours if they were home, but no one came. I crouched down and began covering myself with the camping tarps and sleeping bags. Any second Elek would be here.

I heard Beatrix's balcony door slide open.

"Timea! Where are you, you fucking bitch!" Elek screamed in rage. I stayed as still as I could, holding my breath. My heart was pounding so loudly I feared he would hear it.

"She's not here," Elek yelled to János, who was still inside the apartment. "Let's go!" I didn't move.

A minute or so later, I heard them calling me from the ground below. They had come around to the parking lot at the back of the building to look for me. I didn't move. What if they had guns and shot up at all the balconies from below?

I stayed still, but I could see the parking lot through a rip in the tarp that was covering me. Elek and János were standing next to "our" SUV.

"You're dead, Timea! You're dead!" Elek screamed out, his words echoing against the big buildings in the complex. I couldn't stop shaking. Then they got in the car and drove away. I exhaled slowly.

I stayed on the balcony for several more minutes to make sure they had really gone. What was I going to do now?

First, I had to try to get back over to Beatrix's apartment, but with my adrenaline quickly draining away, I needed to act swiftly. I climbed over the edge of the balcony and leapt back. The apartment looked the same—Elek and János hadn't damaged anything except the door frame, where they'd forced the chain lock off. I hadn't turned the deadbolt. I was sitting on the couch, shaking like a leaf, when Beatrix arrived home from her errands about twenty minutes later. I told her what had happened and asked her if she knew how they had found me. She sat down next to me and put her arm around me.

"The only thing I can guess," she offered apologetically, "is that they were calling here to find my boyfriend. He used to deal weed to them, but I didn't think they were still in touch."

"I can't stay here anymore," I said, stating the obvious.

"No, definitely not. We need to move you now," she said. "Let me call Sergei. He's tough on the outside but he's good to girls. The guys will never go near him."

Sergei agreed to let me stay with him until my flight four days later, and came to pick me up right away. He even told me that he'd drive me back and forth to his club every day so that I could work. I would sleep on a couch like I had been at Beatrix's because his guest room was occupied by a woman named Christine, who used to bartend for him. Christine was older than me and had been in Canada for many years. That night, we talked at length—I told her what had happened to me (except what Tony did to me)—and, like my friends, she tried to get me to believe that I had been intentionally extorted.

"Don't you see that you are a victim of crime, Timea?" she asked. "Organized crime. These guys brought you here and took advantage of you on purpose." I had a hard time understanding this. While I certainly knew Elek, János and Natasa were not the helpers they'd made themselves out to be in the beginning, part of me still believed they ran an agency and that I'd screwed it all up at the beginning by messing up my entry visa and saying I was going to be a babysitter, not an exotic dancer. Everything could have been different if I hadn't been so stupid.

"It wasn't your fault," she insisted. "You need to tell the police in Hungary what happened to you. You need to stop this from happening to other girls." Maybe she was right, but first I needed to protect myself.

"I need to get some money to Elek, to pay him off so he'll leave me alone," I explained.

"You'll never get rid of them that way, Timea," Christine said firmly. "They'll always say you owe more. No, the only way is to scare them. I'll tell Sergei what's happened and he'll send one of his mafia guys to find them and make sure they leave you alone." I nodded. She was probably right.

"Keep your money for yourself," she said. "You earned it."

After my few days at Fantasia and shifts at Lucky's, I had about $3,500 to take home with me. I called Julius to tell him that Elek had found me, and that now I was at Sergei's. He asked if he could come and take me to the airport for my flight back to Hungary, and to say goodbye. It was strange to think that there was actually someone I was going to miss from this whole ordeal. I said yes, gratefully.

On the day of my flight, I woke up with a raging fever and the beginning of a flu. I worried I wouldn't be allowed to fly in my condition. On the way to the airport, Julius stopped at a drugstore to buy me medication to get me through the flight. It was the first real store I'd ever walked through in Canada. The only other store I'd set foot in was the little convenience mart where we bought smokes back at the first motel. Even through my aches and fever, I was amazed by what I saw—row upon row of every product imaginable, from diapers to shampoo to chocolates. Julius asked me if I needed anything else for the flight and I said perhaps some snacks, so he grabbed a bag of nuts and a chocolate bar and paid for everything at the checkout.

At the airport, I was a nervous, feverish wreck. Julius accompanied me through check-in and all the way to security, where he hugged me hard and kissed me softly. I couldn't handle a more emotional goodbye and he seemed to sense that. I said that I hoped somehow I might see him again, in some better time, and he nodded before hugging me again and waving as I walked through the doors.

The security line was long but I went through it without incident, clutching my precious passport to my chest. I needed to throw up, but was afraid of the automatic toilets so I chose a sink in the bathroom instead. Then I splashed some cold water on my face, went to the gate, spread my Pink Panther shirt on the floor next to my duffle bag, and put my head down until my flight was called.

On the plane, I felt like a completely different person than I'd been before coming to Canada. These three months had turned everything I knew and understood about myself and the world inside out. I didn't know who I was anymore or where I belonged. I looked around at the other travellers, half expecting them to be staring at me—as though everything I was thinking and feeling on the inside was visible from the outside.

No one was staring at me. The flight attendants treated me like everyone else, offering me drinks, pillows and even a cold towel for my forehead. I was coughing and my cheeks were flushed, so my fever must have been evident. These simple acts of kindness, together with those of the new friends I'd made in the last few weeks, kept me convinced that good must triumph over evil, and as I tried to get comfortable and sleep, I thought over and over about what Christine had said the other night—that I had to find a way to help the other girls and women being recruited. I pictured the girls I knew, still trapped, and those who'd lost their lives, Zsófia and maybe Hanna. I thought of all the girls on their way over from Hungary and other countries with their hopes and dreams, and what a nightmare awaited them.

I decided to tell everything to the police when I landed in Budapest so they could arrest Elek and János when they arrived two days after me. They would protect me and my family, I was sure, and then maybe we could help other girls.

23 | Betrayal

RESOLVED TO SPEAK to the authorities when I landed, I felt calm and determined emotionally, but I was a wreck physically. By the time the plane touched down in Budapest I was so sick I could barely walk. I was sweating with fever and every muscle in my body ached. I wished I was just coming home from a vacation, or from my wonderful summer as a babysitter in Canada, and that my family would be there to greet me. Instead, no one even knew where I was.

As I approached customs, I began to worry that Elek, János and Natasa would have someone else from the agency—or even the mafia—waiting for me on the other side. I glanced around to see if anyone looked suspicious or if they were watching me, like I had so often at Fantasia. I imagined someone pulling out a gun and shooting me, or kidnapping me at knifepoint. I didn't go into the bathroom in case someone was waiting for me in there. Soon, calm had dissolved completely, and I rushed to the customs line so I could tell the truth and bring my nightmare to an end.

The customs guard asked for my passport and I handed it to him. My head and heart were both pounding, my head from the flu and my heart from fear. *Is this the person I should confess everything to?* I had only determination, not an exact plan. He flipped through my passport a couple of times and looked hard at the page with my photo. Then he looked at me.

"It's a fake," I blurted out, unable to contain myself any longer. He looked at me with disbelief. Then he called another officer over, and I was escorted to a waiting room. After about twenty minutes, two officers came in, one tall with dark hair and the other shorter with blond hair.

"What's your real name?" the tall one asked.

"Timea Nagy," I said.

"You're not Andrea Hernuss, like it says on your passport?" the blond asked.

"No, I'm not."

"But this is a picture of you?"

"Yes, it is."

"Where did you get this passport?"

"It was given to me by the recruiter from the agency that hired me to go to Canada to work as a babysitter. I went to Canada first with my own passport but I was sent back because they wouldn't give a work permit as a babysitter, only an exotic dancer." My story began spilling out. The agents stared at me, expressionless, while I went on explaining. "Then the agency told me I owed them a lot of money and if I didn't go back and work for them, they would hurt my family, so they gave me this passport and I had to go back."

"Why are you reporting this to us?" the tall officer asked. "Do you understand that you are admitting to having committed serious crimes—fraud, impersonation and identity theft?"

I took a deep breath. "Yes, I do," I said. "I'm telling you because I need your help. The agents are after me. I had to escape them and come back and try to get help protecting my family. Will you help me, please?"

"Wait here," the blond officer said, and then they left together. I sat in an uncomfortable plastic chair, alternately sweating and then shaking with chills. I remembered all the times I was sick as a little girl and how my mom could be so nurturing, bringing me clean pyjamas and changing my sheets. I longed to go back in time and be a little girl again, or forward in time to when this moment was in the past. The officers finally returned over an hour later and escorted me to a large interview room where I was told to sit down at a table. Four male officers and one female officer were sitting on the other side. *Thank God. They are going to help me.*

"Why don't you start at the beginning?" the female officer invited, opening up a notebook and picking up a pen. She was polite, but not warm. I started by sharing the money problems my brother and I had, and how a friend had showed me an ad for young women wanted to work in Canada, and how English wasn't necessary. I told them about my interview with Natasa, and how I wanted to be a babysitter, and how she'd said there were a lot of nice, Hungarian families in Canada who needed child care in the summer. I described my arrival in Canada, and how I was taken to the club and forced to dance, but I didn't tell them about what Tony did to me, because I was too ashamed and confused about that. I told them why I had to go back to Canada on the fake passport, and how I had to dance for sixteen to twenty hours a day. I even told them about the massage parlour. I explained how many other girls there were like me, how we couldn't leave, how we were starved and sleep deprived, and threatened constantly. How the agents took all of our money. I told them about the big boss Sasha, who was probably mafia, and the stories we girls heard about him and how he had branches of the agency all over Europe. I even told them about Elek and János, and that they were coming back to Budapest in two days. I promised that I would testify to everything in court, and asked them to please arrest Elek and János when they got off the plane. I said everything in what felt like one breath, but it had taken close to two hours.

When I finished, the female officer looked at me with disgust and disbelief. She had stopped taking notes a while ago and now put down her pen.

"So let me get this straight—you went to Canada, you worked as a prostitute and you didn't get paid. Is that right?" Her tone was harsh. I was speechless at the simplistic, incriminating conclusion she'd drawn after hearing my whole story. *She doesn't believe me.* The male officers were all stone-faced and silent.

"And now you want us to help you?" she asked. I tried to pull my thoughts together and plead my case.

"Yes, but not just me—all the girls. Please."

"Before you went to Canada, you were a music video director, right? A little TV star." They had clearly done some research while I'd been waiting in the other room. "So you like to come up with stories. Is this one of your stories?" She didn't stop there. "Your mother is a police officer, correct?" My heart stopped. Did she know my mom? I gave a small nod. I wanted to beg the officer not to tell her, but I couldn't get a word in.

"Shame on you! Is this what your mother taught you—to be a hooker?" I immediately felt that shame to my core. The way she said it was so black-and-white—there was nothing of the detail or context I'd described. *Maybe she was right—maybe I am just a hooker, a hooker with bad luck. A stupid, foolish, dirty girl. Or maybe I'm just blowing this whole thing out of proportion because I'm so tired.* I looked across the table at the faces of each of the five officers, none of them showing any concern for my well-being. A few of them joined the female officer in her judgment and made similar shaming comments. I wanted the floor to open up and swallow me.

Finally, the female officer pushed back her chair and stood up.

"I've heard enough," she said sternly. "You're being charged with impersonation and fraud. Once we get the people who made you that passport, you'll all be in trouble." Another officer stood up, came over to my chair and handcuffed me.

"Your mother will be thrilled to see you in jail," he hissed. "Well done!"

Of everything I feared, my mother's shame was the worst, and I was going to experience it now. For so many months I had tried to stop this from happening, but I'd failed. And now I was done fighting, running and hiding. I was done trying to make things right. Soon, everyone would know everything: Mom, Zoli, Ádám, everyone at the TV station, everyone on Csepel Island. I would probably be in the newspaper, and there'd be a picture of me too. It would make it easy for Elek, János and Sasha to find my family. And I was going to jail. Me, Timea Nagy, daughter of a police officer. Award-winning, badge-earning Little Drummer and Trailblazer, former Pierrot Fan Club chair, host of the popular TV show *Fresh*. I was none of those things anymore.

The blond officer led me out of the room, down a hall, down some stairs and over into a separate building where I was told we had to finish some paperwork before I'd be released on a recognizance order, with the promise to appear in court. I was going to need a lawyer, but I didn't know how to get one, much less how I was going to pay for one. I needed to use the money I'd come back with to pay off my debts. In all the scenarios I'd played out in my mind, confessing and not being believed was never one of them. Nor was what happened next.

The officer led me into an interview room and left me there, sitting in a chair across from a desk with an old typewriter on it. After about half an hour, a new officer arrived to conduct my interview. He was in his midthirties, with dark hair and eyes, a goatee, and a serious look on his face. He put a file folder with forms in it down on the desk, and then sat down and introduced himself as Istvan.

"Now Timea, I've read your report but why don't you start at the beginning again? Give me your address here in Budapest." I was silent. What was my address? Had my brother been able to keep the apartment somehow? I didn't even know where he was living right now. I didn't want to give my mother's address, or Ádám's, so I gave him the address of our apartment. Then he asked me for some more basic details, like my real birthdate, height, weight and any prior charges or convictions. Then I had to retell my story.

As I talked, Istvan typed. After a while, he stopped and looked up at me. He hadn't asked me to sit down so I was still standing, handcuffed. He had a look in his eyes that I recognized, and it filled me with dread.

"So, you were a dancer, huh?" he asked, almost playfully. I felt my body go numb.

"Yes, I was forced to be," I said, my voice sounding a little weak. I didn't like how he was talking to me.

"Well, for me to write a proper report I need to know more details about that. Can you explain how it works? The dancing?" I knew exactly where he was going with this. I knew that it would be just a matter of time before I'd be naked again. I prayed for the other officer to come back and interrupt. I prayed for the female officer to come back, as mean and disbelieving as she'd been.

"You sign up with the DJ, you choose your songs and you go on stage when you get called," I answered in a monotone voice, looking at my shoes. I stopped talking when I didn't hear the typewriter. Istvan encouraged me to go on. "Then you go on stage and you dance three songs."

"When do you take off your clothes?"

"During the third song," I said.

He got up, walked around the desk and over to me, and took off my handcuffs. "Can you show me some moves? If I'm to write an honest account of your story, I need to believe that you were a real dancer."

I couldn't move, frozen in fear.

"I'm sorry, I'm really not feeling well. Can you please just write what I told you?" I tried to sound firm but it wasn't how I felt. I knew I was powerless—far away from the main offices in a room without windows or a video camera, at the mercy of a man in uniform. He knew it too. He turned me around by my shoulders and pushed me toward the side of the room and told me to stay there, with my arms up and my hands on the wall. I thought he was going to pat me down for weapons or drugs. I'd seen that happen at my mom's police station many times. Then I heard the door open and the blond officer came back in. I thought I was saved, but I was wrong. He locked the door behind him.

"You're just in time," Istvan said to his partner. "We're going to see this little hooker do her thing." He pulled my shirt up and over my head. I was sweating from the fever and my skin was hot to the touch, but that only seemed to turn him on. He reached around my waist, undid my jeans, and pulled them down and off me.

"No, please no," I pleaded. But he ignored me. I wanted to die. I heard him undo his pants and put his gun, holster and belt on the desk. The next thing I knew, he was forcing himself inside me from behind. The pain was excruciating. I wanted to scream but I knew better; I knew I just had to stay quiet. No one was going to help me. I squeezed my eyes closed and tried to go to my safe place but I couldn't find it. He was saying things—dirty things—to turn himself on more, and to humiliate me, and I understood every word. Having sex forced on me in Hungarian was different than when it happened in English or another language. It hurt way more. It wasn't only my body that was being ravaged, but also my identity, my soul. I didn't have a name for everything else that happened to me, but this— without a doubt—was rape.

When he finished, he passed me a tissue and told me to clean myself up but not move.

"We're not done yet," he said. "We have to be fair, for the report. My partner here needs to get the information for himself." I heard the other officer step closer to me. I felt something cold and hard touch my bum.

"Spread your legs and bend over," he ordered. *Not this, please.* He spanked me a few times, but I didn't hear him undo his pants. Then all of a sudden I felt a searing, unbearable pain and I couldn't help but scream. Something was being shoved into me and all I could picture was a curling iron, but afterwards I realized it was a gun. The officer put his hand over my mouth to quiet me, and then I could hardly breathe.

"This should loosen you up," the officer growled, "although you're probably already loose, you fucking whore." He moved the gun in and out, causing agonizing pain. All I could do was lean on the wall for strength. Next I felt his penis inside me. For the first time in my life, I prayed to die.

I must've lost consciousness, because the next thing I knew I was in a chair, slumped over to one side, unable to sit properly. I was in so much pain. I looked down. My shirt was back on me, but my jeans were still on the floor. There was blood on the chair and all over my legs.

Istvan sat back down in the chair behind the desk and lit a cigarette. He had enough information to finish the report, he said. The blond officer told me to put my pants on, and then he led me out of the room and down the hall to a bathroom. I couldn't think; I couldn't speak. I could hardly walk. I tried to wash myself off and catch my breath. I came out of the bathroom and the officer took me back into the room where Istvan was typing as though absolutely nothing had happened. The other officer left, saying he was going to get a car. Istvan pulled the paper out of the typewriter, ripped off a carbon copy and gave it to me, and put the other two copies in a file folder.

"Listen," Istvan said, "you seem like a nice girl who got caught up in a wrong crowd. I want to help you." I thought I was going crazy.

How could he possibly be saying this after what he'd just done to me?

"You're in a pretty bad situation here. You can't leave the country and you're not going to be able to leave your home if these guys are after you, like you say. In fact, you're probably not even safe in your apartment. But just so you know, this report is probably not going to get into the system for two weeks, so you've got some time to apply for a new passport—a real one—and try to leave on that one. Just get out of here."

I was stunned. Was he suggesting that I run from the law? Maybe he was afraid I would report him and the other officer, so he was pushing me to leave. I couldn't think straight—I was so ill and in so much pain. I just needed to get somewhere safe so I could rest. I wanted to go home, but I didn't know if I still had a home.

"You have a lot to think about," Istvan said. "So we're going to drive you home and come back in a few days to check on you." He stood up and we walked out of the room, down the hall and outside. The other officer was waiting in a squad car in the parking lot. He'd gotten my duffle bag from somewhere and put it in the backseat. They put me in the back of the car and we drove through Budapest and over the bridge to Csepel Island. Even though it was the middle of the night, I sank down low in my seat so no one could see me, and leaned on one side to try to help manage the pain. Probably no one would recognize me anyway—I'd lost more than thirty pounds; my face was sallow and my eyes hollow. I spent the drive praying for two things: that my key still worked in the apartment door, and that my brother wasn't home.

As I walked up to the door of my building, and the squad car with my rapists in it drove away, I looked around to see if anyone from the agency or the mafia was watching me. I pictured smaller European versions of the black SUVs like the ones the agency had in Canada, but the street was empty. I fumbled to find my key in the bottom of my bag and then to try it in the apartment door, praying hard. Both of my prayers were answered.

I opened the door to find it empty except for my two cats, who rushed over to me, rubbed up against my legs and looked longingly at me to pat them. But I couldn't. I felt disgusting and I didn't want to get my filth all over them. I called out for Zoli, but there was no answer. While on one hand I was scared to see him and have to begin explaining, on the other hand I was desperate to see the face of someone I loved and who loved me. In Canada, I hadn't allowed myself to think about missing anyone because I wouldn't have been able to handle it, but now that I was home and safe for at least a little while, all my emotions rose to the surface, and I realized how much I missed Zoli. I began crying. I went into the bathroom, where I saw his laundry in the laundry basket, and I cried more. I wished I could go back to a time when we argued over who had used the last clean towel or when he yelled at me for eating his favourite yogurt.

I took off my clothes and turned on the water in the shower and let it get really hot. While I was waiting, I took some painkillers I found in the medicine cabinet. Then I stepped in and let my tears flow over me and be washed away by the water. All of a sudden, I felt enormous grief. My old life was gone; the old me was gone. I wished I'd never left Hungary to go to Canada, that I'd done anything but answer that ad in the newspaper. Now I was a broken and used person. I was a whore, just like the police had said. For months I'd dreamed of this moment, of coming home, putting on my pyjamas and curling up in bed and being myself again. Now I couldn't do any of that. I was too disgusting. I went into my bedroom and closed the door behind me, leaving my cats out in the living room. I put on a fresh pair of underwear and a menstrual pad, since I was still bleeding from the assault. Then I pulled a T-shirt and leggings from my drawer and lay down on the floor in my room. I lay as still as I could, trying to will away the pain and my fever.

I didn't know what to do. I thought I should see a doctor, but I couldn't imagine leaving the apartment. I wanted to call my mom, just to tell her I was home and sick and ask her to come and take care of me, but it was so much more complicated than that and I didn't know how to begin to tell her what had happened in a way that wouldn't destroy her. Maybe if I tried to sleep and get some rest, I would know what to do next. I knew I would have to tell Zoli something when he came home. The clock told me it was 6:30 a.m., but I wasn't quite sure what day it was. Everything was completely mixed up.

I slept on and off all day, troubled by violent dreams. When I was awake, everything, especially what had happened at the airport with the customs officers, played out in my mind, over and over. I got up, ate a few crackers from the cupboard, and then went back to lying on the floor. I stayed there for hours. Then, finally, I heard a key in the front door. *Zoli.* After a minute, he called out to me. He must have seen my bag. I eased myself up to sitting, and then standing. The pain was still intense. I slowly walked into the living room where he threw his arms around me.

"Why didn't you call me?" he asked. "Where were you? Everyone has been worried sick about you! We've heard all kinds of rumours." His eyes were wide with worry, but there was also a trace of the anger I expected. I didn't know where to begin.

"I'm sorry," I said. "It wasn't what I expected. I went to Canada but I wasn't able to make any money." I'd listened to what Christine had said and decided not to leave any money behind for the agents, so I had close to $3,500 in my little bunny backpack; it was a miracle the officers hadn't gone through it at customs. I just couldn't give it all to Zoli right away in case Elek, János, Natasa or Sasha came for me. I would need it to buy the lives of my family, and my life. I was also going to need a lawyer. I could only hope it would be enough.

"What the fuck were you doing there?" he demanded. The happy part of our reunion was already over. "Do you know what kind of rumours are going around about you?" I shook my head, but I could imagine. Natasa had alluded to things people were saying, but I'd hoped she was just trying to scare me.

"Someone sent a fax to the TV station saying that you were a hooker and you got involved with drugs and that they shouldn't hire you back."

"That's not true," I protested. Outright denial was all I could come up with. Zoli didn't seem like he was in any mood to try to understand a big, long, painful story.

"Mom is furious with you, and Ádám—even though he told me you broke up—is sick with worry. How could you just not call us?"

"I'm sorry, Zoli, but if you calm down I can try to explain."

"Calm down? Do you have any fucking idea how hard I've had to work to keep this apartment? I've been working three jobs! I managed to get it for another two months, but that's it." Furious with me, Zoli left, slamming the door behind him. I understood his feelings. I felt angry too, but mostly scared and traumatized. I wanted to explain but I couldn't. I didn't even know if he would believe me over what the police report said, and what I'd been charged with.

As bad as things had been in Canada, I'd still believed I was going to find a way out of everything I was trapped in. Now that hope was gone. I thought about just giving Zoli the money from my bag and then throwing myself over the balcony. I thought about taking a handful of painkillers and ending it all. But I couldn't leave Zoli and my mother to deal with what was coming. They would still be chased down by the agency. They would have to deal with my suicide and find out that their tomboy Timea really was a hooker and a whore. They would have to deal with the fact that I was a wanted criminal, and that I'd been arrested and charged. They would have to deal with how absolutely stupid and naive I'd been, going to Canada against everyone's advice in the first place.

Then there were all those girls back in Canada, and the ones who were here, about to leave and go to work for the agency. What happened to me would happen to them and their families. There was no easy way out of this. I went into my room, lay back down on the floor and bit my nails until my fingertips were completely raw and red.

Two days later, while I was nibbling some crackers and drinking tea at the kitchen table, and trying to figure out what to do, the phone rang.

"You stupid little bitch!" I recognized Natasa's voice immediately. She was livid. "What the fuck did you do? You spilled the beans to the police? Are you fucking kidding me?" I didn't breathe, didn't say a word. I just listened, terrified.

"Elek and János are in jail!" she raged on. "If you show up in court and tell them where you got that passport, I swear we will kill you. You are going to pay for this, you little cunt. Just you wait! We will start with your mother, and then your brother, and we will leave you until last, so you can feel their pain. One day—and trust me, that day will come just when you stop looking over your shoulder—we will cut your fucking throat too!" And then she hung up.

Panic rose in my throat and I felt like it had already been cut. Before I had a moment to think, the phone rang again. I didn't want to answer, worried it could be Natasa again, but it kept ringing and ringing. Finally I picked it up.

"Timea?" It was my mom, her voice shrill. "Zoli said you're back. Where the hell were you? I wrote you letters every week but had no address to send them to. I had the police in Canada looking for you! Why didn't you call? I told you a hundred times to call me when you got there. I will strangle you when I'll see you! You promised! And you didn't even call me when you got home. What the hell is going on?"

Like with Zoli, I didn't know where to begin, but I didn't have a chance anyway.

"A man called me a few days ago to say that you owe him $5,000 and that if I don't pay, they will burn my house down. What the hell did you get yourself into over there?"

"I'm sorry, Mom. I'm so sorry," I finally said. "I can explain everything, but I'm really sick right now. I have a terrible flu." I faintly hoped that disclosing an illness to her would soften her heart toward me, even if it were just temporarily. It had always worked when I was a child.

"Okay, fine," her tone softened slightly. "Go back to bed, take two Kalmopyrin and sleep. I will come later with some soup and we will talk."

"It's okay, Mom. I will come and see you tomorrow when I'm better." I needed to buy myself some time to try to fix this, to come up with a plan. Now that Elek and János were in jail, maybe that meant that someone, somewhere believed my side of the story— that they were the criminals and I'd been taken advantage of. All I could do was hope.

"I'm sorry, Mom," I said again. "I love you." I said the words in case they were the last ones I was able to say for a while, or forever. It had been a long time since I'd told her I loved her.

"I love you too, Timike."

24 | Trapped

THE PHONE IN OUR APARTMENT was still one of those old rotary phones, even though it was 1998. In the three days since I'd been back, it had been the source of bad news or intimidation every time it rang. It was always Natasa's voice, and she was always making threats. I stopped answering. I just sat there in the apartment, thinking through things again and again, and trying to figure out a way to fix everything. I bought time with my mom, calling her to say I was feeling better, fixing a few things, and that I'd come for a visit soon.

Then there was a loud knock at the door, which made me panic. I stood up quickly but silently and walked in my sock feet to the kitchen where I grabbed a knife. More knocking. *This is it*, I thought. *It's Sasha or other agents here to kill me. This is the end.* I looked at my wrists and thought of slitting them, but then a deep, loud voice came from the other side of the door.

"Police! Open up!" *The police?* I broke out in a sweat, fearing the officers who'd raped me at the airport. Were they here to rape me again, or to take me into custody? I looked out through the peephole and saw two young men in plain clothes. They didn't look like how I pictured Sasha, mafia guys or hitmen, but then what did I know? Elek had always presented himself as a friend, a brother, but look how that had turned out. I slowly unlocked the deadbolt, keeping the chain lock on, and opened the door a crack. Both officers flashed their badges.

"Are you Timea Nagy?" one of them asked. I nodded. "You're not in trouble," he said to my relief, but also my surprise. "But we need to talk to you. Can we come inside?" They seemed genuine, but they were also wearing guns. I was accustomed to officers with guns from growing up in my mother's police station, but after what had happened at the airport, just the sight of a gun made me feel like I was going to be sick. The men sensed my hesitation and repeated that I wasn't in trouble. I opened the door wider, slid off the chain and let them in.

As they stepped inside, the first officer, who was tall and blond with a baby face, introduced himself as Lukacs Fekete, from the National Police Service. The other one was Viktor Kis. They were both detectives on an international crime team, and my report from the airport had come across their desk.

"We know that the officers at immigration didn't believe your story, Timea," Officer Fekete said, "but we do."

"And we'd like to know more," Officer Kis said. "Specifically about Sasha. He's someone we've been trying to get for a while. You could help us." All the blood drained out of my face and head and I felt faint. So Sasha *was* a real person, a real criminal. I'd started to doubt his existence, after Maria at Fantasia had tried to tell me that Elek and János had made him up just to scare me.

"I can talk to you," I said. "But not here." I just didn't feel comfortable inviting them in to have a long conversation when my brother could show up any minute, or even my mother.

"Would you feel more comfortable talking to us in our car?" Fekete asked. "We could just drive around." I didn't feel comfortable at all, going anywhere with unknown men, so I just hoped I would be safe—that these officers were who they said they were, and cared like they said they did. Besides, we couldn't really go anywhere like a café or a park to talk. If I was being followed by Sasha and a team of mafia thugs, it was better that I stay out of view and not go anywhere I could be an easy target.

"Okay," I said. "I guess I could do that." Surely, there were still good people in the world.

I grabbed my purse and went downstairs with them, and out to an unmarked white car.

"I don't know where to start," I said. "What do you want to know about Sasha?"

"Why don't you start from the beginning?" Fekete suggested. He pulled out his notepad and pen to take notes while Kis drove. As we headed off Csepel Island and toward the Buda side of the city, I started talking, beginning again with why I'd needed money so badly and how Bianka had showed me the ad in the newspaper. I hadn't mentioned her back at the airport, only because she seemed like an insignificant detail. I also didn't think it looked too good for my character to say I was friends with a professional prostitute, but after how I'd been treated at the airport, I no longer knew if it was better or worse for me to tell the truth to the authorities. I decided on the truth, for the moment.

"Do you think she worked for the agency?" Fekete asked me.

The thought had never crossed my mind. It didn't make sense to me. She had a child. She had her own difficulties. "No," I said with confidence. "She was my friend." I wondered when I would see her again. I guessed that she was in Sweden and I had some time to make amends.

"So you think it was just a coincidence that you were befriended by a prostitute who then encouraged you to apply to this agency that, it turns out, is involved in the sex trade?" His tone was one of genuine interest, although when he put it that way, I felt uneasy.

"Yes, I do," I said, although a little less confidently. "She helped me a lot, and she even came with me to try to change her life by just dancing until I ruined her opportunity. In fact, I still owe her for my return plane ticket." The officer nodded and made some notes.

Over the next couple of hours, as we drove all over the city, I got my whole story out, ending with the fact that Natasa had called that morning and made death threats. I finally began crying when I told them who my mother was, and I begged them not to tell her anything.

"Please just let's figure this out so she never has to know," I begged. "I'll do whatever you say I have to, but my mother can't find out."

"You are an adult under the law, Timea," they reminded me, "so your mom doesn't have to know about your charges, but we do have to investigate the legitimacy of these threats and monitor phone calls to your house and her house to make sure all of you are safe. Hopefully, with all this information, we'll finally be able to bring these criminals to justice. We've been looking for Sasha and his guys for a long time. They are an organized crime ring that we've been trying to break. Timea, you're a victim, not a criminal."

I cried again when I heard that, but I didn't quite believe it. I still saw myself as a stupid, naive girl who had gotten herself into a whole lot of trouble. On some level, I believed I deserved what happened to me.

"You've already helped us a lot," Fekete said. "Your report flagged Elek and János, and they were arrested when they came through customs yesterday on their way back from Canada." So Natasa had been speaking the truth.

"When their suitcases were searched," he continued, "officers found several passports and copies of passports, including a copy of your fake one, as well as work permits and a notebook with amounts of money they collected from each girl they had working for them. None of the names matched the passports, so we figure they are code names. What's your name in the book, Timea?"

"Allison is my stage name," I said. "Andrea is the name on my passport." He wrote that down.

The more I learned from the police, the more validated I felt, but the more scared I became. It was overwhelming, having the layers of my life over the last few months peeled back and finding at the core something even worse than I'd understood: a professional, organized crime ring. That meant that everything I'd heard about Sasha was probably true. I needed to tell Fekete and Kis everything I'd ever heard about him, even if none of it would help them trace him.

"Sasha is an animal," I blurted out. "He set houses on fire. He killed girls in Turkey and other countries." I told the officers everything I'd heard from Elek, but they didn't look shocked. They just nodded.

"Yes, we know. And you can help us to put out an international warrant for his arrest by telling us everything you heard, and about what his 'employees' did to you. Can you please come and testify for us? If you do, we will drop the impersonation and fraud charges against you." There it was. Of course they wanted something from me. Everything always had to be an exchange of some kind. But at least this time it wasn't sinister. Still, I hesitated to respond.

"If you don't help us, Timea, we may have to proceed with the charges on the order of our supervisor." Fekete's tone wasn't unkind or manipulative, but it was clear and firm. I understood that he was making a deal and agreed to testify.

On the drive back to my apartment, Fekete gave me a card with his badge and phone numbers and asked me to call him if I remembered anything else. He would be in touch about when I needed to meet them at the courthouse for my testimony in front of a judge. In the meantime, they would keep an unmarked car in front of my building and my mom's building to watch out for Sasha or any of his henchmen.

I walked up to my apartment overwhelmed by everything I had just learned. Inside, I passed the time by pacing. I found a pack of cigarettes in my dresser drawer and smoked them all. My cats were crying for my attention but I could barely even pat them. Later that evening, Zoli finally came home. He had calmed down, and wanted to talk to me to figure out what we were going to do about the debts still owing. I didn't have the heart to tell him that now money was the least of our troubles, that our lives were in danger. I told him I needed to sleep and that we could talk in the morning.

Zoli went out onto the balcony and I went to my room and curled up on my bed, on top of the blankets. Then, all of a sudden, he ran into my room, excited.

"Timi, come, look! Something big is going down outside. Someone is in deep shit!" He pulled me by the elbow out of my room and onto the balcony, which overlooked the back of the building.

"Look," he said, pointing down at a black Mercedes. "That's a mafia car." Then he pulled me over to the kitchen window and pointed down to the street at the side of the building. "And that white car is an unmarked cop car," he said. "They are watching someone. Whoever it is probably lives in our building."

I suddenly felt hot all over, but I knew I had to play it cool. Was the black car Sasha's people? Or Sasha himself? I knew who was in the white car. "Oh, wow," I said. "That can't be good."

We watched for a while but nothing happened. The whole time, my stomach was churning. I went back to my room and stayed up all night, worrying about what would happen now that the police were involved and I had told them everything. Again, I was a prisoner, but this time it was in my own home. I thought about calling Ádám, but Zoli had said he was furious with me for never writing or calling, so I didn't. The next morning, though, he arrived at my door.

"Timea, why didn't you call or write to me? Do you have any idea how worried I've been?" His eyes looked hurt but his tone was cold and demanding. "What were you doing in Canada—do you know what kind of rumours are going around here about you?"

"I'm sorry, Ádám, I'm sorry," was all I could say. I couldn't give him the answers he demanded until he calmed down, or until I was

ready to talk about it again. I was physically and emotionally traumatized, and I didn't know how Ádám would react to my story. "I know
I should have been in touch but some things went really wrong." My
tone was soft, and it calmed him down slightly.

"Do you know that I was planning to propose to you when you
got back? That I missed you more than I ever thought I would?"
His hurt was palpable. He sat down on the sofa and put his head in
his hands. I stayed standing, feeling terribly guilty.

"Can I please try to explain?" I asked gently. I started into a version
of my story that I thought he could handle, leaving out the acts of sex
and violence that had occurred. I made it sound like I'd been forced
into go-go dancing, working for a corrupt agency.

"Then you're an idiot," he decided. "And it's all your fault. I can't
even look at you anymore." With that, he got up and left. I didn't have
the energy to try to stop him or to defend myself. But I knew for
certain that there was no life for me in Budapest anymore. I didn't trust
that the police could protect me—if this was the big international ring
of criminals they said it was, then Sasha must have many agents after
me, and I would always be looking over my shoulder. If I testified
against the agency, I would only be in more danger, even if some of the
agents went to jail. I would never work here again because of my sul-
lied reputation. I had to leave.

The only place in the world where I knew anyone outside of
Budapest was Toronto. I thought about Julius, Maria, Chris the DJ,
and even Sergei, the owner of Lucky's. They had all offered me help
before. If they were still willing, I could try to get back to Canada. I
called them, one by one, keeping our conversations short because of
the high long-distance cost. Maria said she could write me an invitation letter and that I might be able to get a visitor visa for six months.
I wouldn't legally be allowed to work, but Sergei said I could work
under the table at Lucky's. At this point, now that I was a wanted
criminal, I didn't care about working illegally; all I cared about was
getting away from this mess and being able to start over. But to do

any of that, I was going to need a new passport. Beatrix suggested I just apply for a new one, in my real name.

"Tell them your original passport was lost," she suggested. "The order not to return for eighteen months was stamped in your old passport by the Canadian border guards, right? I've heard that they don't even keep track of those orders in their system, and Hungary doesn't care who threw you out. You're Hungarian, after all. You can get thrown out of every other country, but not your own." I was skeptical, but I decided that I would try anything. I remembered, too, that Istvan—the officer who raped me—had told me he wouldn't file my report for two weeks, so Hungarian officials wouldn't yet know that I had charges against me. I could go to the passport office to pick up the forms, get photos taken, and then complete and submit my application. I also needed to buy a plane ticket back to Toronto with the money I'd saved, and then I could give Zoli some money. All of this had to happen within two days.

I had to get out of the apartment and on the train to downtown without being seen by either the mafia or the undercover cops. There was no way I could ask the detectives to escort me, since they couldn't know that I was planning to get a passport and leave before I testified against Sasha in court. And I had to make sure none of Elek's or Sasha's people figured out what I was doing. As if on cue, the phone rang; it was Natasa again, reminding me that if I helped the police in any way, my family and I would be killed.

I used to go to the rooftop to sunbathe in my early teens, and I remembered that there was a way to get from my rooftop to the rooftop of the next building, across a small utility worker's bridge. I could exit out the back door of that building, where no one would see me. The next morning, I tried my escape route. Pumped up on adrenaline, but still sick and in pain, I managed to get out and onto the train. At the passport office, I filled out the forms and paid extra to have my passport ready in three days and mailed to me special delivery.

"Is there any reason it wouldn't come in three days?" I asked, just to be sure the fee was worth it.

"Only if you're a criminal!" the clerk answered cheerfully. If only she knew.

I went across the street to a travel agency and booked myself a ticket for Wednesday, September 2, 1998, at 6:30 a.m.—four days away—paying out of the cash I had. It was expensive: not only was it last minute, but because I was travelling on a visitor visa, the ticket had to be two-way. The passport was scheduled to arrive the day before I left, and I prayed that it would. There was no margin for error.

Over the next day or so, Natasa called several times to threaten me. Each time I answered, I hoped it would be one of my friends in Toronto. I hung up when I heard her voice.

I decided to tell my brother and my mother that I was going back to Canada—that I'd been invited to fulfill another contract, but with a different agency, a much better one. One that friends worked for and told me I could trust. I told them some of the good things I knew about Toronto, like the big tower and the lake and how clean the airport was. I told them about a couple of friends I'd made. I asked them to try to understand and they did. In spite of how angry they still were at me, they seemed to understand that I needed a fresh start.

My mom said she wanted to see me before I went, and she offered to come over and make dinner. It could be a proper goodbye, which in some way I knew I needed. I had no idea if I'd ever see her or anyone else again. I was afraid, though, that Sasha's mafia car would still be at the back of the building, where the visitor parking was, so I told her to park on the street and come through the front doors because there was painting going on at the back. I asked her if she could bring me some of the old clothes I had stored at her house, ones that were a smaller size.

"I lost a lot of weight in Canada," I explained. "The food was really strange." I described the grilled cheese and egg salad sandwiches.

"That's not good, Timea," she sympathized. "You need some of my homemade soup. I'll bring it along with your old clothes." She spoke softly and with care, like she always had when I was sick, and I soaked it up like a dry sponge. I'd been starving in more ways than one.

I accepted her offer and planned for her to come over that night with her boyfriend, as well as a cousin I hadn't seen for a long time. When I opened the door, she seemed shocked by my appearance and hugged my thin frame strongly.

"Don't worry, Mom, when I go back I'm going to be living with some Hungarian girls and we're going to cook all the foods we love. Maybe you can give me the recipe for your soup?" She nodded. My cousin hugged me next, and then my mom's boyfriend.

"I made bread," he said warmly, passing me a loaf, "and I can give you the recipe for it too." We smiled at each other. I could see why he'd had a great effect on my mom's happiness.

That night, we had the closest thing we'd ever had to a real family dinner, even taking a picture in which we are all smiling. I wondered if it would be the last one we ever took. The future was completely uncertain.

25 | Searching for Safety

THE NEXT TWO DAYS went by slowly while I waited to go to the post office and receive my passport. I did my laundry, packed a small suitcase and waited. On the second evening, there was a knock at the door. Through the peephole I saw the face of Istvan, one of the officers from the airport, and my heart filled with terror. What was he doing here?

"Timea," he called through the door. "I know you're in there." I could see him smiling. I didn't know what to do.

"I have some news about your passport," he said. How did he know I'd applied for a passport? "Open the door," he said firmly. I did as he asked, terrified.

"So, you took me up on my offer?" he asked coyly.

"What offer?"

"To get a new passport before I file your paperwork in the court. I have a close friend in immigration. Where are you going this time?"

"Nowhere," I lied.

266 | OUT OF THE SHADOWS

"Well, I wasn't sure what your plans were so I did file your paper-work, and now I have a subpoena for your court date in two weeks. But you're not planning to show up, are you?" He was onto me. I didn't respond.

"Do you know that I can have my friend approve or reject your passport application?" he said. I shook my head. "But you're a nice girl. I want you to be safe. I like you." His words made me want to vomit. He looked away from me, as though he was considering some-thing, and then looked back.

"I'll tell you what, Timea, why don't you come with me to my house, we will have a nice evening and I will make sure your passport is at the office tomorrow. What do you think?"

I was so scared I couldn't think at all, other than about exactly what he wanted to do to me at his house. I clicked into Allison mode. *What's another night of abuse if it's my last night here, and if it gets me away from all this?* The other options were to stay and live a life of fear, be killed by Sasha and his men if I testified, or be arrested and go to jail if I didn't. I looked at Istvan and nodded, asking only if I could change first. I'm sure he imagined I was going to put on something sexy for him, like the little prostitute I was, but all I did was go to the bathroom and put some cream inside and outside of my vagina, hop-ing to ease the pain I was still in, and that I knew I'd be put through again in some way. Then we left out the front door of the apartment. Now I hoped that one of the cars would see me and follow me, but for the first time in days, they weren't there.

We drove about an hour away from Csepel Island to the Pest side of the city, where Istvan lived in an apartment with his mother, who was old and couldn't hear well. In his bedroom, he got undressed, revealing a hairy belly. Then he ripped my clothes off of me, threw me on his bed, turned me over and entered me hard from behind. I refused to show him my pain; I just wanted it to be over so I could get my passport.

But he wanted more than just that. I endured three more rounds, each punctuated by him smoking a cigarette in between. All I could do was try my best to pretend I was Allison and to picture my safe place—the beautiful field of flowers—but it was almost impossible. He kept talking to me, insulting me and using the dirtiest words I'd ever heard in Hungarian.

Finally, after more than five hours, he'd had enough. He pushed me off the bed and onto the ground. "Get your shit together, get dressed and get out of my house. Don't ever tell anybody about this or I'll kill you. Do you understand?" I nodded. I pulled on my clothes and ran out of the apartment and into the street. It was too late for buses to be running so I started walking. I eventually lay down on a bench in a bus shelter and waited until the first bus came at 6 a.m.

At home in my apartment, I showered and put on more cream to ease the pain. Then I took some painkillers and lay down for a few hours. At noon, I went to the post office. I passed an old church on the way, and for the first time in my life, I talked to God.

"Are you watching this?" I asked. "Can you hear me? Why are you doing this to me?"

Then I apologized for what a terrible, bad girl I was, and began begging. *Please, please. I need to get out of here.*

My passport was there, in my real name; I would never know if Istvan had helped or if what I'd endured at his hands was for nothing. I called for a cab to the airport at 3 a.m., and put a small amount of cash in an envelope for Zoli, plus the money I owed to my friend at the TV station with a note. I didn't leave anything for Bianka—I thought I had time. I had almost $2,000 left to bring with me to Canada, along with the invitation letter I'd received from Maria. She'd let me know that I could be asked at the border to show that I had enough money to be a visitor for six months without working. It wasn't even close to enough, but it was something. Then I dragged my suitcase over the rooftop and out the back door of the other building so neither the mafia car nor the cop car could see me, if they were even there. I was a bundle of nervous energy, filled with fears: fear of being arrested, fear that Natasa would find me, fear that Elek and János had been let out on bail and would be waiting for me at the airport, and fear that I would encounter Istvan. I wouldn't be able to relax until I was back up above the clouds. Then I still had to get through Canadian border security, get a visitor visa stamped in my passport, get to Maria's house and start working—illegally.

At the airport, I faced an unexpected challenge: Air Canada pilots had just gone on strike and all the airline's flights were cancelled until further notice. Luckily, after a couple hours of uncertainty about whether I would be able to leave, I was put on a different flight to London. I buckled myself into my seat on the plane, sweaty and nauseous. I looked out the window and thought I saw a police car on the tarmac. I pictured it coming to get me, of being dragged off the plane in handcuffs. I bit my nails until they bled, and only stopped when I felt the plane start to move. Even as we taxied out to the runway, I pictured the police car chasing us. It was only once we were through the grey, rain-filled clouds that I finally exhaled. And then I said goodbye to my homeland—the place I'd once belonged, but which had betrayed me in so many ways, and which I had betrayed too.

In London it was complete chaos, with Air Canada passengers stranded everywhere. There were lots of announcements but I couldn't understand a thing. Everyone looked stressed. Some people were yelling at the staff. I was so relieved to have made it this far that nothing could bother me, and I was glad to at least have my suitcase, although I wished I had packed some food. I was hungry, but I had to save the money I had with me to show at customs and to start my new life in Canada. I watched airline staff run around, looking for passengers and handing them some papers. Then the passengers would leave in groups. This went on for hours, and I started to worry that I would be stuck here with no place to sleep and no food to eat. I bought a phone card and called Maria to let her know I was held up in London, since she was picking me up at the airport in Toronto. I called my mom to let her know I was safe. I called Julius just to say hi. Then I found a seat in the food court, and began people-watching to distract myself. I saw travellers stuffing their faces with big, fat juicy burgers, chocolate puddings, and sandwiches, and it made me even hungrier. I also noticed how much food they were leaving behind on their trays, not even bothering to throw it away. I decided to help the airport and myself at the same time. I began clearing trays, snatching some fries, a fruit cup, some Coke and half a burger for myself.

I spent that night in the airport. The next day—with the help of a fellow Hungarian passenger who translated between the airline staff and me—I was sent to a hotel paid for by the airline. At first, haunted by the terrible things that had happened to me in the motels in Toronto, I was scared to be in a hotel room alone, but by the second night, I was able to enjoy the experience a bit. There was a buffet in the restaurant downstairs, and in the room I was able to rest and watch TV. I called Maria again to let her know I was still delayed. It was good to hear her voice and to know she was waiting for me, ready to help me make a fresh start. Then I updated my mom. I spent four nights in the hotel, and then finally I got a flight to Toronto. I was happy to be headed to my new life, but also sad to leave the little bubble of hotel life for whatever reality awaited me in Canada.

On the plane, my fears ramped up again. What if customs deported me? What if I got arrested? I thought about God again, and decided to ask for help. I put my hands together and prayed. *Please help me to get into Canada. I promise on my mom's life that I will be good. I promise you that I will volunteer and help pick up the garbage on the streets; I will help anyone and everyone. Would you please just give me a second chance? I promise I will prove myself to you. I will not let you down. I'm sorry for all my terrible choices.*

It was a turbulent flight—so bumpy that many people put their hands together and prayed for a safe landing. I was praying for a whole new life.

———

Immigration was a mob scene. All the officers looked tired, so I lined up in front of the one that looked the most tired, the one least likely to question me. When it was my turn, she asked me the purpose of my trip, and I said "visitor," and held out the invitation letter Maria had faxed me. Then I smiled a big smile and said, "CN Tower, Niagara Falls!" She glanced at my passport, stamped it, wrote a letter *V* on it and a six-month expiry date. She didn't even ask to see my money. On the other side of the exit doors, by the baggage carousel, I dropped to my knees and kissed the floor like I pictured a Muslim arriving at Mecca would do. *Thank you, God!*

Part IV | FREEDOM

26 | Getting Help

THERE WERE FRESH FLOWERS by my bed at Maria's house, and I looked to them for comfort when I awoke from the nightmares that now plagued me—of Elek chasing me, of Tony forcing himself on me, of calling for help but no one hearing me. Maria was a good cook, and made familiar foods for me, but I had trouble putting on weight. I didn't know what post-traumatic stress disorder was at the time, let alone how to treat it, but I know now that I was suffering from it. I did my best to distract myself with work and adjusting to life in Toronto.

At Lucky's, the work was easy—I danced and cleaned for the first month until Beatrix asked me if I wanted to learn to be a "shooter girl," which meant passing around trays of alcohol shots to guys and getting lots of tips. Soon, I was behind the bar with her, which was sometimes fun. The club was getting much busier, but it still had the feeling of being small and much safer than Fantasia or Temptations. I never saw any of the girls from my group and could only assume they'd been put into the hands of other agents, through Tony, now that Elek and János were jailed in Hungary. The money wasn't nearly the same as what I'd made at Fantasia, but at least I got to keep all but a fair cut for the club. I set what I could aside to eventually send to Zoli, but it was never very much.

Zoli and I spoke only once on the phone, and he said that the mafia car and the unmarked police car had disappeared from around our apartment, and my mom hadn't received any more threatening phone calls demanding money. I didn't ask if the police had come looking for me when I missed my court date—if he didn't mention it, then it must have happened when he wasn't home. I didn't call home anymore after that. I just couldn't handle knowing about any troubles there—like if Bianka came for her money or the police contacted my mom—when I had so much weighing on me here: I could be discovered as an illegal worker; I could run out of time on my visitor visa before I could save enough money to give Zoli; I could discover that I wasn't able to make ends meet in Toronto. I wanted to stay in Canada forever, but I had no idea if that was possible. I had escaped the agency and the terror of that life, but I didn't have enough security or stability in my new life to even begin processing all that had happened to me, let alone why.

I began to find the hour-and-a-half commute from Maria's to the club too taxing, so I asked around for another place to live. The day manager at Lucky's offered me the couch at her apartment in exchange for a bit of rent, which I gratefully accepted. It was in the Jane and Finch area, and I had no idea that it was a neighbourhood known for gangs, drugs and gun violence. My language barrier, and perhaps the violence I had already endured, put me in a bubble, and I wasn't aware of my surroundings. I routinely passed by groups of what many might consider to be intimidating men, but as long as they didn't look like the men who had taken advantage of me, I wasn't scared. One night, I passed by a group of guys wearing red bandanas and I smiled at them. Later, I found out that they were members of the notorious west-coast gang called The Bloods. They smiled back.

I had changed inside. I was frightened of things I shouldn't have been, like taking taxis, but then I wasn't scared of things I should have been scared of, like running into the gang. My "normal" fear radar no longer worked because the people who had hurt me the most weren't scary-looking gang members, they were people I should have been able to trust: a female HR recruiter for a babysitting agency, a guy I knew from home who'd been in the army, and people in police and customs uniforms—public servants. I had to figure out who I was now, and if I could ever be normal again.

A few more months went by and I worked as hard as I could, but there was never quite enough for rent, transportation and food. I survived my first Canadian winter by putting plastic bags inside a pair of worn boots I bought at a thrift store, and made it through my first Christmas alone. Everyone had warned me about Canadian winters, but it wasn't possible to truly understand exactly how cold it got and how long it lasted until I experienced it myself. It was gruelling. That winter was the worst in twenty years, and the mayor called in the army to remove the snow.

I saw Julius from time to time—we'd meet up for a walk or for a coffee—but when he told me he planned to go back to school to become a police officer, I told him it was best that he not be associated with me in any way. He reluctantly agreed. After all, I'd fled criminal charges in Hungary, I was working in Canada on a visitor visa, and for all I knew I would soon be an illegal immigrant, because my visa was going to run out soon and I didn't have plans to go back home. A couple of girls at the club suggested I apply for refugee status, but I would need a lawyer to help me do that, which I couldn't afford, nor could I trust I would find one who would believe my story. I had to consider going somewhere else, but the only neighbouring country was the United States, and everyone said the border was impossible to get across. I had no connections there, or anywhere except in Toronto, so I stayed put. In March 1999, my status changed from "visitor" to "illegal alien," and I held shame in my heart about it. Fear of being arrested—the same fear I'd had when working for the agency—returned and made me feel anxious. I didn't know how I would ever be able to change my status, get a good job or build a solid foundation for a real life. I tried to stay focused on day-to-day tasks and hope things would work out somehow.

Over time, my English improved, and I could understand about 30 percent of what customers said to me. I knew every kind of beer and alcohol there was, and the rest of my English came from watching *Friends* reruns late at night when I got home. I was never home early enough on a Thursday to watch the current season, but I could decipher the entertainment magazine headlines in the grocery store and I couldn't wait to find out what happened to Ross and Rachel's relationship. I still dreamed of the day when I'd be in my own apartment with the big, colourful mugs I loved so much. I spoke English as much as I could when I went to the grocery store and pharmacy, and when I rode the bus. Although I had changed a lot, becoming more introverted and quiet, there was still a little bit left of the outgoing TV station interviewer in me, and I wasn't shy about talking to anyone.

I couldn't yet write anything in English, which kept me from preparing a résumé and getting a second job, but in the meantime, Sergei promoted me to head bartender when Beatrix took a position in another club. I loved being given more responsibilities, like cashing out at the end of the night and making the schedule for the waitresses. It was empowering, and I was able to make a bit more money. Unlike Elek, Sergei was good to me and treated me with respect. I brought him his coffee every morning, as he liked to sit and read the paper at his desk before all the dancers and clients started arriving. I spent a few minutes with him then, teaching myself to read

English. Though his business wasn't an admirable one, I was so grateful to have a job there.

One morning, he showed me the headline of the paper he was reading: PROJECT ALMONZO RAIDS TORONTO NIGHTCLUBS, STRIP CLUBS. I understood every word except *Almonzo*. It was the name the police gave the operation, Sergei told me.

"We're going to have to be very careful, Allison," he said. "They're arresting illegal workers." I nodded, immediately tense. He gave me the newspaper to read, but I needed a dictionary and more time, so I asked to take it home with me. Working through the article line by line, I learned that police and immigration officers were busting nightclubs all over the city. More than eighty people had been charged, including a few dancers, and several clubs had been either closed temporarily or shut down completely. Now investigators were following suspects to Hungary, Romania, Bulgaria and Mexico to watch them recruit women to come to Canada to work as exotic dancers, housecleaners or babysitters. The operation had begun a little over a year ago, in June 1998, right in the middle of my time with the agency. I wondered if it had been behind the bust at Fantasia.

As I decoded each sentence and matched it up to my own story, my heart pounded in my chest. On the one hand, I felt a sense of victory that something was being done to put guys like Elek and János out of work. On the other hand, when I read that dancers were being arrested, charged and even held in custody, it frightened me. I read through the charges and realized that I could have faced all of them—and still could: being found in a common "bawdy house," a Canadian legal term that Sergei said meant *brothel*, "living off the avails of prostitution," "performing an indecent act," forgery, and illegally entering and working in Canada. But what stood out for me the most was the way the journalist pointed out the unfairness of criminalizing people who were really victims of exploitation. Seeing it there in black and white made it hit me: I had been *exploited*. I had been a victim—just like Christine, who I'd met that night at Sergei's, had tried to convince me.

But that was in the past, and there wasn't anything I could do about it anyway, except deal with my present situation. I didn't want to get arrested, and neither did anyone else at the club, so we established a code to use if anyone suspected that we were going to be busted. Sergei would have the DJ announce playfully, "The sky is really cloudy today!" and that would be the cue for any of us at risk of arrest to run out the back door. I was back to feeling on edge, like I had when I was working for Elek and when I was back in Budapest. I could never let my guard down.

Months went by and it was almost winter again before I heard the DJ announce the state of the skies. I dropped the cloth I was using and ran outside into the cold night wearing only a halter top, a miniskirt and high-heeled sandals. I went into the Greek restaurant next door and hid in the bathroom, trying to warm up under the hand dryer. Eventually, the DJ came over to let me know it was a false alarm and that I could go back. There were three more false alarms over the next few weeks, and I knew I couldn't take the anxiety much longer. As the world's calendar approached the start of a new millennium, I couldn't help but reflect: I was twenty-two years old, I worked in a strip club, and though I wasn't a stripper anymore, I had nothing to my name, not even a bank account. As I looked ahead, I felt pretty down about the state of my life.

I had heard from some of the girls at the club that there was a Hungarian neighbourhood downtown with Hungarian stores and restaurants, so I explored and found a hair salon close by that was hiring. I got a job sweeping the floor, and was soon trained in how to wash hair by the warm, caring and vibrant owners, Maryann and Eve, who told me they hired me because my shoes were clean. My instincts told me that somehow they knew I needed them as much as they needed me. They turned a blind eye toward my illegal-worker status and paid me in cash. They weren't Hungarian, but they had a lot of Hungarian clients, so I was able to practise my English and speak my mother tongue as well. I worked there during the day and at Lucky's at night, and after a month I had enough money to move closer to the salon. I left Jane and Finch and moved to a tiny studio apartment in a beautiful neighbourhood with lots of trees called the Annex. The place was unfurnished, but I quickly filled it up with treasures I scavenged from the ends of people's driveways: a couch still wrapped in its original plastic, a microwave, a side table, a reading lamp, plates, cups and utensils—I simply couldn't believe what people threw out at the curb in this city. Now that I was paying for my own apartment, it was harder to save money for whatever my next step would be, let alone to send back home, but if I didn't think too far into the future and forgot about the fact that I was in Canada illegally, I was actually starting to feel happy. I had a sense of purpose and belonging, and more energy—like when I was younger, before I got into all the debt. The salon was a great place to be, and I felt like I had big sisters there looking after me. Soon, Eve taught me how to cut hair, and before too long I had my first customer.

Lazlo was an older, fatherly sort of Hungarian man with kind brown eyes and a big, old-fashioned moustache. He agreed to have an amateur cut his hair, and said that it could easily grow back if I messed it up. We laughed, which helped me relax enough to take the scissors and start snipping. As I was working away carefully, he made small talk, asking how long I'd been in Canada and if I'd come with my family. These kinds of questions made me nervous, since I had so much to hide. Then he asked a very pointed question, which caught me off-guard.

"How did you get a work permit to be here?" He sounded genuinely curious.

"It's complicated," I said, hoping he wouldn't press me further.

"Is something wrong?" he whispered. "Do they not treat you well here? You know there are laws against exploiting workers, right?" I didn't know that.

"They are amazing here," I said. Eve and Maryann were mentors to me, generous and respectful. "But my previous employers weren't so nice."

"Were they Hungarian?" he asked. It was as though he knew, or at least had a sense that I'd gotten mixed up with the wrong kind of people at some point. I didn't know if I could trust him, nor why I would share any of my story with him, so I changed the subject to the weather. I'd learned that all Canadians—newcomers or those born here—loved to talk about the weather.

I finished the cut and the man passed me a $10 bill for my tip, along with his business card. His name read Lesley Lakos, and he explained that Lesley was an Anglicized version of Lazlo. Under his name was his title: "investigative translator."

"I work for the police and immigration," he said. "So keep this in case you ever need anything, or if you'd just like a friend to go for coffee with." My instincts told me I could trust him, but still I was timid. What if he reported me to the police? For the rest of the day, all I thought about was if I had done anything to put myself or Eve and Maryann in jeopardy.

About a week later, Lazlo returned to the salon and asked for me. "I was in the neighbourhood, and I'm going to a Hungarian restaurant down the street," he said. "Do you want to come with me, for schnitzels?"

I wanted to know more about the work he did before I shared anything with him, and I was quite hungry, so I agreed. At the restaurant, the familiar smells, tastes, language, and Lazlo's easy-going nature made me relax quickly. We chatted about Toronto and Budapest, comparing notes—he'd been in Canada for many years. He told me about how so many Hungarians and former Eastern Bloc people came to Canada for jobs that didn't really exist, and then struggled to make ends meet while they figured out how to stay longer. I could tell he was trying to gain my trust by telling me about himself, and it was working. He seemed truly kind, and my gut feeling was good. He had a gut feeling about me too.

"Can we meet for coffee tomorrow?" he asked kindly. "I think you have a story to tell. I can just listen, or maybe I can help."

I did need help: to get my life together, to heal from my trauma, and to take some steps forward to legal status, so I agreed. Over coffee the next day, after work, I opened up about how I came to Canada. I couldn't bring myself to provide all the details—I was still so ashamed, and felt responsible for a lot of what had happened—but I shared what I could.

Lazlo listened intently as I spoke. I glossed over the details and stuck to the basic facts. I didn't want to become emotional with someone I barely knew. I still hadn't cried over *everything* that happened and I didn't want to start now, in a café.

"How did you come to be working in the salon?" he asked.

"I met some people in a club who helped me get away from the agents and back to Budapest, but the agents found out and followed me there, threatening my life and the lives of my family. I escaped back here and managed to get a visitor visa, but now it's expired, so I'm a criminal, working illegally. I don't know how to get out of this mess." Telling him had left me completely drained, and yet there was so much more. I kept it inside for the time being.

Lazlo reached his hand across the table and touched mine gently. His face was both concerned and compassionate.

"Have you heard about Project Almonzo? The police and immigration have been raiding clubs and bars, trying to find underage and illegal workers."

"Yes," I said, nodding. "And I'm so anxious all the time. It's just a matter of time before they bust Lucky's."

"I am the main translator for the operation. The police are not trying to throw you girls in jail—the project was actually created to rescue you. Do you have any idea how many girls are in your shoes?" He pulled a newspaper clipping out of his pocket, unfolded it and gave it to me. It was from a national newspaper. "Can you read in English?" he asked. I said I could, although it was still hard for me. I had to ask him to help me at some points. The article explained that another club had been busted as part of Project Almonzo, and that owners were charged with everything from sexual assault, prostitution-related offences, and "procuring foreign women."

It made me think about Tony. I continued reading about the bust, which sounded exactly like how it had happened at Fantasia. I imagined Tony one day being arrested, and that image made me feel good. I was relieved to read that while many of the dancers had been charged, they were also offered help—food and clothing. Translators had been on site with the police during the bust.

"Were you one of the translators?" I asked Lazlo, looking up from the article. He nodded. The last line was a quote from a lead investigator, Mike Josifovic of the Toronto Police Service's Morality Citywide Investigative Unit. He spoke of the dancers and sex workers—girls just like me—saying that they are not criminals, they are victims of exploitation and needed to be treated as victims. There was a phone number where he could be reached if anyone who had a similar story needed help.

"If you want to come forward," Lazlo said gently, "I will support you. You won't be deported."

It was hard to trust after having my trust broken so many times, by so many people, but in my heart, I knew coming forward to tell my story was the right thing to do. This time I would be okay.

27 | Stepping Forward

THE NEXT EVENING, after my shift at the salon, Lazlo accompanied me to the police station where he'd made an appointment for me to speak with Detective Josifovic, with himself as translator.

We were shown into an interview room with a couple of chairs and a small couch. My palms were sweating and I bit my nails. Lazlo patted me on the shoulder to calm me down. A few moments later, the detective came in. He was dressed in plain clothes: a light-green and brown checkered shirt, jeans and running shoes. He appeared to be in his late thirties, and had wavy brown hair, big hazel eyes and a goatee. There was nothing intimidating about him whatsoever. I relaxed a little. He put his hand out and smiled.

"I'm Detective Josifovic, but please call me Mike. Thank you for being here."

"I'm Allison," I said, using my stage name, just in case.

"Can I get you anything, Allison?" he asked slowly, so I could understand perfectly. "Some water?" I nodded and he poured a glass from a carafe on the table.

"Before we begin," he said, "I want you to understand that you are about to give a legal statement, so everything must be the truth. If you ever have to go to court and it is found out that anything you said is a lie, you could face criminal charges."

I nodded. I understood.

"So please tell me your name again."

"Timea. Timea Eva Nagy." Then I offered my real date of birth without being asked, June 5, 1977.

We went through everything slowly and gently, starting with my background and what had led me to need money so badly, and how I'd applied to the agency. The questions were like the ones I was asked when I was interviewed in Hungary, but the atmosphere was completely different. Instead of being under arrest, I was seen and treated as a victim—someone who needed help, and who could help the police too.

Though I had shared my story a few times now, it was still so painful to say everything aloud. I felt shame, guilt and embarrassment, as well as confusion and a bit of anger—mostly at myself. Recounting my story made me relive it and all the feelings I had felt at the time, as well as the ones I'd shut down. Whenever I felt overwhelmed, Mike or Lazlo would tell me I was doing great. Before I knew it, it was after midnight. We'd been in the interview room for over six hours, with just a few short smoke and bathroom breaks. Mike asked me if I could come back the next day and if we could continue. I'd only gotten to the point of leaving Fantasia and going to Chris the DJ's house. There was still so much more. Mike assured me that I was not going to be arrested. I agreed to return.

The next morning, Mike once again met Lazlo and me at the front entrance of the big police headquarters downtown. It wasn't the same station I'd been taken to after the bust at Fantasia, but it was just as impressive. I hadn't paid too much attention in the darkness the night before, but I appreciated it now in broad daylight. Lazlo went inside to say hello to some other officers, and Mike suggested he and I go across the road to a coffee shop called Tim Hortons, which he told me was named after a famous hockey player. I'd seen the franchises all over the city but had never gone into one, which Mike couldn't believe. As soon as we walked through the door I was in love. It smelled like fresh coffee and doughnuts.

"Tim Hortons coffee and doughnuts are practically our national dish!" Mike said with a laugh, and then showed me how to hold the cup from base to lid to avoid getting burned. I liked him more and more. He spoke slowly so I could understand, was warm and funny, and he didn't treat me differently after all he'd heard. There was no judgment. I knew he believed everything I told him.

Back at the station we continued the interview for several more hours. Some details were difficult to get through, and I skipped or held back on some of them—like how I was raped by the Hungarian police, and some of the stuff Tony had done to me. I could share those details later if I had to. It was hard to talk to Mike through Lazlo, even though I liked Lazlo too. There was also another detective in the room, as well as a camera, which triggered feelings of vulnerability and the memory of being constantly watched.

At the end, Mike asked me if I'd like to see a doctor—he must have been concerned for my physical well-being after learning of how I'd been starved, sleep deprived and exposed to no end of sexually transmitted diseases—but I declined. I didn't have a health card, but moreover, I just couldn't imagine talking through my "sexual history" with anyone else. Some other time, maybe. I wore a heavy blanket of shame on my shoulders, and it was hard to shake off.

"We do need to go to immigration for an interview, though," Mike told me. "We plan to lay charges against Tony Verudi, the owner of Temptations, and we also want to raid Lucky's. We will need your help on both matters, and we will arrange a special visa for you to stay in Canada because you will be a witness in a court process."

I was happy to hear that charges would be laid against Tony, and that I might get to stay in Canada legally, but I was conflicted about helping the police raid Lucky's. I'd been treated so well there, and I liked Sergei, his grandmother and all the staff. What would happen to them? After all the times I'd been betrayed, I didn't want to become the betrayer.

At immigration, I was met by a very kind and understanding officer named Mario Catenaccio. Like Mike, he believed everything I told him and wanted to help. After the interview, Mike drove me home, and as we said goodbye he gave me his card with his pager number.

"I'll let you know when we get the next appointment at immigration, and I'll call you back to talk more about Lucky's, but in the meantime, you can call me anytime, for anything. Understand?"

I nodded and thanked him. I went inside and sat down to think long and hard about what was being asked of me. I thought about my mom—the police officer—and what she would tell me to do. I had to help the police, and see the big picture and the issues—not just think about my own friends.

A couple of weeks later, Mike took me to see a psychiatrist for an assessment, a resource he helped me access through Victim Services. He worried about all I'd gone through and how it was affecting me, and he wanted me to be supported through what would likely be a lengthy legal process. During the session, the doctor asked me— through a translator—all about my childhood, which brought up a lot of painful memories. I thought that the purpose of the appointment was to discuss what had happened in Canada, not before, and I didn't feel prepared to go into watching my parents fight, dealing with the poverty and, ultimately, my father abandoning us. I hadn't even real-ized that those things could have affected me. But the doctor probed so I talked, and as I did, my anxiety mounted. Eventually we got to my life in Canada—the dancing, starvation and sleep deprivation; the threats, the assaults, the unwanted sex. Being watched and controlled, and also being so alone in a new country. And then, finally, the worst part: what happened when I returned to Hungary, at the airport. Sharing that made me feel totally exposed, like I was being raped all over again.

By the time we finished the two-hour session I was nauseous. The doctor said we'd meet again to talk, but I didn't want to. I didn't see how it could help when I felt so much worse instead of better. I left his office and took the stairs instead of the elevator. My legs felt as if they weighed a hundred pounds, and I collapsed in the stairwell and cried like I'd never cried before. I heaved and gasped for air as tears flowed from my eyes, down my face and onto my T-shirt and jeans. All my pain, suffering and loneliness came up from deep inside. I could feel my entire body shaking, and I couldn't make it stop. I wiped my nose on my sleeve and tried to slow my breathing. I just wanted to go home and curl up in bed, but it was an hour by subway and bus. Mike had said I could call him for a ride, but I didn't want to see him or anyone. On the bus, I turned my face to the window and let more tears fall. I could see my reflection and I hardly recognized myself.

That day changed me. It was hard to function at work, and I started slacking off at both the salon and at Lucky's, showing up late for shifts, neglecting my regular duties and being less friendly with the customers. Mike had said to call him whenever I needed help, but what could he do about my sadness? It was so deep I felt like I was drowning in it—water so deep and dark that I couldn't feel the bottom. I called him sometimes just to hear his voice—he was always calm and made me feel safe—but I kept our conversation to surface-level topics, like how things were going at the salon or what his kids were up to. Our friendship helped, but it couldn't save me.

I got a horrible tooth infection and could hardly eat anything for weeks. Maryann and Eve sent me to their dentist, with their credit card.

He said I had six badly infected cavities at the back, and that I should
have come in two years ago. He couldn't even imagine what the last
two years of my life had been like. It would cost close to $2,000 to treat
these infections, so I asked if he could just pull my teeth out instead.

"You're too young, Timea," he said.

"I can't owe that much money to anyone," I said firmly. I just
couldn't, not after everything I'd been through.

So he pulled them all out.

Finally, about three months later, the time for my immigration
interview came. I was riddled with anxiety. Because of my experience in Hungary and all the fear that Elek and János had instilled
in me, I expected to walk into a room full of monsters. Instead, with
Mike by my side, I walked into a room of serious but welcoming
faces. There were members of the Royal Canadian Mounted Police
(RCMP), the Ontario Provincial Police (OPP), Canada Customs and
Revenue, Canadian Citizenship and Immigration, and a translator.
Mario was one of the immigration officers, and he had his partner
with him, a female officer I'd never met. She introduced herself and
explained that she'd be leading the interview.

The questions were thorough. The female officer was quite tough,
and the way she questioned me made me feel small, like I was lying,
but Mario was softer. I couldn't tell if anyone believed my story so I
kept looking at Mike for reassurance. I said that I was sorry for breaking the law and that I would do anything to make up for it. No one
seemed to understand why I didn't just stay in Hungary, so I shared
how I was arrested there, and how if I testified against Elek and János,
Sasha would find and kill me and my family, and how if I didn't I
would go to jail as part of their ring. I couldn't talk about the rapes
by the officers because I hadn't told Mike about that, and I didn't
want to lose his trust. Besides, it didn't matter to my case, only to me.

A couple of weeks later, I got a call from Mario asking me to come
into the immigration office. He couldn't tell me anything over the
phone. At the office, I was fingerprinted and photographed, and I was

sure I was about to be deported, but then he handed me papers that said, "Temporary Work Permit." He explained that the police were going to arrest Tony soon, which meant that he'd be on trial within the next few months. I was being granted a special status to stay in the country for the length of his court case—and I could work *legally*. I wouldn't have access to health care and I couldn't go to school, but what I did have was more time to build my life and hopefully apply for permanent status. I was beyond grateful.

I surrendered my passport to Mario, as was protocol, and he gave me an identity card to carry with me instead. This meant I couldn't leave the country, but I was free to travel anywhere within it. Two years of suffering, running and hiding had finally come to an end. Anxiety floated away and my heart lifted in my chest for the first time in ages. I smiled broadly and hugged Mario hard. What lay ahead, I didn't know, but for the moment I could celebrate. I called Mike and we went to Tim Hortons.

On February 24, 2000, Mike called to let me know that Tony had been arrested.

"We carried out a search of his home, his office and the whole club, and while I can't tell you everything we found, I can tell you that we found copies of both your original and your fake passport, as well as your first work permit and the second one. We also found dozens more passports of other girls. He is in custody and his bail hearing is in a couple of days." Mike said more, but I couldn't understand everything—partly because of my still-limited English, but also because my emotions were so high.

"What do I do now?" I asked. My heart was racing.

"Nothing—we just wait for the bail hearing. Your safety is not in danger. There is nothing you need to do. I just wanted you to know."

The next day, the front page of a Toronto newspaper featured a picture of Mike taking Tony out of the club in handcuffs. Just seeing him again scared me and brought back a flood of painful memories, including all our sexual interactions, but I also felt a sense of satisfaction that our roles were reversed: now he was powerless and controlled instead of me.

Tony was charged for multiple offences between April 6, 1998, when Natasa first presented me with my agency contract back in Budapest, and August 16, 1998, when I escaped. The charges included one count of "attempt to live on the avails of prostitution," one count of "keeping a common bawdy house," two counts of "exercising control," and three counts of sexual assault against me. Tony had assaulted me so many more times than the three for which he was being charged, but I couldn't waste my energy caring about the details. The most important thing was that charges had been laid. I felt validated, but also exposed—especially when I learned a few days later that he had been granted bail. What if he tried to find me? I quickly shrugged off that worry. I knew I could call Mike.

All I could do was put one foot in front of the other until the trial, when Tony would be convicted and go to jail. Then I could only hope there would be a way for me to stay in Canada.

28 | Striving for Justice

PROJECT ALMONZO CONTINUED to carry out raids on clubs all over the city into the summer of 2000, including Charlie T's, a club right next door to Lucky's. Sergei and my co-workers worried that we would be next, but I knew it for a fact. Mike, Mario and a few of their colleagues had asked me to help them plan the raid by providing inside information about how the club operated, what time of day they should carry it out, and who they should look to arrest. I didn't think they would find anything too bad—Lucky's was nothing like Tony's club, let alone Fantasia—but then, I didn't know everything that went on there. For the last while, my focus had been away from dancing and on bartending, which I was getting quite good at, earning extra money in tips.

I felt guilty about my new job as a mole—especially since Sergei had been so good to me, and the money I earned there was most of what I lived on—but my greater loyalty was now to the police and immigration officers who were helping me stay in Canada and working so hard to break up the criminal rings that were exploiting young women like me.

Mike didn't tell me when the raid would be carried out, but he did say that he would stage my arrest in order to protect me from ever being found out by Sergei, or anyone else. One Sunday afternoon in July, I arrived at the club and began setting up the bar as I always did, cutting up limes and laying out cocktail napkins. About ten girls arrived to start dancing, and a couple of drivers ordered drinks. A few regular customers showed up, followed by a big group of construction workers. They ordered a round of drinks, and some of them went into the VIP rooms where they ordered more. Soon after, some guys in suits came in, and then another group in street clothes. It was getting really busy, really fast, which wasn't usual for a Sunday. I had to jump in to serve tables because there weren't enough waitresses.

I was on the phone asking the manager to call in extra staff when the front door was kicked wide open. The surprised security guard jumped out of the way and about two dozen uniformed and plain-clothes police officers rushed in, shouting, "Police! No one move! This is a raid!" They ran in single-file and spread themselves all around the club, two of them heading straight for the DJ booth to cut the music and turn all the lights on. The DJ put his hands up, and the girls on stage screamed and huddled together. Several men at the tables stood up and tried to leave but they were stopped. My feet were frozen to the ground as I watched the scene unfold. I could hear my manager through the phone, frantically asking what was happening, but all I could say was, "We're being busted." I hung up. Even though I'd known the raid was coming at some point, I got caught up in the panic of the situation. It was like watching a scene in a movie I'd already seen before and still feeling scared, even though I knew it ended well.

I saw Mario run by me with a jacket that said "IMMIGRATION," and then Mike with a jacket that said "POLICE." Both of them were holding handcuffs. To my great surprise, all the construction workers and the guys in suits stood up and pulled out badges, which hung around their necks on chains under their clothing, as well as hand-cuffs. I never would have guessed that they were undercover cops. They must have dumped the drinks I made them, although they still tipped me. What had they done in the VIP rooms? Tried to get the girls to talk, I imagined.

The officers escorted the DJ out of the booth and got all the girls out of the change room and the VIP rooms, lining them up on the stage like I'd been lined up on the stage at Fantasia. I could feel their fear. Every man in the place, from customer to driver to DJ, was told to line up along one wall. It was a scene of organized chaos, and I stayed off to the side of it, behind the bar. I looked for Mike but I couldn't find him yet. A few moments later, I saw him come out of a VIP room and look around. Our eyes met and he winked, and then he called out in a tough voice, "You! You by the phone!" He pointed at me as he walked over swiftly. "Don't move." He grabbed me by the arm. Everyone I worked with looked over, feeling sorry for me. No one knew I was now on a legal work permit, so they all thought I was going to be deported. I saw Mario looking at me too, and he gave a quick wink.

"Are you in charge of the bar?" Mike asked. I nodded, my face grave. "Yes, sir."

"Step away from it, and sit at that table over there." He pointed to an empty table and I did as I was told. As I walked over to the table, I saw a couple of women wearing police jackets with "CRISIS WORKER" on the back talking to the girls. I wondered what they were saying, but I knew what the response would be from all the dancers. *We're working here because we want to be working here.* I knew from my own experience that they couldn't say anything else. They wouldn't reveal if they were underage, illegal aliens or being forced to do work they didn't want to do. If they did, they risked criminal charges, deportation and the loss of their livelihood. They wouldn't give up the names of their agents, or pimps, if they had them either. If they did that, their lives would be at risk.

Next, Sergei was pulled out of his office by two officers, pushed against a wall and patted down. They found a gun, which I wasn't expecting. I'd always thought of Lucky's as a somewhat innocent, sleepy kind of club. They handcuffed him and told him he was under arrest. Sergei showed no emotion or resistance; he just co-operated. I felt like I'd betrayed him and I was shaken up. Yet at the same time— with Mike and Mario there, and knowing that this was all part of an important plan—I reassured myself that it was the right thing.

Over the course of the next hour or so, I watched customers get arrested for possession of drugs and soliciting sex acts and be taken away in handcuffs. One dancer was arrested for carrying a weapon— a pocket knife—and for possession of heroin. Another had cocaine in her bag. I knew the girls to see them and say hello, but I had no idea what they were involved in other than dancing and taking clients into the VIP rooms. I honestly thought the bar was as clean as could be. Even after all this time, and all I'd seen, I was still naive. I watched a group of uniformed officers go upstairs to the storage room, along with a few of the officers in suits. They came back with a couple of boxes. Sergei was taken away then, and I found out later from newspaper reports that he was into weapons dealing and that those boxes were filled with guns or receipts for guns. I was shocked, but the discovery also alleviated some of my guilt. Sergei didn't only dress like a mafia guy, he was a mafia guy. I'd just been on his good side.

Mike came over and pretended to check my ID and arrest me. He took me out to a cruiser, but instead of driving me to the station, he took me to my apartment. As we drove away from the club, I said goodbye to my life there and vowed to leave it all behind forever.

After the raid, Lucky's closed for good, and I had to find a new night job right away. I couldn't earn enough just working at the salon and I didn't want to fall behind on my rent. That was the terrifying reality that had brought me to Canada in the first place! I quickly got a job pulling pints at an Irish pub right below the salon, and I easily found my place there amidst the music, fun crowds watching sports, and co-workers who got along really well. Staff meetings were more like family meetings, though nothing like the family meetings I'd been through with the agency.

To save even more money, I moved into a house with three other girls, all university students. It was the closest I would come to fulfilling my dream of living in an apartment like on *Friends*, but the girls were very busy with their classes and I worked so many shifts that I hardly saw them. Instead, I befriended a cat and took him in, naming him Mario after the immigration officer who helped me stay in Canada. I was getting comfortable in my new life.

One night after the pub closed, I was walking home when a guy stopped me a few blocks from my apartment. First he made a comment about my uniform, which was a kilt and a T-shirt with the pub logo on it, and I thought he was a customer. But then he leaned in close.

"You think you're through, huh?" he sneered. "You thought we wouldn't find you?" I felt my body go cold. "Consider this a friendly reminder to keep your mouth shut when you go to court. Tony is a good friend. You are fucking up his life." With that, he walked away, leaving me frozen to the pavement in fear.

I hurried home, frequently checking to make sure I wasn't being followed, and called Mike immediately. We met at the station an hour later and I gave a statement, but with only a vague description of the guy to go on, there wasn't much he could do. I began having nightmares again—dreams in which Tony, Elek, János, Sasha and the Hungarian police were all chasing me. I almost stopped sleeping altogether, choosing to work every shift I could instead.

By 2002, two years after Tony's arrest, there was still no news about his trial, but I was consumed by thoughts about what I would say on the stand. I worried about the blurriest part of my story—the part where I knew that the agency employed dancers, and where Natasa had encouraged me to try it out since it was so much more lucrative than babysitting. I hadn't agreed, but had I disagreed? Worse was that when I came back to Canada, I asked for an exotic dancing visa and knew that I would have to dance for a few days or a week when I first arrived, until a babysitting job was found. I didn't think I had been clear with Mike about that in my statement. I was too ashamed. I believed that if I'd agreed to dance, it made everything my fault. While Mike wholeheartedly believed that I was a victim, there was a part of me that still wasn't sure. I certainly wasn't a "perfect" victim, and this kept me up at night. What if I was discredited in the trial, and what if that meant that Tony would walk free? If that happened, I was sure Canada would send me back to Hungary. I had no idea what had happened to Elek or János, or even Sasha. For all I knew, they could be out of jail, waiting for me. And I still had outstanding charges.

What I longed for most during this time was a friend. I sometimes thought about calling Mike or Mario, just to talk, but I knew that they weren't really my friends, and I didn't want to cross a line. I liked the people I worked with at the pub, but I hadn't really connected with any of them in a way that would allow me to open up. Once in a while, I talked to God. I prayed that he would send me a friend.

My prayer was answered when I got a job interview at a tourist attraction called Medieval Times, down on the Canadian National Exhibition grounds by the waterfront. It was a football-field-sized arena set up as a castle where people went to eat a meal with their hands, watch a knights-in-armour jousting show and other medieval traditions. It was funny to me, since there was nothing at all medieval about the city of Toronto. Everything was so young here, compared to Europe. I did well in the interview and was hired to be a wench, a medieval waitress. The pay was good, and the job was full-time, which meant that I could leave both the pub and the salon and put all my energy into one gig. I ran down to a park by the lake and rolled on the grass, giggling. Then I found a pay phone and called Mike to tell him the good news. He sounded really proud of me, and he reminded me to call Mario too. Both of them had to know where I was at all times.

During that call, he gave me an update on Tony's case: the first court date was set for a year from now, in 2003. It was a long wait, and while I didn't like being in the limbo of a court process, I knew that, ultimately, it was good news. The more time I had in Canada, the more chance I had of making a real life here and maybe—just maybe— keeping it.

I felt like I fit in at Medieval Times—in our costumes, we were all pretending to be someone we weren't. Some of the people I worked with were aspiring actors or singers, so they easily put on a British accent. I was still working on my English and trying to sound more Canadian, but I loved the drama and musical aspects of the job; it reconnected me to my past working in TV, making videos and singing in chorus. My clothes were covered in grease by the end of every shift, but I didn't care. I got to see the show and be in a castle. It was a fun atmosphere, which helped me feel like my real age—twenty-four—instead of years and years older.

Eventually, I started to form friendships with my co-workers. Then a guy named Brad—a squire—asked me out on a date. That was a big step for me. I'd had my brief relationship with Julius, but since then, nothing. I'd had so many terrifying experiences with men that I didn't know if I could ever have a normal relationship, let alone sex, so I had to go slow. Brad and I took the bus together, went for walks and got to know each other. He was kind and respectful. It was nice to feel a bit normal, even though I knew I wasn't really. I didn't tell him my story for fear it would change how he felt about me.

Most of the staff members, including Brad, were around my age, but management tended to be a little older and more experienced. Everyone's favourite manager was Dan, who was in charge of the show. In his early thirties, he was not only mature but also gorgeous, with long blond hair. His voice was deep and dramatic—perfect for making all the announcements during the performance. He was a mentor to many, someone we could talk to at any time. His wife came to the show every so often, when she could get a babysitter for their two small children. He seemed like someone I might talk to, someday.

I knew deep down that I had a lot of stuff to work through, but I wasn't ready yet, and I didn't know where to start. Instead, I grew more trusting day by day, at my own pace. After a few months, Mario the cat and I moved in with Brad, into a sweet basement apartment in High Park. I bought a bicycle and started riding to work along the lakeshore path. We had friends, and a routine. He took me to his parents' farm in the country—the first time since going to Chris the DJ's house that I ever saw any part of Canada outside the city—and I fell in love with the big, open fields, red-brick farmhouses and roads that seemed to go on forever. It was also the first time I'd really experienced a family in Canada, and I fell in love with them too. I kept my story a secret so it wouldn't get in the way of them loving me back.

For the first time in a long time, since Ádám, I became emotionally attached to someone else. Though I couldn't fully let Brad in, I brought him in as much as I could. I felt like I was beginning to be normal.

But my story was always with me, and it was ongoing, because there were trial delays for all kinds of reasons—from paperwork issues to lawyers' schedules to Tony's health. Finally, a trial date was set for February 23, 2004. Suddenly, the bubble I'd been living in for almost five years burst. I was paranoid that I would be sent back to Hungary after the trial, and that I'd be discredited on the stand. All my confidence in myself and the life I'd built in Canada disappeared, and I reverted back to the unsure, frightened, sad Timea I'd been before. I could hardly concentrate on work, friendships or my relationship. I missed shifts at Medieval Times and had trouble managing my finances. I drifted away from Brad, telling him that my visa was going to expire and that I would probably be leaving. In the almost two years we'd been together, I'd not told him about my past, or about the trial. I didn't know where to begin, I didn't know how my story was going to end, and there was so much in the middle that I didn't fully understand. I could hardly hope that he would. With Mike, Lazlo and Mario, I'd been able to recount the facts of all that had happened to me, but not the feelings. Getting into the feelings would be like opening a giant can of worms.

Soon, Brad broke up with me, and he was quickly with another girl, a co-worker. I couldn't bear seeing them every day, so I quit my job. It was just before Christmas, and I was so distressed and felt so alone that I contemplated ending my life. What stopped me was the knowledge that Mike was counting on me for the trial. After that, I would have to see if there was a life for me that was worth living.

On the morning of the trial, I woke early and dressed as if I were going for a job interview, in black dress pants, a black turtleneck and a grey blazer, all of which I'd picked up at a second-hand store. I'd found the perfect pair of conservative black pumps there too, for $3. They had a small hole in the bottom, but I couldn't afford better and I hoped I'd only have to wear them once. No one would be looking at the bottom of my shoes.

Mike met me on the steps of the courthouse, which was a regular-looking office building near Sherway Gardens and Motel 27, where I'd been kept for more than two months. Temptations—the scene of the crimes Tony was about to be tried for—was somewhere in the area too, but I didn't know exactly where and I never tried to find it. I'd learned through the court process that Tony had changed the name. Maybe I'd drive by it one day, but right now the thought was still too traumatic.

Mario arrived next, and he and Mike put me in the hands of the Crown attorney and went to sit in the gallery. Both men cared about me genuinely, and had confidence in my testimony. Mike in particular felt the gravity of the proceedings—I was "his victim," and he had been with me since day one. He wanted victory as much as I did. The Crown attorney didn't seem to have the same passion for the case, nor the same confidence in me, although he was set to prosecute. We'd barely spent any time together in preparation, and it showed when I was on the stand. For hours that day and the next, Tony's defence lawyer shredded me to pieces. He called me a liar over and over again, accused me of making up the whole story so that I could stay in Canada, and suggested that I was mentally ill and that the whole case was a waste of taxpayers' money. The unprepared Crown attorney had virtually no comebacks. Mike and Mario watched, horrified and helpless. Tony sat in the accused box with a smirk on his face, while his brother sat in the gallery of the courtroom and made throat-slitting motions at me while I was on the stand, when no one was looking. I looked away from them and at Mike and Mario, who I knew believed me. The judge barely looked at me at all.

Tony was on the stand for two days after me, but I didn't attend. I didn't want to hear him lie and deny everything he'd done to me, not to mention all the other charges. He'd been exploiting girls like me for years. He had lots of pimps like Elek and János supplying him with strippers from all over the world and he was making a good living off of our forced labour, or so Mike told me his investigation had shown. But he also had a wife (a former dancer) and another dancer who worked for him testify as character witnesses, denying that he was capable of any type of exploitation or assault. I had no one to stand up for me.

The judgment was scheduled for two and a half weeks later, on March 8, 2004, but I couldn't go to court to hear the ruling because I had to work at the new job I'd just gotten. Mike promised he'd call me once the verdict was announced.

He called me after it was over and let me know that we'd lost. Tony had been acquitted of all charges. There had simply not been enough hard evidence, as I would come to learn is so often the reality in sexual assault cases. It's "he said, she said," or in my case, "They said, I said." Tony had walked out triumphant, likely right back into his regular work. I hung up the phone, utterly defeated, and with my future completely up in the air.

Mario encouraged me to apply for permanent residency status in Canada, since my temporary work permit would expire sixty days following the end of the trial. I had now been in Canada for almost six years, had fulfilled my duty to the Crown as a witness, learned English, and was supporting myself—I was a good candidate for permanent residency. He offered to help me fill out the basic paperwork, but I needed to get an immigration lawyer and was put on a legal aid wait list. I was in limbo, just surviving from day to day. I didn't know how much more I could take.

My Medieval Times manager called to invite me to the staff Christmas party. He told me Brad had moved on to another job and wouldn't be coming, so I said I would. I was glad to go and see my old friends and co-workers. At the party, I met a fun-loving guy named Wayne and we shared an instant attraction. We began dating, and our relationship quickly became serious. We moved in together and in such constant and close proximity, I soon realized that neither of us was at a particularly good time in our lives, and that Wayne had problems that were as deep as mine. I came to this conclusion not because we confided in one another but because I saw him struggle with depression and drug use. He could also be quite jealous and insecure. One day while I was out on a summer bike ride, he searched through my belongings and found all my court and immigration documents (my work permit had been given an extension while I waited for the results of the permanent residence application). I came home to find him sitting on the bed, head in hands, and my papers all around him. He stood up in a rage and began yelling at me, unable to cope with the truth about my life, let alone all my lies. I tried to explain and to apologize but he was too upset, and he left.

The next day I called him over and over again, but he didn't answer, so I stayed at my friend Rob's house for a night to give Wayne more time to calm down. The next morning, I went home; instantly, I knew something was wrong. The TV shelf was moved out from the wall and the cables were cut off, their ends hanging out. Mario the cat was crying and tried to bite my feet as I walked toward the back of the apartment, my heart in my throat. I found Wayne's body hanging from the shower curtain rod in the bathroom. I froze in horror, chills running through my entire body. I walked slowly back to the living room and called 911. When the operator asked what my emergency was, I could barely say the words. She asked me to check him for a pulse, but I knew I didn't need to.

I was traumatized. I took time off from work, and I wanted to call Mike but didn't feel I should. After all, the trial was over and I wasn't his victim anymore. In fact, I wasn't a victim at all—so it felt the judge had ruled when he let Tony walk free. If anything, people were victims of me—of all I had done, all the mistakes I'd made, my absolute foolishness and selfishness. The greatest proof of that was Wayne. I was responsible for his death.

I couldn't go back to the apartment I'd shared with Wayne, so I continued to stay with Rob. I either acted like a zombie or like a terrified kitten, and I was unable to work. I couldn't go into a bathroom alone and I didn't want to have a shower. I told Rob about the trial, and about Wayne, but nothing about all that led up to the trial—it would be too much for me to tell and for him to hear, I was sure. Rob called our co-worker Jessica to come over and help me bathe and get changed. As winter began, I fantasized about going outside, falling asleep in the snow and freezing to death. The only thing that stopped me was my cat, Mario. He loved me unconditionally.

One spring day, Rob came home and said he'd brought a visitor. It was Dan, the kind, handsome manager from Medieval Times. He'd asked Rob my whereabouts and Rob had filled him in on the basics, so Dan wanted to see how I was doing. His gentle, caring energy seemed to fill up the room, and I was able to absorb some of it. His warm, encouraging words of wisdom helped me feel as if I could breathe again. I told him a little bit of my story; if he was going to reject me, it was better he do it sooner than later.

"You're a good person, Timea," he said. "We all care about you. You will feel better. You're not responsible for Wayne." Before he left, he handed me a gift—a journal. The next day, I got out of bed and went for a walk down by the lake, taking the journal with me. In it, I wrote that I was going to get my life together for real, and that I was going to get healthy somehow. I meant it, and I believed it. I also realized that I was going to need help. I needed an immigration lawyer, a doctor, a therapist, a good job and a real home. I needed proper boots before winter struck again. I had resolve, but I didn't have support.

Because my immigration status was in limbo, I couldn't access any resources. Under my temporary work permit, I didn't qualify for anything—not social assistance, public housing or health care. For months, all I heard in my search for help was the word *no*, and I hated it. I started to feel anger—deep-seated anger—and it motivated me. If I wasn't allowed to do anything legally, fine. I would do whatever it took to make my own money, in whatever way I could. I called the number listed in a newspaper ad and signed up with an escort agency, which I knew meant full-fledged prostitution.

I was right back where I started, and in the middle of what I'd tried so hard to escape: selling myself. This time, though, instead of being scared and victimized, I was indignant. I was the roughest, toughest version of Allison, with no emotions at all. Over the course of the winter, spring and into the summer, I serviced dozens of clients a week at motels, rooming houses, apartments and private parties.

There were no security guards to protect me, and the clients could be mean and nasty, not like the men at Lucky's or even at Fantasia. There was nothing they didn't want me to do. When pain, fear or sadness came up from within me, I used the energy of my anger to shove them back down, deep inside. I stopped calling Mike and Mario and disappeared underground, avoiding everyone I knew. I left my cats with Rob and went to stay with our friend Jessica, telling her I was working night shifts as a cleaner in a hospital. The only person I spoke to was my driver from the escort agency.

The escort agency was nothing like Elek's operation, and I kept all my money except for a relatively small fee. I believed that I could make all the money I wanted and then buy myself a better life. I finally had free will, I told myself. I could make my own decisions instead of being a victim to all the things that had held me down in my life: a communist government, a fallen economy, a mother I could never please, a father who had abandoned me, an agency that had exploited me, men who had used me, the Hungarian police officers who raped me, a justice system that failed me, a boyfriend who'd blamed me, a brother who was angry at me and even my own naïveté.

But absolute free will, as I see it now, is more illusory than any of us might like to think. We make decisions based on our past experiences, knowledge, self-concept and state of mental and physical health. We make them within societal systems that may be structured against us, particularly if we are women, immigrants, ethnic minorities, uneducated, poor or in any other way disadvantaged. When we feel worthless and fearful, choosing the devil we know over the devil we don't know makes sense to us, because the unknown is frightfully overwhelming. In trauma, we want to feel safe, yet we have to search for that safety through shattered lenses. We may also have developed a trauma bond to a person or situation, one that feels unbreakable. This is often true for victims of domestic violence, who return time and again to their violent spouses. It was true for me when I chose to return to sex work *of my own free will*. It would take me a long time to forgive myself for that "choice."

I soon discovered that, like life with Elek's agency, the life of an escort is a dangerous one. I spent six months calling the shots and being fearless, until one day a client pulled a gun on me. The experience immediately snapped me out of the trance-like state of trauma and anger I was in, and back to a reality that involved a renewed sense of self-worth. I was twenty-seven years old—too young for my life to end. I had to start over, again.

29 | Saving Myself

FALL BECAME MY FAVOURITE SEASON the year I was thirteen, when I was released from my lengthy hospital stay after my gymnastics accident, but Canadian falls were especially beautiful. In fall 2006, I dug down as deep as I could for the courage to change the course of my life for good. I drew my inspiration from the maple leaves that turned as red as the one on the Canadian flag. I decided I had to let go of my anger and do my part for Canada, like I'd promised God long ago I would if I was given the chance to stay. If I made good on my side of the deal, maybe one day I could even become a full-fledged citizen.

I got back in touch with Mario, who told me that my work permit had been extended again and that I could apply for permanent residency as a protected person, and I finally got a lawyer through provincial legal aid. I'd made a lot of money in my six months as an escort, so I sent some of it home to my brother and mother, and put some of it toward first and last month's rent on a new apartment in

High Park. I joined a suicide support group to help me heal the trauma of Wayne's death, and it started me on a path to healing from everything that had happened over the last seven years.

My support group facilitator encouraged me to do work that actually made me feel good about myself, and to try using some of my life experience to help others. I signed up to work a crisis line, which involved an eight-week suicide-intervention training course. It was the first real education I'd had in ten years, and it felt good. I felt my brain come back to life in a new way. I was inspired by the trainers and by my fellow volunteers. I was told I had a gift for being with people who needed help, and I realized that it was because I knew how they felt. I understood helplessness and hopelessness. I had survived many horrible things, yet somehow I was still here on the planet. I realized there must be a reason for that.

Before Christmas, I received a letter from Citizenship and Immigration Canada. I was a nervous wreck, my hands shaking as they held the unopened envelope. Whatever was inside would determine the course of my life from this moment forward. I took a deep breath as I gingerly opened it, praying. When I read the words *You have been granted permanent residency*, I whooped aloud and jumped for joy— and then I fell to my knees and kissed the ground like I had in the Toronto airport seven years earlier, when I escaped Hungary. I called Mike first, and then Mario, crying with joy through both phone calls. I could now do everything all Canadians could do—except vote. I had to wait to be a citizen to do that.

I immediately went out and bought my first real wallet because I now had things to put in it: a health card, a residency card and a social insurance card. I opened my first bank account. For all these years, all I'd had was cash, which I kept stuffed in a little coin purse. I got my G1 driver's licence—the first step in learning how to drive. I was becoming a real, valid person again. I was filled with new energy and excitement for life, and I felt unstoppable. Being granted legal status didn't just give me permission to stay in Canada, it gave me permission to dream dreams and have a real chance of seeing them come true. I started right away.

I got a new job at a sandwich shop, saved some money, and by the next summer had enough to bring my mom to Canada for a visit. Despite all our problems over the years, she was my mom, and after eight years apart with only occasional phone calls and letters, I missed her. I wanted her to see this dynamic, diverse city and this beautiful country. I also felt that if I could give her something—the gift of time and new memories—it might start to make up for her disappointment, for all I had done wrong. She came in the spring of 2006, and Mike and I took her to Niagara Falls and to the Toronto Police Service Headquarters. I'm not sure which impressed her more!

I didn't talk much about the past with her, and I noticed a decline in her mental functioning. She seemed to forget things, and her behaviour and mannerisms were slightly different. I chalked it up to aging. I taught her a little bit about using the internet, which was new for her, and we set up Skype accounts and Facebook profiles so we could stay in touch. She told me more about my brother than he had ever shared, but not much of it was good news. He was struggling financially, and emotionally too. He couldn't keep a relationship or a job. He partied a lot and went to every soccer game he could, often getting into fights. She described him as "lost." I didn't know how to help. I felt I was the cause of many of his problems, and it would be years before we would sit down together and talk through everything, from childhood all the way to the time I first went to Canada. I was finding myself, but I couldn't find him at the same time.

I practised driving and eventually got my full licence, and then a car. I learned that no car needs an oil change every week, and that when it did need one, it would cost $50, not $350. Driving alone was the most unbelievable freedom I'd ever experienced, and I started going on road trips outside the city on my days off. I was stunned at the beauty of Ontario, and its massive size. I drove to Ottawa, five hours away, where I saw the beautiful Parliament of Canada for the first time, and was awestruck by the Peace Tower and the eternal flame. I drove to Tobermory at the tip of the Bruce Peninsula on Lake Huron, where the water is green like a tropical sea. I drove to Niagara-on-the-Lake and other quaint, historical towns, falling in love with each one.

Sometimes seeing all the beauty of the landscape, and myself in it, was bittersweet. I'd lost a lot of my youth to horrific trauma, and then to the struggle of limbo—years that should have been for education, friendship, family, romance and building a career. I felt sad for the little Hungarian girl and young woman I'd been before everything went wrong, and I missed her. But the stronger and more free I felt, the more I came to terms with who I was now and all the opportunities that awaited me in the future as an almost-Canadian.

I wanted to make a difference, and the idea of working with the police began to really interest me. Maybe it was because I'd been raised by a cop, but I think mainly it was because of Mike. After all the years of him being my support person and me being his victim, our relationship had evolved into more of a mentorship. He told me how to apply to become a volunteer with police victim services, and he offered to be a reference. It was a competitive program, with only fifty of more than three hundred applicants accepted every year. I was thrilled to be chosen.

The training was intense, long and comprehensive. I learned a lot about policing, crime and the law. I absolutely loved the victim services model, and learning all about how they worked with other support organizations to help people. Sometimes there were guest speakers during the sessions, often called "survivors" instead of victims. They'd been through all kinds of horrible criminal experiences: rape, child abuse, violent assault and more. Now they were using their experiences for good, to help others. I felt so inspired by their bravery, and although I related closely to the horror of what they'd gone through, I didn't quite see myself as I saw them. For the most part, in my mind and heart I was still just a person who had made bad choices, messed up my family and deserved what I got. There were still a lot of unresolved issues, questions and loose ends about what had even happened.

I didn't yet see my potential to help others as a fellow survivor, but I did see my potential to become a police officer. Maybe, by wearing a badge, and knowing how to defend myself physically and serve the public, I could truly clear my conscience, end the guilt I still felt about why and how I came to Canada, and say goodbye to my shame once and for all. And maybe, if I followed in my mother's footsteps and became a police officer, she would finally be proud of me. I could do one thing to make her happy before she died. I got so excited by this idea that I called Mike right away and told him of my plan. The next day, I quit smoking, joined a gym, hired a personal trainer and got a daytime job at an inner-city homeless shelter. Our clients were very vulnerable and faced no end of challenges to their survival and well-being. I understood them deeply.

One day, a few of us were having lunch in the shelter kitchen and I picked up a newspaper that was on the table. There was a huge article on the front page about Canada's new law against human trafficking. *Human trafficking.* What did that mean? I'd heard of drug trafficking, but not human trafficking. I read further and learned that it meant buying and selling people, luring them with empty promises, then forcing them to work like slaves. I felt a knot in my stomach. I'd been exploited and taken advantage of, but had I been trafficked? The article talked about what a big problem the issue was in Toronto and other cities, with people being brought in from all over the world and made to work in terrible conditions, from housekeeping and office cleaning to the sex trade, with no pay.

There was a second article about a group of Russian girls who'd been lured to Toronto with promises of high-paying work as baby-sitters, housekeepers and go-go dancers. My stomach hurt. The police said that the victims were hard to work with because they would not give up information about the people who had brought them to Canada—their traffickers. *Traffickers.* I felt light-headed, but I couldn't stop reading. The article said many of the Russian girls feared jail sentences, as they had illegal passports or no documentation to speak of. They were starved, made to work at clubs for up to twenty hours a day, and forced into prostitution. All their money was taken by pimps who the girls believed were their "agents." They had to work when they were sick. They were constantly threatened. They had been found by police on the side of a highway, *escaping*.

I put the paper down; it suddenly felt too heavy for me to hold. It was as though I was reading my own story. Every detail—from the promises Natasa made me to the long days I worked with no food or rest—was accurate. I couldn't ignore the realization that I had been trafficked. *I was a victim of human trafficking.*

None of this had come up in Tony's trial. It was entirely about trying to prove that he had sexually assaulted me, in a club that he owned where I was employed, and at a motel, where I was staying. How I came to be working at the club, let alone how I came to Canada, was never brought up. At one point in his testimony, Tony denied knowing me altogether. The copies of my passports hadn't even gone into evidence, and there was no explanation as to why— just some legal reason that defied common sense. Reading this article, I finally understood why. Until now, Canada hadn't had laws dealing with human trafficking. Like slavery, it wasn't commonly known as a modern-day problem. I didn't know if Tony had been working directly with Elek, János and Sasha, and I honestly hadn't thought too much about it, but now it was all coming together. It was organized crime—a big ring of sinister criminals disguised as recruiters, agents, managers and even boyfriends—and it was far bigger than I'd ever thought.

———

Now that I had a name for what had happened to me, I felt the need to re-examine my story—every detail of it—this time using my new knowledge to gain a different perspective. For the first time, I truly looked at myself as a victim—and a survivor. This gave me the gift of self-compassion, and I used it to help me heal and to motivate me to help other victims.

30 | Saving Others

AS HUMAN TRAFFICKING was named and exposed as a current issue in Canada, my co-workers at the shelter became concerned that they might not know how to handle victims if they came through the doors in need of help. I'd sensed the same concern with the police, based on what was described in the articles I read. I knew that what victims like me felt toward police was abject fear. The police and front-line workers needed someone to help them understand that, and to figure out what to say and not say. Maybe I could help.

My credibility was in my experience, so I knew I would have to be able to talk about it in order to help others. As fortune would have it, a friend gave me a ticket to New York to attend a storytelling and writing conference he couldn't make it to, and it changed my life. I had the chance to try sharing my story in front of small groups, and I found it incredibly healing to speak out, be accepted and move people just by the fact that I'd survived. One group member was a police investigator in Kansas. He asked me to develop a presentation to train his force and crisis workers, and flew me out there for a few days' work. I came back inspired and motivated by knowing I could help attack the issue of human trafficking, and I told Mike all about it. He recommended me as a speaker at a Toronto police conference, and from there I was asked to develop a training session for police in Canada to help identify and reach potential trafficking victims. Learning how to work with people who'd been brainwashed, starved and traumatized was delicate work, and the police embraced and valued my inside knowledge.

Before long, I was invited to speak to other police forces in the province, and over the next few years I travelled extensively. The work helped me continue to heal from PTSD because it gave me purpose, and because the more I talked about what happened the more I released the hurt I'd endured. Just before Christmas 2009, I gave a talk to five hundred police officers at a training conference just west of Toronto. As was my custom, I told my story, shared some of my work and invited officers to call me if they needed more detail or help on a specific case. A month after my event, a call came in—one that would change my thinking about the scope of human trafficking and involve me in a nationwide bust.

"Timea Nagy? I'm Constable Lepa Jankovic with the Niagara RCMP detachment. My partner, Constable Husam Farah, heard your talk last month and we've got a case we need your help with. Do you have a few minutes to talk?"

"Absolutely," I told her.

"We've got thirteen men here at a homeless shelter in St. Catharines who we believe were trafficked. One of them escaped from a local restaurant where he and the men were being held. He led us to the rest so we could rescue them. They're in pretty bad shape—they've been forced to work in construction and treated terribly," she explained. I was taken aback—I hadn't heard of men being trafficked.

"They only speak Hungarian," she continued. "We're having trouble finding someone who can interpret and also handle the difficulty of the situation. We're hoping you can talk to them. We know they'll trust you."

"I'll come right away," I told her.

When I arrived at the shelter in St. Catharines a couple of hours later, Constable Jankovic was there to meet me. She was a striking woman at least a foot taller than me, dressed in plain clothes. "Call me Lepa," she said right away.

"Please call me Timea," I said, "but with the victims please call me Christina. Lots of victims return to their traffickers out of fear and intimidation, or because they are indebted to them. If that happens, I wouldn't want the traffickers to be able to find me." I'd thought about this on the drive, and chosen my alias after Christine—the woman who first told me I was a victim, not a criminal.

"You got it," Lepa said, nodding. "Ready to go in?"

Lepa led me to the room where her partner, Husam, was waiting outside the door. He opened it and ushered me in. There were thirteen men, all skin and bones, with deep, dark circles under their eyes. They looked so ill it was as if they'd just come up from underground. They grew quiet when I entered, and eyed me curiously.

"My name is Christina," I said in Hungarian. "I'm here to help you."

The men took turns introducing themselves. "We're hungry," one man said. "Do you have any food?" All I had were cigarettes I'd bought for a trafficked escort I'd helped at a police station a few weeks prior. I passed them around and the men quickly became comfortable with me. One by one, they told me their stories.

Most were poor tradesmen from small villages outside Budapest, and they had been tricked into coming to Canada with promises of good, high-paying construction work that would allow them to support their families at home. They had been taught a single English word—*refugee*—to say at customs when they held out the visa applications from their agency.

Each of the applications had made a different false claim for refugee status—one pretended he was homosexual and stigmatized; another claimed to be a target of the Hungarian mafia. Upon arrival to Canada, their Hungarian traffickers sent the men to different rented homes. They kept them in basements with little light, offered no change of clothing or access to showers, and fed them one meal per day. From dawn until dusk they worked at residential construction sites—right alongside bona fide workers who were unaware of the men's plight. At night, their captors forced them to shoplift at malls and hand over the goods to be hocked for more profit. They were allowed just four hours of sleep each night. All of the proceeds from the construction and the thieving went to "pay back" the debt the traffickers claimed the men owed for their flights, agency fees, food, lodging and construction materials.

The men were also forced to fill out applications for refugee assistance funds under various false names so that each had four or five active files. Matching bank accounts were set up for each file. When the cheques arrived, the funds were deposited and withdrawn by the agents—thousands of dollars each month.

The victims were threatened and beaten, and told their families' throats would be cut if they tried to escape. As they spoke, in my first language, I saw myself in them. While they had not been sold into sexual slavery as I had, their shame and guilt was just as strong. They believed they were criminals, that this situation was all their fault because they had failed to make enough money. Some couldn't even look me in the eye. "I couldn't escape," one man said. "I was too afraid. They told me I'd be put in a black garbage bag and thrown in Lake Ontario." I'd heard those exact words before.

"I can still hear his voice," he confided in a whisper. "The voice of the man who said this to me."

I listened to them until three o'clock in the morning. I took down their names, their ages—eighteen to sixty-two—and their stories. They asked me if I could come back the next day to talk some more, and if I could get them some food or a change of clothes. I promised I would return the next day and do whatever I could to help them. I pulled on my jacket, said goodbye, and walked to my car. I was far too tired to drive back to Toronto, so instead I drove to the parking lot of a Tim Hortons close by and rested. I had just closed my eyes to sleep a little when a powerful feeling overtook me. *This is why I was trafficked—so I could help other victims.* It hadn't totally hit me until that moment. I could almost feel a switch flip inside me, changing me from survivor to advocate. I realized that the issue of trafficking was even bigger than I thought, not limited only to the trafficking of female sex workers but to men and women performing all kinds of forced labour.

Over the following weeks and months, I made many trips from my home in Toronto to where the thirteen men were sheltered. The police were searching for the traffickers and had put warrants out for their arrest, and the traffickers were searching for the victims— hunting them down like I'd been hunted. The police named their investigation OPAPA, O for the jurisdiction of Ontario, then for Pápa, the small town in Hungary where most of the men had been recruited. It was the biggest investigation into human trafficking in Canadian history, led heroically and tirelessly by Constables Jankovic and Farah. I became part of the team by supporting the victims as they were rescued, making sure they had shelter, food, clothing, and by offering emotional support. I called their families with updates, and bought phone cards so they could call their families themselves when they were ready. Some were overcome by shame over having been duped, others were overwhelmed by all the questions they couldn't yet answer, and all were suffering from the effects of trauma.

By May 2010 the RCMP had twenty-three victims and statements from each one. They faced some close calls as the traffickers nearly found them, and I helped relocate the group twice within St. Catharines before we finally moved them to another community, a few hours away. I travelled with them, helped them settle in, and then went back to working with the police until they finally found and arrested the traffickers in twos and threes. In the end, they had eighteen suspects in custody, charged and awaiting trial. The Crown attorney who took the case on, Toni Skarica, was small in stature but titanic in passion, skills and intellect, never wavering in his commitment to getting the case to court and winning. Where other prosecutors might reduce the number of accused, he stood firm. Where charges might be dropped to simplify the case, he increased them and welcomed the complexities of the investigation. I saw in him another hero in the fight against human trafficking. Inspired by the whole team, I took a translation course and earned my official certification. The more I could offer, the better.

As OPAPA ramped up, word of it spread across the law enforcement network. My name and phone number were shared as someone available to help trafficking victims through post-escape or rescue crisis. It wasn't long before I found myself driving to police detachments all over southern Ontario to meet with new victims. Most of the calls were to help escaped or rescued foreigners like me—forced into dancing and prostitution—but to my surprise, there were also numerous Canadian-born girls and young women who'd been lured into jobs with "agencies" just like I was. I learned that even English-speaking Canadians were at risk. A language barrier is just a bonus for traffickers—another layer of vulnerability they can exploit and use to isolate victims. They used whatever they could.

My work with victims began to fill my whole schedule from Monday to Saturday. There was just one problem: I was working as a volunteer. My livelihood was fragile. There was so much more I wanted to do for victims—like set up a safe house for sex-trafficked women—but I could hardly keep a roof over my own head. Then I met an earth angel.

One Sunday, I gave a talk to a charity group outside of Hamilton. At the end of the presentation, a man approached me to say how moved he was by my story. He was a lawyer, Rob Hooper of Hooper Law Offices, and his wife, Jill Trites, was a businesswoman. He asked if he could give me a little advice.

"First of all, you should never speak for free again. You are probably the best speaker I have ever heard, and I have heard a few." His smile was warm and his tone confident. I laughed.

"Well, then, that'll be $5, please!"

My jovial response caught him off guard, but he quickly recovered and then surprised me back by pressing a $5 bill into my hand.

I turned red and said, "Oh, I'm sorry, I was totally joking!"

"But I'm not," he said. "What help do you need most, Timea?"

My list of needs was long: from paying my huge cell phone bill to paying grocery and clothing bills—victims' expenses I'd taken upon myself in order to help. I shared my list with this man.

He pulled out his chequebook and began to write the words *three thousand five hundred dollars* on a cheque. He signed it and passed it to me with a flourish.

"What? Are you serious?"

"Very," he said. Then he gave me his card and asked me to come and meet him at his office the next day. "I'd like to talk with you about starting a charitable organization." It was an answer to a prayer I hadn't yet put into words.

Rob and Jill became my patrons, supporting me while I set up a charitable organization I named Walk with Me Canada Victim Services. After some time, I had a mandate, a board of directors and a website. I set out seeking donations and public speaking events that would fund me and the organization. I organized volunteers who opened their homes to rescued trafficking victims. These families took in girls twenty-four hours a day, providing care, support and stability. Most of all, they showed these girls that good people existed and that trust was possible.

The more presentations I gave, the more donations I received, and the more family placements I had for victims. By the end of 2011,

Walk with Me had helped rescue almost two hundred victims of human trafficking. I was honoured with awards, but what mattered most to me was my goal of opening a safe house.

I continued to be sought after by police and investigators, who asked me to write a manual based on my experiences. I did so, developing it into a training program for officers to help them identify victims at the border, at clubs and in various other workplaces. Entire police forces bought the book, and I put all the proceeds back into my organization. Eventually, I saved and fundraised enough to open Canada's first safe house for sex-trafficked workers. Together with the amazing volunteers who had come forward after my talks, we found a five-bedroom bungalow with a cute backyard. We greeted the survivors by putting their names on their bedroom doors, drawing them bubble baths, laying out new pyjamas and having our volunteer cooks make their favourite meals. They could stay for up to a week while we worked with the police and other front-line services to make more permanent plans. We held bonfire nights for the girls, and sometimes boys, where we would sit with them, eat some food and then write down negative memories or place symbolic objects from their past into the fire to symbolize a new start. We also worked like a 24/7 mobile crisis team and in some cases, when our house was full or too far away, we would take them to a hotel or a family member's house and stay overnight to help them settle in. The work was hard, but gratifying.

Over the course of the next two years, I continued to share my story over and over, trying to help law enforcement understand the plight of girls just like me, and to raise funds for the safe house. The more that police became aware of how to rescue victims, the more calls I got to shelter them. The safe house was set up to accept eight victims at a time per month, but some months we received two hundred requests. It was overwhelming. Canada's exotic dancing visa program—which I'd learned was intended to help protect sex workers by giving them legal status, but had been twisted into a sinister money-making opportunity by men like Tony and Elek—was slowing down and would be cancelled by the federal government in a few months (I'd been working with a parliamentarian on that matter). The result was that we had fewer foreign trafficking victims but many more domestic victims, particularly from small towns—recruited and brought to big cities. The younger the better, it seemed.

As I found my purpose in life, I stayed single. Just the thought of explaining what I did for a living—let alone why I did it—evoked anxiety. Instead, I kept my focus on new friendships, and used Facebook to reconnect with a few friends from the past. One of those was Dan, the manager from Medieval Times who had been so kind to visit me at one of the darkest points of my life, after Wayne's suicide. It had been years since we talked, and it felt great to be back in touch. I learned that he and his wife had divorced and that it had been hard for the children. As he confided in me, I was able to confide more and more in him too. We went back and forth in online messaging for weeks before switching to long conversations on the phone, deepening our friendship each time. When we finally met in person a few months later, we fell in love. It felt completely right.

Then in February 2012, the Niagara RCMP officers leading OPAPA—the ones who'd asked me to help with the trafficked Hungarian men—gave my name to Deb Kerr at Canadian Border Services Agency, who had first reported to the RCMP an unusual number of Hungarian men immigrating to Canada and settling in the Hamilton area, yet not bringing their families over, leading the RCMP to investigate and uncover the ring. She was now investigating the immigration issues related to the case, and the status of both the victims and the accused. She called to ask for my help.

"We need someone to translate for us, Timea, and also to listen in and help us put a few pieces together," Deb said. "We'd like you to meet us at the Hamilton-Wentworth Detention Centre to interview Ferenc Karádi, one of the higher-ups in the criminal organization and cousin of the kingpin Ferenc Domotor." While I didn't relish the thought, I wanted to do whatever it took to help the investigation and eventual trial.

"Just say when," I responded, trying to sound braver than I felt.

The next day, two immigration officers came to pick me up. We drove to the Hamilton detention facility, where we went through security, walked through a series of locking gates and doors, and entered a closed visiting room. I didn't know quite what to expect. Moments later, a guard opened a door on the other side of the glass dividing wall and in walked Ferenc Karádi, a tall, overweight man in his late-forties with his head shaved, wearing an orange prisoner's jumpsuit. Introductions were made and I translated them, but I didn't give my name. Then Karádi began speaking to me in Hungarian.

"Miss, you look like a nice lady. Please help us. Tell the police we're being tortured in here." He looked me in the eye as he spoke. "You understand, don't you?" he continued. "All the stories those men are telling about us, they never happened. We treated those men like gold."

I couldn't believe what I was hearing. I'd been working with "those men" for two years. I'd been in the room when some of them awoke screaming from nightmares about what had been done to them at the hands of the man in front of me and his family members and partners in crime. They cried spontaneously. They were constantly sick from starvation and I had taken some of them to the doctor. They feared for the lives of their families back in Hungary, and rightfully so. One family had been threatened by the trafficking team back in Pápa and told their house would be burned down if they didn't pay a ransom within twelve hours. Their captors called them *csicskas*—slaves.

I looked at the man sitting across from me—the man responsible for so much suffering. How could he possibly act like the victim? He held his hands out to me, palms up, begging me for help. I wanted to claw his eyes out.

"I'm sorry, there's nothing I can do for you. I'm just here to translate." I took a breath. "Let's continue with the interview."

"This is all a set-up!" he said. "The police and the government put all this together because they don't like us Hungarians. They even have people hiding my employees from me!"

"Really?" I said, feigning surprise, waiting for him to say more.

"Yeah," he said. "The worst is that there is a Hungarian woman called Christina who is behind the whole thing. Do you know her?"

My mouth went dry. Christina was me—the alias I'd chosen.

"I don't know who she is or anything about the investigation," I lied. "I'm just a translator."

"Tell them we're being very badly treated." He nodded toward the investigators. "We're getting three meals a day here, but they're really skimpy. I'm losing weight and I can't sleep well."

I almost jumped out of my skin. *You dare to complain about three meals a day when you barely fed your victims one?* Karádi's life in jail was luxurious compared to the inhuman conditions he'd forced upon his own countrymen. *I hope you never sleep again!* I wanted to scream, but I kept my cool. He and the others would have their day in court, and I was confident they would get what they deserved. I would likely never see my own traffickers behind bars—Elek, János, Tony, Natasa and Sasha—but putting Karádi in jail, and shutting down the whole criminal ring, would bring me great satisfaction.

"Can't you help me?" Karádi pleaded one more time. I remembered how I'd looked to my own translator as my lifeline, all those years ago when I was interrogated the first time I arrived at Pearson airport. I was a twenty-year-old girl who wanted to make some money babysitting. Karádi's kind had preyed upon me. Now he was powerless and I wasn't a victim anymore.

The officers finished asking their questions and I translated. Later, we would debrief, and they would ask me for my insights and impressions. Then we interviewed three more of the accused. Their stories were all the same—bold-faced lies.

In a Hamilton courthouse in April 2012, twenty-two men and women pleaded guilty to all charges against them: human trafficking, conspiracy, assault, identity theft, grand theft and a host of fraud charges. Their convictions formed new case law in human trafficking. The day of sentencing was set and the Crown anticipated prison time.

Until this point, there had been very little media interest in the case, which frustrated me. I knew that if we wanted to end human trafficking, we'd have to start with public awareness. The day before the sentencing hearing, Walk with Me sent out a press release to every media outlet I could think of. I so desperately wanted the media's attention on this issue that I almost considered standing on a street corner and passing out fliers like I did when I was a teenager in Budapest, promoting the Pierrot concert.

The press release worked. The next day, the courtroom was packed with journalists ready to report on the handing down of the first sentences in Canadian history for international human trafficking, and the biggest trafficking case in Canadian history: nine years in a federal prison for the kingpin, Ferenc Domotor, and four to six years for his brother, sister-in-law, cousins (including Karádi) and the rest of the ring. After they were carted away, the prosecutor and one of the victims were interviewed for national news television and the papers. I'd stayed out of the public eye for my own safety through the investigation, but now I could reveal my identity and speak about the case and human trafficking to the press. At one point during the trial, the accused had managed to hire a hit man from Hungary to kill Lepa and Husam, the Crown attorney, the victims and me, but Canada Border Services was able to turn him around.

The federal government began responding to the issue of human trafficking—which had garnered the public's attention with the media coverage—by launching an initiative in June 2012 called the National Action Plan to Combat Human Trafficking. It would introduce aggressive new initiatives to prevent human trafficking, identify victims, protect the most vulnerable and prosecute perpetrators. It felt amazing to see something being done about this critical situation on a national scale. Border Services was now heavily involved in the issues too, changing laws around visitor visas and investing in having me train them to look for potential victims and traffickers at the borders. Ontario Works—the provincial social services agency—examined and adapted their protocols around refugee claims to protect false claims by traffickers and assist those who might be victims of identity theft and extortion. Canada was really tackling the problem, and playing a part in the effort was gratifying.

At some point through all this, I studied for my citizenship test and passed. On July 1, 2012—Canada's 145th birthday—I swore my oath at a beautiful ceremony in Hamilton, with my love, Dan, by my side. Lining the perimeter of the courtroom were officers from OPAPA, there to witness and celebrate with me. Lepa Jankovic was taller than ever in her ceremonial RCMP uniform with stately scarlet serge and iconic wide-brimmed Stetson "Mountie" hat, and beaming beautifully at me. The judge called me forward.

"Ms. Nagy," he said, "I know who you are and all about the work you have done. Thank you. Welcome to Canada." With my citizenship papers clutched to my chest, I could no longer hold back my tears. I finally belonged.

For the next several months, I continued working with the police, helping victims of sex trafficking and assisting with investigations into organized crime rings. I loved my work training police officers, and my program expanded into the United States, where I began training FBI agents and working with major banks and software companies who are forever trying to crack the money-laundering end of the trafficking business. Hearing a personal story of a victim-turned-survivor helped them put a face to the cause and gave them a reason to keep at it. While I sometimes found it difficult to tell my story over and over, the emotional toll was worth it to effect change and influence front-line responders.

Besides, I now had a wonderful home with a loving partner. Dan and I had moved in together, renting a small but pretty house outside

Toronto. It was perfect for the two of us, my cats and his teenage children, who were with us part-time. I was finally Canadian, with a proper home and a family to call my own.

I was preparing for our first Christmas together and on my way home from a shopping trip when my cell phone rang. I pulled over and answered.

"Timea Nagy?" an official-sounding woman's voice asked.

"Yes."

"I'm calling from the Prime Minister's Office." My heart stopped. "You are a finalist for the Prime Minister's Volunteer Award and I just need some information to complete your background check."

An award—from the prime minister? Me? I was speechless.

"But how did this happen?" I asked. "Who nominated me?"

"There is a big package here with the names of some police officers. I'll be in touch once we've made our decision. Oh, and congratulations!"

A few weeks later, I learned that I'd been chosen as one of the twenty winners of the 2012 National Volunteer Award. I went to Parliament to receive it in person from the prime minister at the House of Commons. That day, I remembered the promise I'd made to myself so long ago—that I would be the best Canadian I could possibly be if I were only allowed into the country. I'd made good on my promise. I folded my hands in a silent prayer. *Thank you.*

Epilogue | Into the Light

I WAS TWENTY YEARS OLD when I first came to Canada in 1998, and now I'm forty-one. My life is divided in two: before I was trafficked, and after. No one "gets over" such traumatic experiences, but there are ways to integrate them into your identity and make them meaningful, to fully come to terms with their impact. That has been my healing journey, a journey I know I will always be on, to some degree.

Throughout my years as an advocate, I've been able to help hundreds of trafficking victims reunite with their families and rebuild their lives, but I was never able to fully help my own family come back together. After my mom came to visit me in Canada in 2006, and I set her up with email and Skype, we began to be in regular contact. She sent me a birthday card and Christmas card every year, but we never spoke of the past. She found out about my work—and, therefore, what had really happened to me—when a Hungarian gossip magazine picked up a story about the first talk I gave in Kansas. The cover headline said, "Ex-hooker Speaking Out," and featured a picture of me below it. It was upsetting for her, to say the least, but she was proud that I was working with law enforcement to deal with a serious criminal issue. She was, after all, a police officer first and foremost.

Early in 2015, after an ongoing funding battle, I made a difficult decision, together with the board of directors, to close Walk with Me. Losing it was like losing my firstborn child, and although I hoped to reopen it one day, its closure gave me time to put the last broken pieces of my heart together, starting with an attempt to build a real and deep relationship with my mom. I hadn't been back to Hungary since I'd left that last time, in September 1998, and there were more pieces of my story to heal there, but I decided to bring my mom to Canada again so I could just focus on our relationship. It had been years since I'd seen her. When I called to tell her the news, she told me she was too sick to come. She had bone cancer that had spread from her lungs. "Timi," she said, "please come home."

I booked my flight to Budapest, and breathed deeply through the anxiety of being back in the airport, remembering and reliving what had happened there. I feared I would be detained because of my old criminal charges, but they had either been dropped, had expired or my Canadian passport protected me, because no one said anything when I went through customs. From there I went straight to my mom's bedside. My friends and colleagues in policing had sent me with some little gifts for her, and she especially loved the miniature Peel Regional Police car, showing it off to all the patients in her ward. She was very soft and sweet, and although we had many hours together, she wasn't lucid enough for me to say what I desperately wanted her to hear: *I am sorry. I'm sorry for the big mess I got myself in. I'm sorry I was never the daughter you wanted me to be. I'm sorry I didn't understand you.* Through all my work with trauma victims, I'd developed empathy for my mother, who was a trauma victim herself—losing her father in a war, being raised in poverty and living under communism. Then there was her depression. I felt compassion, and it opened my heart to her in a new way.

My mom's impending death brought me and my brother together, in love and respect, giving us the chance to know each other as adults while we sat at her bedside. He told me about his journey over the years, and I told him about mine. We'd kept up on the basics through emails and texts, but we'd never had really deep conversations. It was helpful to both of us. For so long, guilt and shame had kept us apart. He'd finally been evicted from the apartment we tried so hard to save, and had moved into a tiny flat in a run-down and dangerous area of Budapest. Before he moved, Bianka had sent her mafia ex-husband and a couple of his comrades to get the money I owed her, and when Zoli couldn't produce it, they beat him badly. I was sick at hearing this and begged forgiveness, which he granted. He'd believed I was "living the good life" in Canada, until he saw the same magazine article my mom did. He asked for my forgiveness too, for being unable to protect his little sister. Finally, we were able to understand each other's journeys, and replace the guilt and shame with love. We had missed each other tremendously.

Together, we decided to try to find our father and let him know Mom was dying. After talking with some aunts and uncles, we learned he was living in a little village not far from Budapest, near where he'd grown up. After twenty-eight years without seeing or speaking to him, we showed up in his hometown to find that everyone knew us—Dad had talked about us so much. He was overwhelmed to see us, and we spent hours talking together at a table in a local pub. There was so much to catch up on, so much hurt to dissolve. I told him a little bit about what happened to me in Canada, but not too much. I didn't want to cause him pain. He confessed that when I was in the hospital after my gymnastics accident, he had come to see me. Not wanting to make trouble, he had stayed in the hallway. It meant a lot to know that I hadn't imagined him that day. When we told him about Mom, he broke down crying and confessed that he'd always loved her. We put our arms around him.

Mom died in March 2015, five days before her sixty-fifth birthday. Because Zoli was working a great deal, I became responsible for going through her belongings and making funeral arrangements with my stepfather. I read through her diaries and her medication notes, and sorted through her photo albums. I had so many questions for her and was overwhelmed with grief and longing, realizing how many conversations we would never have. I wanted to know more about myself, but even more, I wanted to know about her. Who was she as a child and a young woman? Why had she become a police officer? What other hopes and dreams did she have, and what happened to them? How had living under communism affected her? Most importantly, what was it like for her to be my mother?

Her funeral was on a beautiful spring day, her favourite season—that much I knew. It was attended by many of her police colleagues, friends, family and people from the community, all people I hadn't seen or talked to in nearly two decades. They were gracious, offering only condolences and not asking questions about what had happened to me. Dad was there too. Though I'd lost my mother, I got my father and brother back.

After the funeral, I returned to Canada, and my dad and I began corresponding through letters. I wrote him pages and pages, with questions I'd wanted to ask my mother but had never had the chance; he wrote asking for forgiveness for his absence in my life. I hoped to visit him again, but he took ill suddenly and died later that year, just a few months after Mom.

––––––––––

The sex trafficking industry has changed dramatically in the years since I was lured into it, and the internet now plays a huge role. Girls and young women are being used to make pornography, to be personal sex slaves and to sell and distribute drugs, in addition to the stripping and prostitution to which I'd been subject. International trafficking now goes two ways—foreign girls are coming into Canada and Canadian girls are shipped out—and domestic trafficking is a huge problem. Sex trafficking has grown into a $150 billion industry worldwide. A Canadian trafficker makes, on average, $300,000 per year for each victim he extorts and exploits. The industry is also further underground now. Advances in technology like the internet, smart phones and even GPS tracking bracelets on victims can present more advantages to traffickers, especially in sex work. It's rarer now to see signage on actual strip clubs, or prostitutes on street corners, but anyone can visit backpage.com and order the sexual service they desire, delivered to a location of their choice, "24/7," like most of the ads offer—ads that are created and managed by pimps.

While the internet makes it easier than ever for pimps and traffickers to sell the services of the victims they control, it can also make it easier for law enforcement—with the help of an informed public who might report suspicious activity in their neighbourhoods and workplaces, and bankers—to find them. In Canada, I began working with a financial technology company, using my insight to help them design software that could help banks address the problems of fraud and money laundering. By attacking the financial side of trafficking, we could access the human side. All of my work training people about the lives of victims—especially those in forced sex work—had helped me figure out patterns of banking transactions that pointed toward the accounts of victims and their traffickers. While I never had a bank account as a victim, most victims today do. Bookings for sex services are most often made on the internet, and fees are paid electronically. It is as easy to go online and order a prostitute to come to your home as it is to order running shoes or a blender.

In 2016, the Canadian Museum of Human Rights created an exhibit about me, and in 2017, I was honoured with the Governor General's Meritorious Service Decoration, as well as interviewed by *The Economist* magazine for a documentary about attacking human trafficking from the financial-crime aspect. I also continued my front-line rescue work with victims, responding to calls at all hours of the day and night, while also training other survivors to become advocates. My work is exhausting but so fulfilling. In June 2017, on the night before I turned forty, Dan proposed and I said, "Yes!" Then we bought our first house together.

Before Dan and I married, I wanted to sort out a few unresolved pieces of my story. In January 2018, I went back to Budapest, this time with the focus on healing, on reuniting for real with extended family and friends, and on understanding how others—particularly my boyfriend Ádám—had been affected by what happened to me. Ádám and I hadn't spoken in twenty years. Learning how much he had suffered with worry and guilt was difficult, and our reunion was imperfect—a raw conversation over the phone from my hotel. In hearing about his painful journey, I came to see him as another victim—his girlfriend had been lured, trafficked and sold into the sex trade. The effect of that on him was tremendous. Spending time with Aniko, my friend from the Pierrot club, was wonderful and restorative, as was meeting with a top producer in the music industry to remake a popular song into a public service advertisement about human trafficking. It was a life-changing journey. Then we began composing and recording an original song with me on vocals: "Life Is Still Beautiful to Me." And it is.

One of the greatest opportunities this trip gave me was the chance to heal my relationship with Hungary itself, my homeland. I had never allowed myself to fully feel the pain I'd experienced over having to leave my culture, my first language and everything that was familiar to me, and over having been betrayed by my own people— Elek, János, Natasa, the police and possibly Bianka. Her role in getting me to sign up with the agency—if she had a role—remains a mystery. When people hear my story, they usually think that Bianka lured me, but I'm still not sure. She did work in the sex industry; she did encourage me to apply for a job in Canada; and she did seem to know Natasa at least loosely, but there are too many puzzle pieces involving her own financial losses for me to think she'd had something to gain by helping to sign me up and by coming to Canada with me. Unless she was lied to as well. Many young women who are charged as traffickers today started off as victims. It's a vicious cycle.

Visiting friends on Csepel Island, I heard that Elek had spent fifteen years in jail and had never shown his face again, but no one knew anything about the others from "the agency." There were moments when I felt fear that they might still be looking for me, but I batted those fears away with the knowledge I'd gained from all the cases I'd worked on—that pimps give up on "lost girls" after six months to a year. I'll never know if Elek targeted me because he knew me, or if he only found out I was coming when he got my agency form from Natasa or saw me at the airport. But I don't need to know. It wouldn't help.

In Budapest on my healing trip, I also spent some time as a tourist, visiting historic landmarks, museums and the old part of the city—just soaking it all up. I cried sometimes, the grief most often triggered by smell or taste, and I also made new memories to replace some of the painful ones. I loved seeing the bridges across the Danube, seeing them as I always have, like stitches sewing two sides together. I was finally sewing my two identities together: Timea the Hungarian and Timea the Canadian.

In 2018, the United Nations announced a new commission on human trafficking, and I was asked to provide my expertise to the global taskforce assembled in New York. I was honoured and filled with hope to know that I had worldwide solidarity on my goal to end human trafficking in my lifetime. It's a huge battle that needs a global response, from individuals to industries to nations. It requires that we do everything from educating our children—boys and girls—on respectful relationships, self-confidence, peer support and trafficking savvy so that they are less vulnerable to being lured, all the way to eliminating the acceptance of sex as a commodity. We need to denormalize using pornography, hosting bachelor parties with strippers, and visiting strip clubs or "massage parlours" as male rights of passage or merely "boys being boys" and then go more deeply into why there is so much demand in our society for sex work. If there wasn't the demand, there wouldn't be the supply.

We must also address the way that many young men in Canada and around the world are groomed as much to be criminals as young women are to be victims, lured as early as middle school into drug trafficking and then "graduating" to human trafficking. We need to educate all industries vulnerable to slave labour (hospitality, construction, agriculture, factories, and sex or "entertainment" venues) on how to detect and report potential victims so the victims can be freed and their traffickers be held accountable and face the consequences of their crimes. Related industries such as banking, real estate and law enforcement are getting on board the fight, too.

The need for funding in the fight against trafficking is overwhelming, so I created a social enterprise called Timea's Cause to fill the void left by Walk with Me and to create revenue for victim-serving initiatives across North America. With the help of volunteers, I train and mentor sex-trafficked survivors, and we provide prevention and education workshops to law enforcement, banks, social service providers, the hotel and tourism industry, real estate agents, youth and parents. We speak, train, and release manuals and text books each year to support our training. We developed a line of organic self-care products and opened an online store called TimeasMarket.com, and we do pop-up shops during the holiday season. Not only are we able to raise funds, but we also employ survivors of sex trafficking, giving them life skills and a place of belonging and purpose. My dream is to grow this company to a point where its revenue is significant enough to allow me to finally reopen the safe house—and many more across Canada—creating a model that can be applied worldwide.

What sustains me through my work, and gives me the greatest joy now, is the new family I have built with Dan. Just a week before I went to the UN, we were married in a beautiful autumn ceremony followed by a Hungarian buffet and garden party, witnessed and supported by so many loved ones. Zoli gave a tearful toast. I was walked down the aisle by my police officer, Mike Josifovic (now a sergeant), and my friend and patron Rob Hooper. Dan and I don't plan to have our own children, but I love my role as stepmother to his children, now young adults. His ex-wife has become a good friend and supporter of my cause, as have his sister and mother, who was a feminist and activist in her younger years and who is one of my biggest cheerleaders today. I feel truly blessed to have them all in my life.

I have a chosen family that includes my "mothers," Eve and Maryann from the hair salon; my "blue brothers and sisters," the police officers who are my allies in the fight against human trafficking; and Rob Hooper and Jill Trites, who helped me to start Walk with Me, supporting me emotionally, intellectually and financially. Rob became my father, uncle and brother all rolled into one, teaching me how not to freak out when I get a bill and how to manage a business with a real office and a filing cabinet. Jill became my combined aunt and big sister, teaching me how to buy a proper bra, how to cook, how to host dinner parties, and so much more. Being trafficked at twenty, and losing my family of origin, I'd missed out on all the normal growth and development experiences a young person should have. My chosen family gave some of that back to me, along with the chance to celebrate holidays, set traditions and feel a wonderful sense of belonging.

I don't know why this all happened to me. I don't know why human beings hurt each other so much, or why terrible things happen. What I do know is that there is always spring after winter, and always sunshine after rain—and also that each of us has a responsibility to take care of one another. We cannot accept that there are millions of people currently trafficked and enslaved worldwide—more than at any other time in history, even when keeping slaves was legal—for none of us has true freedom or prosperity if it comes at the cost of others' freedom, labour and even lives. It needs to end, because the collective freedom of our human family is at stake, especially that of the next generation. We can do it.

ACKNOWLEDGEMENTS

WE ARE GRATEFUL to so many people for helping us bring this project to publication.

Thank you to our marvellous agent, Beverley Slopen, who championed our partnership and project with tenacity, enthusiasm, expertise and confidence. Thank you to our editor, Bhavna Chauhan, and publisher, Amy Black—bright and compassionate women who believed in us from the beginning and guided us through the publishing process. Heartfelt gratitude goes to our entire team at Doubleday Canada for transforming pages into the book of our dreams, and for helping it reach readers: Kristin Cochrane, Val Gow, Emma Ingram, Leah Springate, Terri Nimmo, Allie McHugh and Ward Hawkes. Thank you to copy editor Linda Pruessen, proofreader Erin Kern and lawyer Linda Friedner. Thank you to Nita Pronovost for matchmaking us in the beginning.

—Timea Eva Nagy and Shannon Moroney

From Timea:

I offer thanks from the bottom of my heart:

To the love of my life, Dan Payne, for teaching me what unconditional love is and for accepting me for who I am. Thank you for all your support through my sleepless nights, my work on the front lines, and for never complaining when I put work ahead of our home life. You understand what my work means to me, and your compassion and patience has made it possible for me to continue. Thank you for learning how to cope with my triggers and how to comfort me after a nightmare. I'm honoured to spend my life with you, and look forward to all our years ahead.

To my big brother, Zoltan Nagy, for coming back into my life and giving me back the feeling of belonging. I love you, bro!

To Sergeant Michael Josifovic of the Toronto Police Service for treating me with dignity, for supporting me through the darkest time of my life, and for never giving up on me. I am proud to call you my friend.

To the DJ and staff at Fantasia who helped me escape, and to Julius Hegedus for your friendship and support.

To Claudia Brazil, my best friend, spiritual teacher, mentor and guide, and the woman who encouraged me to share my story with the world. Thank you for being in my life and for your endless support.

To my adopted sister, Eva Gyovai Fontanyi, and your family. Thank you for giving me a home away from home. Thank you for loving me and helping me feel not alone. Thank you for never letting me forget how to speak Hungarian.

To my stepchildren: Thank you for accepting me into your hearts and family, and letting me be your "evil stepmother." I'm not perfect, but I'm working on it. Special thanks to my mom-in-law Juanita Payne, to Maggie Keegan for being a fantastic cheerleader, and to my sister-in-law, Tracy Gamble Payne, for ongoing love and support.

To Rob Hooper and Jill Trites: "Thank you" is simply not enough. Your unconditional love, mentorship and acceptance of me and my cause, and your ongoing support for victims of human trafficking is beyond admirable. You helped me learn to trust and love again, and you nurtured me through my young adulthood. Thank you for creating space in your heart for me. You inspire me every single day, and I hope I make you proud.

To my adopted mothers, Eve and Maryann: Thank you for the kindness you showed me when I was broken, and for taking me in when I was so vulnerable. Thank you for being in my life, for bringing me joy and appreciation for art, and for modelling humility and acceptance.

To "The Originals," my Blue Family: Lepa Jankovic, Husam Farah, Dave Hartless, Graham Hawkins, Craig Labaune, DVA, Mike Viozzi, Phil Groeneveld, Ron Kapuscunski and Deb Kerr, for your dedication to ending human trafficking, your extraordinary work with victims, and for making me feel like part of the team.

To my extended Blue Family that has helped me and other victims for many years: Your sleepless nights and ongoing dedication to victims of crime means the world. Specifically, I thank: DVA and Jimmy Zuccero from Peel Regional Police Drugs and Vice Unit; Julia Sorensen, Paula Rossevy and Rob Enzlin from the OPP, and Tom, Sergei and Matt from the Lindsay detachment; Jeff, Brad and the gang at Kingston Police; members of the Halifax Police, Human Trafficking (HT) unit; the Winnipeg Police Department; Gord Perrier of Hamilton Police HT unit; and the Human Trafficking units of the Halton Police, Waterloo Regional Police, Durham Regional Police (especially Tucker and the gang), Toronto Police Service, London Police (especially rockstars Dana and Ryan), Windsor Police (particularly Peter and team), Calgary Police (shout-out to Paul and team), Montreal Police (especially Dominique and your special dedication to victims), Texas State Police, and San Francisco Bay Area Police. Huge thanks to the Pimping Unit in Las Vegas for your ongoing dedication.

To my Walk with Me family—especially Jennifer Lucking and Kat MacLoud: Thank you for sharing my vision and working for six years to help to ease the pain of rescued survivors.

To every single one of our Walk with Me volunteers from 2009 to 2015, for your dedication and tireless support.

To Shae Invidiata, Randy Phipps and everyone at Free-Them who supported our cause financially with fundraisers and walks, and supported us emotionally and in times of need. Thank you for ALWAYS having our backs and treating us like royalty.

To my Medieval Times family: Jessica Fox, Rob Hillerby, Jamie Lyon, Sarah Klipper, Dave Deslandes, Dezi, Arlene, Catherine, Kirk, Tristan, Adam Brooks, Dave Kinsman, Robin Andrew Dworak, Sean Delaney and Darren G. Smith.

To Rob Hillerby, my big brother during MT years and to this day: Our long conversations and walks during a very complicated time of my life helped me feel normal and grounded. You were—and are— just what the doctor ordered. Thank you for your friendship.

To David Cormican, my dear friend: You showed up in my life when I had no one left. Thank you for the amazing guidance and walks through High Park. You may not realize it, but our time together made a huge impact on my life.

To Peggy Callahan and Lloyd Sutton: Thank you for your friendship, love and mentorship. Thank you for believing in me, for your patience, for always supporting me and for keeping humour alive with your shark gifts.

To Shelly Gilbert and Loly Ricco—the rockstars of social service providers to Ontario's victims of human trafficking.

To survivors and speakers from Voice Found, Simone Bell and Cynthia Bland: Keep up the amazing work!

To Laura and Ian Ross, parents to five beautiful children—thank you for being amazing mentors and very dear friends to us.

To my Lindsay family and everyone at Women's Resources Lindsay for your hard work, advocacy and dedication to victims of human trafficking.

To Doug Didge Vanderhorden for your ongoing advocacy and incredible community mobilization in Kingston.

To every single social service provider who has attended my talks and workshops, and those of other survivors: Your commitment to learning inspires us to continue our work, and the sacrifice of time with your families means a great deal. Thank you for not giving up on victims, even when the work is challenging.

To Simon Haggstom in Sweden: Thank you for your advocacy for victims of human trafficking.

To Detective Constable Ryan Boutin from Lindsay Police: Thank you for catching me the night I fell apart and for your ongoing dedication to victims.

To my mom's colleagues, the officers who practically raised me after school at the police station—János Marticsek, Bela Nemes, Ildiko Marticsek, Laszlo Beviz, Csaba Toth and Gábor Toth: thank you for not letting me get in trouble, and for giving me a foundation in trusting uniforms that I needed.

To Mario Catenaccio for fighting for me to stay in Canada, and for always being just a phone call away. I am forever grateful.

To Joel Oosterman (and your entire family) for being a voice and advocate on Parliament Hill.

To my dear friends in New Mexico at DeliverFund, especially Nic McKinley, Jeremy Mahugh, Tara Bradford, Kara Smith and Michael Fullilove: Your dedication to fighting human trafficking and to saving victims in Batman style is beyond inspiring. Thank you for letting me be part of your operations.

To Peter Warrack at the Bank of Montreal (BMO), who believed in me and my story and decided to bring the banking world together to fight human trafficking and related financial crime. Project Protect is now a leading example in the world because of you!

To Stephen Brent Sargeant and his wife for the generosity they have shown for our victims of human trafficking and for their ongoing advocacy in the financial industry.

To Tania Ferlin for mobilizing the hospitality industry and creating a much-needed awareness. I thank you from the bottom of my heart for your passion and hard work.

To Jeff Lanza, retired FBI agent, for giving me my first speaking opportunity in Kansas City.

To Kevin Bales, founder of the Free the Slaves organization and a mentor to many advocates around the world in the anti-slavery field: Without your work and dedication, we wouldn't be here talking about human trafficking yet. We still wouldn't have laws and stats and an understanding of this epidemic.

To our former justice minister Peter MacKay for standing up for survivors and victims of exploitation and continuing to be our voice.

To David Starr for giving me a brand-new car so that I can drive victims around safely in the Canadian winter, and for your years of support and mentorship.

To my Newfoundland family at Verafin, especially founders Jamie and Brandon who first invited me to share my story. The rest is history. Thank you for spreading the human trafficking message across North America. Your dedication to teaching and trying to bring real change through financial technology and software inspires me every day.

To musicians Balázs Éry and Gérendás Peter—growing up with your songs gave me hope during my darkest hours. Thank you for giving me a chance and thank you for taking up our newest project. Our song, "Life Is Still Beautiful," will help others to learn and to heal. Balázs, thank you for believing in me and for your ongoing friendship and mentorship.

To Pierrot—your music gave me so much more than just favourite melodies to sing through my life. Words can never capture that gratitude I feel for the time I spent with you and the fan club.

To my dear friend Julcsi (Putnoki Langmar Julianna): You are the most amazing childhood friend one could ever dream of. I love you.

To Drayton Entertainment founder Alex Mustakas and the actors, production team and staff: Thank you for what you do. Your shows are world-class and truly part of many healing journeys, including mine.

To Michelle, my little survivor: Thank you for being there for me during some dark times. You are truly transitioning to being an advocate. I'm extremely proud of your strength on your own journey to freedom and happiness.

To my dear co-author Shannon Moroney: Without you this book would never have come to light. I would have never had the strength to get through the writing process. Your passion, your devotion and your spirit are why we made it this far. Thank you for choosing to take on this project and devote your heart and soul to it. Thank you for stepping into my life and walking in my shoes—word by word—through my darkest times, and then picking up your children from school with tears in your eyes from my story. Thank you for helping me to find my voice on the page and for keeping me strong.

To all of you earth angels who showed me kindness when I needed it the most: Lesley Kraus and her family, the Mueller family, the Hegedus family, Mike Yosher and Yosi Shnet, and to the people who came into my life to inspire me, love me, help me and support my cause—Jordana H. Goldlist, Lesley Invidiata, David Morneau, Rob Jalbert, Bob and Linda Vautour, Ric and Marg, Benjamin, Tom, Karen, Victor Young, Natasha Falle, Joy Smith, Amanda Kind, Brenda Halloran, Terry and Lynn Barna, and Sarah Bach.

To all the survivors I have had the honour to work with: Thank you for giving me the honour of being there for you during the darkest hours of your life. I truly hope that you find the love, happiness and hope you deserve. Each and every one of you is worth it. Every single person I meet wants to continue to fight for us, fight for you. That is why I do what I do—because we all deserve a second chance. You too. And it is never, ever too late. Please know that there is an entire army of people out there fighting for your freedom and future. Ashley, Karolina, Karen, Jessica, Markie, Michelle, Shantel, Felicia, Nikki, Nakita, Brianna, Breyane, Alicia, Annie, Pocahontas, Rebecca, Julia, Kayla, Deanna, Erzsébet, Courtney, Ashley Jalbert, Yvette Jalbert, Glendene Grant and Jessie Foster, Tamás Miko and the Hungarian survivors of OPAPA, their families, and many more—you are always in my heart.

And last, but definitely not least, I would like to thank God for never leaving my side in the darkest hours of my life.

From Shannon:

My deepest gratitude goes to Timea, whose bravery, resilience, determination, advocacy and positive energy is inspirational. Thank you for trusting me to write your incredible story, and for opening your heart and mind so fully to me so that I could do so. It is a privilege and honour to have been on this journey with you, and to have had "our baby" together. You are a true friend and soul sister. I'm so proud to know you, and I look forward to all our future work (and fun!) together.

Thank you to my devoted and patient husband, Mike, for being steadfast and stable through my emotional journey working on this book. It wasn't easy! We made it. I love you.

I thank my Golden Circle of family and friends for their unwavering love and support, as always; especially my parents, Pete and Pat Moroney.

Thank you to my dear daughters, Phoebe and Anna, for being pixies, unicorns, fairies and stars through my writing process and bringing me back into the present moment with your hugs, giggles and endless craft projects. I love you all the time, everywhere.

I thank our school friends, teachers and mums for bookending my writing days with laughter, tobogganing, singing, and playdates in Lollipop Park.

I also extend heartfelt thanks to my manuscript readers Lisa McDonald, Kate Love, Laura Rutherford, Rachael Lessmann, Pat Moroney (Mum), Tanis Rideout, Magdalena Rydsky, Heather Love, Mariana Aime, and especially my husband, Mike. Your enthusiasm, tenacity, objectivity and thoughtfulness—not to mention your time and love—were invaluable to this project and to me.

Thank you to RCMP Corporal Lepa Jankovic, RCMP Constable Husam Farah, Detective Constable Mario Catenaccio and Sergeant Mike Josifovic of Toronto Police Service, sexual assault lawyer and advocate Pamela Cross, and Rob Hillerby for valuable conversations and correspondence.

To Timea's wide and wonderful circle: I am so grateful to know you on the page and in person. You're all heroes.

© Abbi Longmire

TIMEA EVA NAGY is a human trafficking survivor, author, educator, inspirational speaker and one of the most recognized advocates against human trafficking in the world. She is the founder of Timea's Cause, a corporation dedicated to the rehabilitation of sex slavery victims and to anti-trafficking education and training for the public, major banks, law enforcement teams and other front-line professionals. Her groundbreaking work has been honoured by the presentation of the Meritorious Service Decoration from the Governor General of Canada (2017), the Prime Minister's Volunteer Award (2012), the Queen Elizabeth Diamond Jubilee Medal (2012), the Frederick Douglass Award from Free the Slaves International (2012), the Attorney General of Ontario's Award for Outstanding Victim Services (2011) and many more. Timea lives outside Toronto with her family. Visit her at www.timeanagy.com.

© Rhea Kent Photography

SHANNON MORONEY is the bestselling author of *Through the Glass*, which chronicles her journey following the violent crimes and incarceration of her first husband. Acknowledged in the top ten list of books at the World Empathy Library, it was also a Canada Reads Top 40 selection and is required reading at numerous universities. Shannon is an internationally recognized advocate of restorative justice, a powerful speaker, one of the "world's 50 most resilient people" (Global Resilience Project), a *New York Times* "Women in the World" recommended writer (2016) and is featured by the international Forgiveness Project. She travels extensively to lead transformative forgiveness and healing retreats for people and communities overcoming trauma. She lives in Toronto with her family. Visit her at www.shannonmoroney.com.